£1-00
SMR

C000185239

CLASSIC COOKS

JANE ASHER

MARY BERRY

TESSA BRAMLEY

PAT CHAPMAN

HELEN CHEN

JOY DAVIES

ANNA DEL CONTE

JILL DUPLEIX

TERRY DURACK

ANTON EDELMANN

ROSE ELLIOT

KAY FAIRFAX

SIMON HOPKINSON

ELISABETH LUARD

PATRICK M^cDONALD

NICK NAIRN

GORDON RAMSAY

ROSAMOND RICHARDSON

NICOLE ROUTHIER

SONIA STEVENSON

ANN AND FRANCO TARUSCHIO

BRIAN TURNER

LESLEY WATERS

ANNE WILLAN

CLASSIC COOKS

250 recipes from the world's top chefs and food writers

PHOTOGRAPHY BY SIMON WHEELER
AND PHILIP WILKINS

WEIDENFELD & NICOLSON
LONDON

First published in 1999 by Weidenfeld & Nicolson

Text copyright © JANE ASHER, MARY BERRY, TESSA BRAMLEY,
PAT CHAPMAN, HELEN CHEN, JOY DAVIES, ANNA DEL CONTE,
JILL DUPLEIX, TERRY DURACK, ANTON EDELMANN, ROSE ELLIOT,
KAY FAIRFAX, SIMON HOPKINSON, ELISABETH LUARD
PATRICK McDONALD, NICK NAIRN, GORDON RAMSAY
ROSAMOND RICHARDSON, NICOLE ROUTHIER
SONIA STEVENSON, ANN AND FRANCO TARUSCHIO
BRIAN TURNER, LESLEY WATERS, ANNE WILLAN

Photographs copyright © Simon Wheeler and Philip Wilkins, 1999

A CIP record for this book is available from the British Library.

ISBN 0 297 82487 2

Designed by Lucy Holmes
Edited by Maggie Ramsay
Photographs by Simon Wheeler and Philip Wilkins
Food styling by Joy Davies and Louise Pickford
Typeset by Tiger Typeset
Index by John Noble

Weidenfeld & Nicolson
The Orion Publishing Group Ltd
5 Upper St Martin's Lane
London WC2H 9EA

CONTENTS

Jane Asher is an actress and writer: she has appeared in plays, films, radio and television productions, and her first novel, *The Longing*, was published in 1996. Her first book, *Jane Asher's Party Cakes*, was published in 1982. Since then she has written more than a dozen books on cakes, parties, cooking for children and entertaining. She runs her own business, Jane Asher Party Cakes Shop and Sugarcraft Centre in Chelsea, London.

Mary Berry is one of Britain's foremost cookery writers and broadcasters. She has written more than 30 cookery books, including the comprehensive *Mary Berry's Complete Cookbook*, and frequently appears on television. The BBC-TV series *Mary Berry's Ultimate Cakes* was accompanied by a best-selling book of the same name and was followed by *Mary Berry at Home*. She lives in Buckinghamshire, where she runs Aga workshops in her beautiful kitchen; 8,000 Aga owners have attended.

Tessa Bramley is chef-patron of the Old Vicarage restaurant in the village of Ridgway, outside Sheffield. Her innovative modern menus have earned her high marks in all the major food guides. In 1996, the Old Vicarage was awarded two stars by the *Egon Ronay Guide*, one of only six restaurants outside London to achieve this status. Tessa is a regular presenter on Channel 4's series *Here's One I Made Earlier*. She also has several of her own TV series to her credit, including *Tessa's Country Kitchen* and *Tessa's Taste Buds*. Tessa is a frequent contributor to newspapers and magazines, and her first book, *The Instinctive Cook*, was published in 1995, followed in 1997 by *A Taste of Tradition* and *Traditional Puddings*.

Pat Chapman's passion for curry was virtually inherited, his ancestors having been in India for 200 years. He founded the world-renowned Curry Club in 1982, leading to the regular publication of the *Good Curry Restaurant Guide*, with its prestigious awards to top restaurants. Pat frequently broadcasts on television and radio, and holds regular cookery courses. He is a consultant chef to a number of UK Indian restaurants and he has appeared as a guest chef for Hilton Hotels, Club Med France and Selfridges Restaurant in London, as well as at Bombay's celebrated Taj Mahal Intercontinental hotel. He has written 30 books, which together have sold more than 1 million copies, including *The Curry Club 250 Favourite Curries and Accompaniments*, *The Balti Curry Cookbook* and *Curry Club Indian Restaurant Cookbook*. His repertoire also includes books on Thai, Chinese, Bangladeshi and Middle Eastern cooking.

Helen Chen was born in Shanghai, China, and learned to cook traditional Shanghai and Beijing dishes from her mother, Joyce Chen, the *grande dame* of Chinese cuisine in the United States. A respected culinary expert in her own right, Helen is the author of several cookbooks, including *Helen Chen's Chinese Home Cooking* (1994). She is also a director of Joyce Chen, Inc, a speciality cookware company. Helen travels regularly to China and the Far East to search for and develop new kitchen products and recipes.

Anna Del Conte was born in Italy and educated at the University of Milan, where she studied history. In the 1950s she married an Englishman and has lived in England ever since. The *Financial Times* has described Anna as 'Britain's most respected writer on Italian food'. Among her widely praised books are *Portrait of Pasta* and the reference book *Gastronomy of Italy*, for which she was awarded the Duchess Maria Luigia di Parma prize in 1988. Her more recent books include *Secrets from an Italian Kitchen*, *Entertaining all'Italiana*, *Anna Del Conte's Italian Kitchen* and *The Classic Food of Northern Italy*, which won the 1996 Guild of Food Writers Book of the Year award in Britain; in Italy it won the Founder's Prize of the Accademia Italiana della Cucina.

Joy Davies began her career in food as principal researcher on *The Good Cook* series for Time-Life books. She has been cookery editor of *Woman* magazine, and was part of the team that created the *BBC Good Food* magazine. She has also been food editor of *She* and *Options* magazines, and has contributed to a number of other publications, including the *Guardian*, the *Daily Telegraph* and *Harpers & Queen*, for which she won the 1992 Glenfiddich Award (Visual Category). Joy has travelled throughout Asia, exploring the markets, kitchens and cooking styles of India, China, Japan, Korea, Thailand, Burma and Indonesia. She lives in London.

Jill Dupleix is one of Australia's most inspirational food writers, with a passion for all things hot and spicy. She is the author of eight cookbooks, including *hot food cool jazz*, a best-selling collection of Malaysian hawker stall recipes accompanied by a CD of modern jazz. She is also the food editor of *The Sydney Morning Herald* and *Elle Australia*, and is a popular food commentator on radio and television. Jill lives in Sydney, Australia, and frequently travels throughout Asia to visit the food markets and collect recipes.

Terry Durack is Australia's most widely read and respected restaurant critic, food writer and noodle lover. As well as writing columns for the *Sydney Morning Herald* and *Australian Gourmet Traveller*, his articles appear regularly in the USA, Canada and Japan. He has written four books on food, including the highly acclaimed *Yum*, an autobiography with recipes. Much of his time is spent in Asia, commenting on food trends, judging food competitions and devouring noodles.

Anton Edelmann was born in Germany, where he began his training as a chef. His route to the top of his profession followed traditional culinary disciplines in some of the top hotel kitchens in Germany and London. In 1982 Anton fulfilled his ambition to head the kitchen in one of the world's most fabled hotels, The Savoy in London. Anton Edelmann's first publication, *The Savoy Food and Drink Book*, marked The Savoy's centenary in 1989. Since then he has written several other books, including *Canapés and Frivolities*, *Creative Cuisine*, *Fast Feasts* and *Christmas Feasts*. He has appeared in the BBC-TV series *Hot Chefs* and as a judge on *Masterchef*, and was a castaway on Radio 4's *Desert Island Discs* in April 1993.

Rose Elliot has written more than 45 books, making her one of the bestselling vegetarian cookery writers in the English-speaking world. Her books include *Not Just a Load of Old Lentils*, which has been continuously in print since it was published in 1972, *The Bean Book*, and more recently *The Classic Vegetarian Cookbook*, *Vegetarian Cookery* (published in a new edition in 1996) and *Learning to Cook Vegetarian*. Though a life-long vegetarian, Rose's main concern is not to convert meat-eaters, but simply to share the delicious flavours of vegetarian food. Her cookery demonstrations are in great demand, and she writes for a variety of newspapers and magazines.

Kay Fairfax is widely known in the world of food and flowers of the southern hemisphere. Her home town for many years was Sydney, Australia, where she ran a catering business, wrote for magazines, made a range of children's toys and appeared on television. She has written books on food, decorative crafts and horticulture, including *Homemade*, *The Australian Christmas Book* and *100 Great Stir-fries*. She now lives in Wiltshire.

Simon Hopkinson grew up in Bury, Lancashire, where his love of eating was established at the kitchen table. He trained as a chef and worked in a number of highly acclaimed restaurants in Britain. After seven years at Bibendum in London, he left the kitchen to concentrate on writing. His first book was the award-winning *Roast Chicken and Other Stories* (both André Simon Memorial and Glenfiddich Food Book of the Year in 1995) which he wrote with the help of Lindsey Bareham. He has a weekly column in *The Independent* newspaper and is a regular contributor to a number of magazines. He has also written another book in collaboration with Lindsey Bareham, entitled *The Prawn Cocktail Years*.

Elisabeth Luard's gastronomic tastes have never been anything but cosmopolitan. After living in Spain and France she published her first cookbook, *European Peasant Cookery*, in 1986. She both wrote and illustrated *Flavours of Andalucia*, which won the Glenfiddich Award for Food Book of the Year in 1992. She has also written two novels, and *Family Life – Birth, Death and the Whole Damn Thing*, an autobiography with recipes. She has a column in *The Sunday Telegraph* and contributes regularly to *House & Garden* and *Country Living*.

Patrick McDonald was born in Northumberland, and discovered his passion for food at an early age, while watching his mother and grandmother cook. He trained under Anton Mosimann at the Dorchester Hotel, and later became head chef of the Manor House Hotel in Wiltshire. His first restaurant, The Epicurean in Cheltenham, Gloucestershire, won a plethora of stars, rosettes and rave reviews in the national press for his innovative and distinctive style of cooking. He now runs The Epicurean at Pershore in the Cotswolds.

Nick Nairn started his career as a Navigating Officer in the Merchant Navy; as he travelled the world he sampled a huge variety of foods. While on leave, he began cooking for friends and discovered a talent that eventually led, in 1986, to his converting an old mill near Aberfoyle in Scotland into Braeval. In 1991, at the age of 32, Nick was awarded a Michelin star which he has retained ever since. Braeval has won many awards and is highly rated in numerous guides, including *Michelin* and *The Good Food Guide*. Nick has also started a cookery school at Braeval. He has made several television appearances: on *Ready Steady Cook, Food and Drink, Who'll Do the Pudding?*, and as a guest judge on *Masterchef* and *Junior Masterchef*. He has presented three of his own cookery series, *Wild Harvest,* and he is the author of the accompanying best-selling BBC books.

Gordon Ramsay won two Michelin stars at his first restaurant, Aubergine in Chelsea. His latest restaurant, Gordon Ramsay, opened in 1998. Fellow chefs from top restaurants voted him the AA Chef's Chef of the Year for 1996. One of his peers commented: 'Gordon continues to come up with innovative and exciting ideas which have had a massive influence on the eating habits of London.' He has appeared on BBC-TV's *Food and Drink* and *Masterchef*. His first book, *A Passion for Flavour*, won the Glenfiddich Award for Food Book of the Year in 1997, and his second book, *A Passion for Seafood*, will be published in 1999.

Rosamond Richardson has written numerous cookery books. *Alfresco*, her book on eating out of doors, won the entertaining category of the James Beard Awards in 1993. *The Great Green Cookbook* has received widespread acclaim, and *Food from Green Places* was published in 1997. Rosamond was also food consultant for Linda McCartney's best-selling books, *Linda's Kitchen* and *Linda McCartney on Tour*. She lives in a small village in the Essex countryside.

Nicole Routhier was born in Vietnam, and trained at the Culinary Institute of America. She is one of the most popular cookery writers in the United States, and is considered the foremost authority on Vietnamese cuisine. She has written several books, including *Cooking Under Wraps*, *Nicole Routhier's Fruit Cookbook* and *The Foods of Vietnam*, which won both The James Beard Foundation and the Institute of American Culinary Professionals Cookbook of the Year awards in 1991. Nicole Routhier lives in Houston, Texas, where she owns a restaurant consulting practice and teaches Southeast Asian cooking.

Sonia Stevenson, a master chef for more than 25 years, founded and ran the Michelin-starred restaurant, The Horn of Plenty at Gulworthy in Devon. She has cooked as the visiting chef at many great restaurants, including Maxim's in Paris, where she was the first woman ever to do so. She now devotes her time to passing on her considerable knowledge through teaching masterclasses, writing and appearing on television. Her books *The Magic of Saucery* and *A Fresh Look at Fish* are best sellers. Her television appearances include BBC-TV's *Masterchef* and Granada's *More Calories Please*.

Franco Taruschio was born in the Marche region of Italy and settled in the Marches of Wales in 1963 when, with his wife Ann, he bought The Walnut Tree Inn at Llandewi Skirrid near Abergavenny. The inn has become internationally known for its superb food. Franco has appeared on several TV food programmes, and the couple have filmed a series for BBC Wales, entitled *Franco and Friends: Food from the Walnut Tree*, accompanied by a book of the same name. They have written three other books: *Leaves from the Walnut Tree* (1993), *Bruschetta, Crostoni, Crostini* (1995) and *Pasta al forno* (1997).

Brian Turner, chef-patron of the highly regarded Turner's in Walton Street, Knightsbridge, is one of Britain's best-known chefs. He is the resident chef with a weekly feature on Granada TV's *This Morning*, he has his own series on Anglia TV called *Out to Lunch with Brian Turner*, and he makes regular appearances on the BBC's popular cookery challenge *Ready Steady Cook*. He has also appeared in the *Food and Drink* series. In addition he is a frequent contributor to national and regional radio programmes, and is often invited to appear as 'guest chef' at leading hotels around the world. He is also Chairman of the Académie Culinaire de France, the professional body of chefs.

Lesley Waters, a former chef, is now a popular television cook. In addition to *GMTV* and *Bazaar,* she has been resident cook for Lifestyle Channel and for UK Living. In 1992 she teamed up with Malcolm Gluck to present the *Superplonk* video, the guide to top supermarket wines. In 1994 she co-presented a 12-part series for Anglia TV about healthy living called *Bodyworks*. During 1996 she was one of the main presenters of *Can't Cook Won't Cook* and she is currently part of the teams on *Ready Steady Cook* for BBC2, *Who'll Do the Pudding?* for BBC1 and *Mixing It* for Channel 5. Her books include *Ready Steady Cook 3* and *Fifteen-Minute Feasts* for BBC Books, *Weight Watchers Carefree Christmas*, *Weight Watchers Storecupboard Cookery* and Sainsbury's *Quick and Easy Food for Friends*.

Anne Willan has more than 30 years experience as a teacher, cookbook author and food columnist. She has written many books, including the influential *Reader's Digest Complete Guide to Cookery* and the 17-volume *Look and Cook* series, which also featured on television in Britain and the USA. Anne Willan founded Ecole de Cuisine La Varenne in Paris in 1975 and continues to direct its culinary programs at the Château du Feÿ in Burgundy and at The Greenbrier in West Virginia. She has also served as the President of the International Association of Culinary Professionals.

SOUPS

When you walk, just walk;
when you eat, just eat.

BUDDHIST WISDOM

WATERCRESS SOUP

**SERVES 2 AS A MEAL,
4 AS A STARTER**

675 g/1½ lb potatoes,
    cut into chunks
900 ml/1½ pints vegetable
    stock, or water and 2
    vegetable stock cubes
100 g/3½ oz watercress, washed
freshly grated nutmeg
salt and pepper
150 ml/5 fl oz single cream
    or milk

Put the potatoes in a saucepan with the stock or water and bring to the boil. Pull off the leaves of the watercress and set aside. Add the stalks – and the stock cubes if using water – to the saucepan and simmer until the potatoes are really tender, about 20 minutes.

Tip the contents of the saucepan into a liquidizer or food processor and blend until smooth, then return to the pan. Chop the watercress leaves finely and add to the soup. Season to taste with nutmeg and pepper: you may not need salt if the stock cubes are salty. Add the cream or milk, heat through and serve hot.

Serve this country soup from Normandy as a warming lunch with French bread and a board of ripe French cheeses. Or, for a winter dinner, serve it as a starter before couscous with spicy leeks and tomatoes (page 141), followed by a dark chocolate mousse (page 311).

POTAGE DE POTIRON ET POIREAUX
Pumpkin and leek soup

SERVES 6

1 kg/2¼ lb pumpkin
1 potato, quartered
4 leeks, about 500 g/1 lb 2 oz
1.2 litres/2 pints water
large pinch of ground nutmeg
salt and pepper
125 ml/4 fl oz crème fraîche or double cream
pinch of sugar (optional)
25 g/1 oz butter, cut into pieces
1–2 tablespoons chopped fresh chives

Peel the pumpkin and discard the seeds and tough fibres. Cut the flesh into pieces the same size as the potato. Halve the leeks lengthways, slice the white and pale green parts into 2.5 cm/ 1 inch pieces and rinse in a colander to wash away the grit.

Put the pumpkin, potato, leeks and water in a large saucepan with the nutmeg, salt and pepper. Cover, bring to the boil and simmer until the vegetables are very tender, about 30 minutes.

Strain the liquid into a large jug and reserve. Work the vegetables through a sieve or food mill back into the saucepan, discarding the fibres from the sieve. Stir in the reserved liquid.

Shortly before serving, reheat the soup in the pan with half the cream, adding more water if the soup is very thick. Taste and adjust the seasoning, adding sugar and more nutmeg if it seems bland. Remove the soup from the heat, add the butter pieces and stir until melted. Spoon into warmed bowls, stir a spoonful of the remaining cream into each bowl and top with a sprinkling of chives.

Butternut squash can be substituted for the pumpkin, onions for the leeks. For an autumnal approach, leave out all but one leek and add an 800 g/1¾ lb can of cooked whole chestnuts in water, drained, just before serving.

Pumpkin soup is perfect before a roast bird – turkey, chicken or game such as pheasant. Baste the bird with butter and make generous amounts of wine gravy. For dessert? Chocolate crème brûlée or vanilla ice cream with chocolate sauce and a sprinkling of toasted hazelnuts would be my choice.

STILTON AND CELERY SOUP

SERVES 4

1 head of celery, tough outer stems removed
15 g/½ oz butter
1 onion, chopped
900 ml/1½ pints vegetable stock
1 teaspoon cornflour
150 ml/5 fl oz single cream
125 g/4 oz Stilton cheese, crumbled
salt and pepper

Wash and chop the celery. Heat the butter in a large saucepan and add the onion; cover and cook gently for 5 minutes, then add the celery. Stir, then cover and cook gently for a further 10 minutes or so – don't let the vegetables brown.

Pour in the stock, then cover the pan and leave to simmer over a low heat for 30 – 40 minutes, or until the celery is very tender.

Purée half the mixture in a liquidizer or food processor, then return it to the saucepan. Mix the cornflour with the cream until smooth and add to the pan, together with the Stilton. Stir over a low heat until the soup has thickened slightly and the cheese has melted – don't let it boil. Season to taste and serve at once.

Serve with warm rolls as a first course to a festive meal: turkey for meat-eaters or mixed mushrooms with wild rice for vegetarians, accompanied by piquant Brussels sprouts with lime zest and juice.

CARROT AND GINGER SOUP

SERVES 4–6

2 tablespoons sunflower or soya oil
1 onion, finely sliced
675 g/1½ lb carrots, finely sliced
2 tablespoons finely slivered fresh ginger
900 ml/1½ pints water
2 tablespoons ginger wine or 1 tablespoon honey
1 tablespoon butter
salt and pepper

To garnish
a slice of fresh ginger, cut into matchsticks

Heat the oil gently in a heavy saucepan, add the onion and cook over a low heat for about 10 minutes, stirring regularly, until it softens – don't let it brown.

Stir in the carrots and ginger, cover and cook gently for another 10 minutes, stirring occasionally to avoid sticking.

Add the water and the ginger wine or honey, bring to the boil, then cover, turn down the heat and leave to simmer for 30 minutes or so, until the carrots are perfectly soft.

Let the soup cool for a minute or two, then add the butter and tip everything into a food processor or use a hand-held liquidizer to blend to a purée.

To serve, reheat gently and season to taste. Don't be tempted to add cream. Serve in hot bowls, scattered with a few matchsticks of ginger.

Delicious accompanied by small croque-monsieurs: cheese and ham sandwiches fried in a little butter and oil, cut into bite-sized triangles. Complete a light meal with a green salad made with mustardy leaves (always good with cheesy things) and a decadent dessert – strawberry tart or lemon meringue pie.

LEEK AND POTATO SOUP
scented with basil

Melt the butter in a deep, heavy-bottomed saucepan, add the leeks and onions and cook over a low heat until soft but not browned. Add the potatoes and stock and simmer until the potatoes are soft and tender.

Add the cream and simmer for a further 5 minutes. Add the basil leaves, then purée in a liquidizer or food processor. Pass through a sieve and season to taste. To serve, reheat gently.

A perfect, simple starter on its own, or serve with tomato crostini. Follow with calves' liver with braised celery, then mango tarte tatin with vanilla ice cream.

SERVES 4

125 g/4 oz butter
400 g/14 oz leeks, chopped
225 g/8 oz onions, chopped
325 g/12 oz Maris Piper potatoes, chopped
1.2 litres/2 pints chicken stock
250 ml/8 fl oz double cream
12 fresh basil leaves
salt and pepper

MEXICAN AVOCADO SOUP

SERVES 4–6

2 perfectly ripe avocados
½ cucumber, peeled and chopped
1 small green chilli, deseeded
    and chopped
1 thick slice of mild onion,
    roughly chopped
1 garlic clove, sliced
juice of 2 limes or 1 lemon
small handful of fresh coriander
    leaves
600 ml/1 pint cold water
    (or hot chicken stock)
salt

To serve
a few coriander leaves
quartered lime or lemon
coarse salt
tortilla chips
chilled tequila (optional)

Halve the avocados, remove the stones and scoop out the flesh. Put the flesh in a liquidizer with the rest of the ingredients and blend thoroughly. Taste and adjust the seasoning, remembering that you will be handing round salt and lime quarters for people to add their own. Chill for at least 30 minutes.

Serve the chilled soup in small bowls, topping each portion with a coriander leaf. Hand the lime quarters, coarse salt and tortilla chips separately.

To make a Mexican splash, accompany with little glasses of very cold tequila, either to sip with a suck of lime and a lick of salt, or to stir directly into the delicate creamy green soup.

The Mexicans also serve this soup hot: use boiling chicken stock instead of cold water, prepare it just before you're ready to serve and don't reheat.

Complete the meal Mexican-style with a grilled fish or chicken and a fiery chilli salsa, served with refried frijoles: cooked black beans squished into a frying pan with oil and garlic and fried to crisp the base, as for a hash. Finish with fresh papaya with lime juice.

QUICK GAZPACHO

SERVES 4–6

300 ml/½ pint tomato juice or vegetable juice
½ slice of white bread, roughly torn
600 ml/1 pint cold water
1 tablespoon wine vinegar
½ green pepper, deseeded and roughly chopped
¼ cucumber, peeled and roughly chopped
1 thick slice of mild Spanish onion, roughly chopped
1 garlic clove, roughly chopped
2 tablespoons olive oil
1 tablespoon sugar
pinch of chilli powder or a dash of Tabasco sauce
pinch of celery salt
4 ice cubes

To garnish

1 thick slice of onion, finely chopped
¼ cucumber, diced small
2 ripe tomatoes, diced small
½ green pepper, deseeded and diced small
1 hard-boiled egg, chopped (optional)
1 slice of serrano or Parma ham, diced (optional)
2 slices of bread, diced and fried in olive oil until crisp

In a liquidizer or food processor, blend all the soup ingredients, including the ice, until quite smooth. Taste and adjust the seasoning – cold food needs to be highly seasoned.

Serve in bowls you have rinsed round with ice to cool them. Put the garnishes in separate small bowls, so each person can choose what to sprinkle on his or her soup. Fry the croûtons at the last minute: they should be so hot they sizzle when they hit the soup.

Complete the meal lightly with a classic Spanish tortilla, or more substantially with a chicken roasted with lots of garlic and olive oil. Finish with some fresh juicy fruit – strawberries, peaches, grapes, melon. Gazpacho is the national dish of Andalusia, where the natives rarely serve anything but fruit after a meal.

You could make double quantities of the gazpacho and keep half in the refrigerator to be diluted with more iced water and served (without its garnishes) as a refreshing summer drink. Omit the onion if you're going to keep it for more than a couple of days, as onion ferments easily.

BROAD BEAN AVGOLEMONO
with lovage

SERVES 4–6

450 g/1 lb shelled fresh broad beans or 225 g/8 oz
    dried broad beans (fava), soaked overnight
    and drained
1 onion, chopped
1 stalk of lovage (or fennel or celery), finely shredded
1 teaspoon grated lemon zest
juice of ½ lemon
2 tablespoons olive oil
1 litre/1¾ pints vegetable or chicken stock or water
1 glass dry white wine
salt and pepper

To finish
2 small eggs
juice of ½ lemon
4 spring onions, chopped
2 tablespoons chopped fresh parsley
lemon quarters

Pick over the broad beans. If they are elderly or dried-out, nick out the little black 'key' and skin them. If they are young and tender include some of the young pods (de-stringed and chopped) – these have a lovely asparagus-like flavour.

Put all the soup ingredients in a large saucepan and bring to the boil. Cover and simmer for about 30 minutes (or at least 1 hour if using dried beans), until the beans are quite tender.

To finish, remove the soup from the heat. Whisk the eggs with the lemon juice in a small bowl. Whisk a ladleful of the hot soup into the egg-and-lemon mixture and stir this back into the soup. Don't reboil the soup or it will curdle. Serve immediately, sprinkled with chopped spring onions and parsley, accompanied by quartered lemons and plenty of bread to mop up the broth.

This is the Greek method of thickening soups and sauces: avgolemono means egg-and-lemon. Begin the meal with a salad of roughly chunked tomatoes, cucumber and mild onion dressed with fresh oregano, olive oil, salt and black olives. Grilled meat can follow if you're hungry, or maybe a shoulder of lamb baked in the oven with garlic and oregano. To finish in high Hellenic style, serve baclava or thick sheep's milk yogurt with honey and nuts.

BULGARIAN MONASTERY SOUP

SERVES 4 AS A MAIN COURSE

85 g/3 oz round rice
    ('pudding' or risotto)
4 tablespoons corn oil
1 garlic clove, finely chopped
1 green pepper, deseeded
    and chopped
1 small green chilli, deseeded
    and chopped
1 fat leek, trimmed and finely
    sliced (with its green parts)
1 small lettuce, shredded
a sprig of thyme
2 bay leaves
1.2 litres/2 pints water
salt and pepper

To finish
150 ml/5 fl oz thick
    creamy yogurt
1 egg
1 tablespoon chopped
    fresh parsley
1 tablespoon chopped fresh dill
pickled cucumbers

Pick over the rice and remove any small stones.

Warm the oil in a large saucepan and add the garlic, green pepper and chilli. Let the vegetables cook gently until soft but not browned. Stir the rice into the fragrant oil. When the grains turn opaque, add the sliced leek, the lettuce and the herbs, pour in the water and bring to the boil. Turn the heat down, cover loosely and simmer very gently for about 30 minutes, until the rice is tender.

To finish, remove the soup from the heat. Whisk the yogurt and egg with a ladleful of the hot soup, and stir it back into the soup. Let it stand for a minute to allow the egg to set a little. Taste and adjust the seasoning.

Serve in hot soup plates, sprinkled with parsley and dill. Accompany with pickled cucumbers and dark bread – black rye bread with caraway seeds for ethnic correctness.

This is a Bulgarian recipe, and the Bulgarians are famous not only for their yogurt, but also for being the best gardeners in eastern Europe. An apple tart or peach cobbler will complete the meal authentically.

SPANISH CHICKPEA AND PEPPER SOUP

SERVES 4 AS A MAIN COURSE

225 g/8 oz dried chickpeas,
  soaked overnight in enough
  water to cover, or 450 g/1 lb
  canned chickpeas
1 litre/1¾ pints water
2–3 garlic cloves
2 tablespoons olive oil
1 ham bone or 2–3 slices of
  bacon, chopped
1 bay leaf
½ teaspoon coriander seeds
¼ teaspoon black peppercorns,
  crushed
1 onion, roughly chopped
4 tablespoons chopped
  fresh parsley
2 tablespoons chopped
  fresh mint
1 teaspoon oregano or marjoram
  (fresh or dried)
1 large potato, sliced
large handful of spinach,
  shredded
salt

To finish

1 red pepper, deseeded and cut
  into strips
2 tablespoons olive oil
1 garlic clove, roughly sliced
chopped fresh parsley

If using soaked dried chickpeas, drain them and put them in a saucepan with the water and bring to the boil. Skim off the foam as it rises. Stick the garlic cloves on the point of a knife and hold them in a flame until the papery covering blackens at the edges. Drop the singed garlic cloves in with the chickpeas. Add the olive oil, ham bone or bacon, bay leaf, coriander, peppercorns, onion and herbs. Bring back to the boil, then turn down the heat, cover and cook for 1½–2 hours, until the chickpeas are quite soft. Keep the liquid at a rapid simmer, don't add salt, and if you need to add more water, make sure it's boiling.

If using tinned chickpeas, drain, add to the water with all the flavourings, and cook for 30 minutes.

When the chickpeas are tender and well-flavoured, remove the ham bone if using, add the sliced potato and cook until tender. Stir in the spinach and bring back to the boil. Add salt to taste.

Meanwhile, fry the strips of pepper in the olive oil with the garlic until the peppers soften and caramelize a little.

Serve the soup piping hot, with a spoonful of the peppers and their oily and garlicky juices in each serving. Sprinkle with parsley and serve with plenty of rough country bread rubbed with tomato and garlic.

A salad of cos lettuce, chunks of cucumber, quartered hard-boiled eggs and sliced mild onion dressed with olive oil, salt and vinegar completes the meal in proper Spanish style.

CATALAN 'BULLIT'

SERVES 4 AS A MAIN COURSE

1 tablespoon olive oil
1 large onion, finely chopped
½ green or red pepper, deseeded
    and chopped
1 stick of celery, chopped
225 g/8 oz small new potatoes,
    scrubbed and cut into bite-
    sized pieces
1 litre/1¾ pints water
salt
1 small courgette, diced
125 g/4 oz young green beans,
    topped and tailed,
      or 125 g/4 oz shelled peas
      (fresh or frozen)
handful of spinach or Swiss
    chard, shredded

To finish
2 tablespoons olive oil
3–4 spring onions, finely sliced
4 tablespoons chopped
    fresh parsley
2 tablespoons chopped
    fresh marjoram
grated zest of 1 lemon
1 garlic clove, finely chopped
salt and pepper

To serve
aïoli (page 373)

Warm the oil in a large saucepan or casserole. Add the onion and fry gently for a few minutes. Add the chopped pepper and celery and let everything sizzle until soft but not browned. Add the potatoes, water and 1 teaspoon salt and bring to the boil. Turn down the heat, cover and leave to simmer for 15–20 minutes.

Add the courgette and beans and cook for a further 8–10 minutes; stir in the spinach a few minutes before the end of the cooking time. The potatoes should be tender and the consistency of the dish should be midway between a stew and a soup.

To finish, just before serving stir in the oil (olive oil is used here both as a seasoning and a thickening), spring onions and herbs, lemon zest and garlic. Bring back to a full boil to amalgamate the oil, then taste and add freshly ground black pepper and extra salt if necessary.

For a more substantial dish, poach eggs in the broth: drop them into hollows between the vegetables and spoon hot broth over until the whites set. Accompany with plenty of rough country bread and a bowl of aïoli.

The bullit, like a minestrone, is a meal-in-a-bowl — substantial and delicious. Follow with fruit and cheese.

PASTA IN BRODO

Pasta in chicken broth

SERVES 4

1.5–1.8 kg/3–4 lb free-range chicken
1 carrot, halved
1 onion, halved
few sprigs of thyme
few sprigs of parsley
1 bay leaf
3 strips of lemon zest
6 black peppercorns
salt
125 g/4 oz dried farfalline, stelle or other soup pasta

To serve
fresh chervil leaves
freshly ground black pepper
freshly grated Parmesan cheese

Pull away any fat from inside the chicken. Remove the legs, thighs and breasts. Separate the ribs from the back and chop into large pieces. Put the chicken bones and meat into a large, heavy-bottomed saucepan with the carrot and onion. Cover with cold water and bring slowly to the boil. Skim off any scum. Add a few tablespoons of cold water to encourage more scum to be released, then skim every few minutes until no more scum appears. Add the herbs, lemon zest and peppercorns, partially cover the pan and simmer for 3 hours, topping up with boiling water.

When the chicken meat is tasteless, the broth is ready. Strain into a jug or bowl, then pour through a fine sieve into the cleaned pan. Bring back to the boil and reduce to 1.5 litres/2½ pints. Add salt to taste.

To serve, add the pasta to the boiling broth and simmer until cooked, about 5–6 minutes. Serve with chervil, pepper and Parmesan.

For a main course, serve roast chicken with some sautéed wild and cultivated mushrooms.

PASTA E FAGIOLI

Pasta and bean soup

SERVES 4–6

150 g/5 oz dried borlotti beans,
    soaked overnight in cold water
5 tablespoons extra virgin olive oil
1 cm/½ inch thick slice of pancetta,
    cut into lardons
2 sticks of celery, chopped
2 carrots, chopped
2 onions, chopped
4 tomatoes, seeded and finely chopped
2 sprigs of thyme
1 bay leaf
125 g/4 oz macaroni

To serve
salt and freshly ground black pepper
Parmesan cheese
extra virgin olive oil

Drain the soaked beans and rinse thoroughly.

Heat the olive oil in a frying pan, add the pancetta and sauté until golden. Remove the pancetta with a slotted spoon and add the celery, carrots and onions. Sauté for 5 minutes or until softened.

Put the drained beans, pancetta and vegetables, with the tomatoes, in a large, heavy-bottomed saucepan. Add the herbs and cover with water. Bring to the boil and boil rapidly for 10 minutes. Reduce the heat, partially cover the pan and simmer very gently for about 2 hours. At the end of this time the beans should be tender. If the soup becomes too dry, top up with boiling water.

Remove two-thirds of the soup and pass through a food mill or blend in a liquidizer. Return the purée to the soup, add some boiling water and bring back to the boil. Add the macaroni and simmer until tender, about 10 minutes, stirring well to prevent the pasta from sticking. Leave to stand for 10 minutes.

Serve in soup dishes, with salt and black pepper, shavings of Parmesan and a swirl of your best olive oil, accompanied by some ciabatta or other good Italian bread, lightly toasted and rubbed with a cut garlic clove and a dribble of olive oil.

Follow with another classic Venetian dish, fegato alla Veneziana: fine slices of calves' liver fried with thinly sliced onions (page 266). A salad of slightly bitter leaves, such as curly endive, would be a good finale.

PUMPKIN MINESTRONE

SERVES 4 AS A MAIN COURSE

2 tablespoons olive oil
1 large leek, finely sliced
1 stick of celery, finely sliced
1 large carrot, diced
2–3 tomatoes, skinned and diced
1.2 litres/2 pints boiling water
225 g/8 oz slice of pumpkin,
    peeled, deseeded and diced
1 large potato, diced
bouquet garni
50 g/2 oz macaroni or other
    tubular pasta
1 tablespoon pesto (page 374)
salt and pepper

To finish

4 slices of day-old rough
    country bread
1 garlic clove, halved
Parmesan cheese, grated
olive oil

Heat the oil gently in a large saucepan, add the leek, celery and carrot and cook over a low heat for about 10 minutes, until softened but not browned. Add the tomatoes and then the boiling water, the diced pumpkin and potato, and bring back to the boil. Tuck in the bouquet garni and simmer for about 20 minutes or until the vegetables are nearly tender.

Stir in the pasta and cook for another 12–15 minutes, until the pasta is tender.

Stir in a generous spoonful of pesto, then taste and adjust the seasoning.

To finish, rub the bread with the garlic and place a slice in the bottom of four hot soup plates. Ladle on the soup and serve hot. Hand grated cheese and extra olive oil separately.

The country people of northern Italy, whose traditional midday meal this is, will tell you a minestrone can be made with whatever vegetables happen to be in season, and should be so thick a wooden spoon will stand up in it. A piece of fruit and perhaps an almond cake will complete the meal in northern Italian style.

HUNGARIAN PAPRIKA SOUP

SERVES 4 AS A MAIN COURSE

3 tablespoons lard
   (or oil plus a rasher or two
   of bacon, chopped)
450 g/1 lb onions, finely sliced
salt
1 carrot, diced small
½ red pepper, deseeded and
   diced small
1 potato, diced
1 teaspoon caraway seeds
2 heaped tablespoons
   sweet paprika
1 litre/1¾ pints water
1 glass red wine
1 tablespoon tomato purée
2 bay leaves
1 teaspoon chopped marjoram
50 g/2 oz pasta bows or shells
pinch of sugar

To finish

1 fresh red or green chilli,
   deseeded and finely chopped,
   or 1 teaspoon chilli powder
soured cream (or thick yogurt)

Heat the lard (or oil and bacon) gently in a heavy saucepan and cook the onions until they soften and turn golden – sprinkle with a little salt to draw the water and speed up the process. It's this preliminary light roasting that gives the flavour to all Hungarian soups and stews.

Push the onions to one side and add the diced carrot, red pepper and potato. Sprinkle with the caraway seeds and a little more salt. Let the vegetables sizzle for a minute or two, then stir in the paprika – it should just soak up the oil rather than fry. Add the water, wine, tomato purée, bay leaves and marjoram. Stir, bring to a rolling boil, then turn down the heat. Cover loosely and leave to simmer gently for 15 minutes, until the vegetables soften.

Add the pasta, bring back to the boil, then turn down the heat, cover and leave to simmer for another 12–15 minutes, until everything is tender. Taste and adjust the seasoning.

To finish, transfer a ladleful of the hot soup to a small bowl and stir in the finely chopped fresh chilli or chilli powder. Hand this chilli mixture separately, along with soured cream, so that each person can control the pepperiness and creaminess of the soup. The colder the day, the more welcome the chilli – an excellent source of sniffle-defying vitamin C in winter.

A cherry or plum-stuffed strudel will complete the meal in true Magyar style.

JAMAICAN SPLIT PEA SOUP
with sweetcorn

SERVES 4–6

175 g/6 oz yellow split peas
2 tablespoons butter or ghee (clarified butter)
1 onion, finely chopped
1 garlic clove, sliced
1 teaspoon curry powder
   (Bols is the favourite brand in Jamaica)
1 teaspoon ground cumin
1 litre/1¾ pints water
salt and pepper

To finish
4 tablespoons cooked sweetcorn kernels
a little butter
1 fresh red chilli, deseeded and finely diced
chopped fresh coriander

Rinse the split peas in a sieve under cold running water. Drain well.

Melt the butter or ghee in a large saucepan and add the onion and garlic. Fry for about 2 minutes, then sprinkle in the curry powder and cumin and fry for a further minute or so. Add the split peas and stir well, then add the water and bring to the boil. Turn down the heat and simmer, loosely covered, for 1½–2 hours, until the split peas are almost puréed. Give it a stir every now and again – peas may stick and burn. Top up with boiling water if necessary.

To finish, heat the sweetcorn in a little butter. Taste the soup and adjust the seasoning. Serve hot in bowls, and top each serving with a spoonful of sweetcorn and a sprinkling of diced chilli and chopped coriander.

Delicious with fresh soft rolls or 'bakes': bread-dough balls flattened and fried like doughnuts. To make a meal of it, follow with something really Jamaican such as ackee and saltfish, crab patties or jerk pork. Finish with papaya with lime juice – or maybe a granita made with crushed fresh pineapple. Sunny days be with you.

MULLIGATAWNY

Melt the butter in a large saucepan, add the onion and fry until it is lightly caramelized. Stir in the curry powder or paste. Add the rest of the vegetables and the lentils, along with the stock or water. Bring to the boil, cover loosely, turn down the heat and simmer for 30–40 minutes, until the vegetables and lentils are perfectly tender.

Tip half the soup into a food processor or liquidizer and blend to a purée. Return to the saucepan, taste and adjust the seasoning and reheat until boiling.

Serve hot, sprinkled with coriander and a ring or two of green chilli. Serve the remaining garnishes in small bowls, to be stirred into this thick soup, or spooned on top. Accompany with any of the Indian breads: naan, paratha, chappati.

You will not need anything too sturdy after a soup like this. Maybe something from the tandoori oven – a joint of chicken or a skewerful of spiced prawns with a few crisp lettuce leaves. A coconut ice or a fresh mango will refresh the palate after all those spices.

SERVES 4–6

50 g/2 oz butter

1 onion, chopped

2 tablespoons curry powder or paste

1 small turnip, diced

1 parsnip, diced

1 carrot, diced

1 potato, diced

85 g/3 oz orange lentils (masoor dal)

1 litre/1¾ pints vegetable stock or water

salt and pepper

To garnish

chopped fresh coriander (or parsley and a pinch of
    ground coriander)

1 green chilli, deseeded and finely sliced

thick yogurt stirred with mint or grated cucumber

toasted grated coconut

toasted flaked almonds

chopped raw onion and apple dressed with lemon juice

chopped tomato spiked with a little chilli

chutney

poppadums

FRESH SHELLFISH SOUP

SERVES 4

150 g/5 oz fresh winkles

150 g/5 oz fresh cockles

150 g/5 oz fresh clams

2 tablespoons olive oil

1 shallot, chopped

1 stalk of lemongrass, peeled and chopped

bouquet garni

2 tablespoons Noilly Prat or dry vermouth

600 ml/1 pint fish stock

salt and pepper

3 large basil leaves

To garnish

1 small carrot, cut into thin sticks

½ small courgette, cut into thin sticks

3 tablespoons cooked or canned cannellini beans

Put the shellfish into a large saucepan with 1 tablespoon of the oil. Heat with the lid on for about 5 minutes, shaking the pan occasionally until the cockle and clam shells have opened. Any that haven't opened should be discarded. Strain into a small bowl and reserve the juices. Remove the flesh from the shells and set aside.

Add the remaining oil to the saucepan, add the shallot, lemongrass and bouquet garni and cook gently for 5 minutes or until softened. Add the reserved shellfish juices, the vermouth and stock. Season to taste and bring to the boil, then simmer for 10 minutes.

Remove from the heat, add the basil leaves and leave to infuse for 10 minutes. Strain through a sieve into a bowl, discard the solids, then return the stock to the pan and add the shellfish flesh.

For the garnish, blanch the carrot and courgette sticks in boiling water for 1 minute, then drain and rinse under cold water.

To serve, add the blanched vegetables and the beans to the soup and return to a light boil. Taste and adjust the seasoning and serve immediately.

For a main course, serve a juicy grilled steak, chunky homemade chips and a creamy mushroom sauce. Complete the meal with a light chocolate mousse and a few fresh raspberries.

MUSSEL AND SAFFRON SOUP

SERVES 4

3 tablespoons olive oil
½ yellow pepper, finely chopped
½ red pepper, finely chopped
2 shallots, finely chopped
2 small sticks of celery, finely chopped
good pinch of saffron strands
4 tablespoons dry white wine
1 kg/2¼ lb fresh mussels, scrubbed
   and debearded
1 litre/1¾ pints fish stock
salt and pepper
3 tablespoons cream
2 teaspoons chopped fresh tarragon

In a large saucepan, heat the oil, then add the peppers, shallots, celery and saffron. Cover and fry gently for about 10 minutes, shaking the pan occasionally.

Add the wine and cook uncovered for a minute or two, then stir in the mussels. Cover the pan and cook for 3–5 minutes or until all the mussels have opened. Any that haven't opened should be discarded. Lift out the mussels using a slotted spoon, remove them from their shells and set aside. Throw away the shells.

Add the stock to the saucepan and bring to the boil, cover and simmer for 10 minutes.

Reserve about 2 tablespoons of mussels for garnishing and add the rest to the stock. Season to taste and simmer for a further 5 minutes.

Blend the stock and mussels in a liquidizer or food processor, then pass through a sieve, rubbing the mussels through with the back of a ladle. Return to the pan, add the cream and reheat to just below boiling point. Taste and adjust the seasoning, then ladle into four warmed soup plates. Garnish with the reserved mussels and chopped tarragon and serve immediately.

Stay in the Mediterranean mood and follow the soup with a salade niçoise made with freshly grilled tuna. For pudding, try a French-style dark chocolate tart or thin slices of chocolate torte.

CHINESE MUSHROOM SOUP

SERVES 4–6

25 g/1 oz dried Chinese
    mushrooms (shiitake,
    wood ears)
1 litre/1¾ pints homemade
    chicken stock (page 372)
6 spring onions (white parts only
    – use the green parts for the
    garnish), sliced
2–3 slices of fresh ginger, cut
    into matchsticks
1–2 star anise
pinch of sugar
1 tablespoon soy sauce
1 small glass Chinese rice wine
    or dry sherry or white wine

To finish

50 g/2 oz Chinese transparent
    noodles (vermicelli)
6 spring onions (green parts),
    finely sliced on the diagonal
small bunch of watercress
    or a handful of fresh spinach,
    shredded
dash of wine vinegar
salt
fresh coriander leaves

Put the dried mushrooms in a small bowl, cover with hot water and leave to soak and swell for 10 minutes. Drain, reserving the soaking water, and trim off the tough stalks.

Put the mushrooms into a saucepan with their soaking water (leaving behind any sandy deposit) and add the stock, spring onions, ginger, star anise, sugar, soy sauce and wine. Bring to the boil. Skim off any foam, turn down the heat, cover and simmer for 30 minutes.

Meanwhile, put the noodles in a small bowl and cover with boiling water. Leave to soak for 5 minutes, then rinse in cold water (or follow the instructions on the packet).

Strain the soup into a clean bowl. Pick the mushrooms out of the strainer, slice or tear into shreds, and return them to the broth.

To serve, bring the broth back to the boil. Stir in the soaked noodles, the finely sliced spring onions, the watercress or spinach and the vinegar. Taste and add salt if necessary. Serve in small bowls, with a sprinkling of fresh coriander.

This is nice with a few small spring rolls or crispy won tons to nibble, and a few rosy radishes.

The Chinese take clear soup as a refreshment during the meal rather than as a starter, so your soup can feature in any Chinese meal – even a takeaway. As a rough rule of thumb, serve as many dishes for sharing as you have diners, plus rice. Think about the balance of the meal – something crisp, something soft, something saucy, something dry.

LAKSA LEMAK
Curry noodle soup

SERVES 4

100 g/3½ oz dried rice vermicelli
4 cubes of fried beancurd puffs
2 tablespoons vegetable oil
1.5 litres/2½ pints chicken stock
2 teaspoons palm sugar
    or brown sugar
1 teaspoon salt
500 ml/16 fl oz coconut milk
meat from half a cooked chicken,
    sliced
8 fish balls
8 uncooked prawns, peeled
200 g/7 oz fresh egg noodles
    (Hokkien noodles)
150 g/5 oz beansprouts
½ cucumber, peeled and cut
    into matchsticks
sprigs of fresh mint and coriander

Laksa paste
1 onion, finely chopped
1 tablespoon grated fresh ginger
1 tablespoon grated fresh
    galangal
2 garlic cloves, chopped
2 stalks of lemongrass, white
    part only, sliced
6 dried red chillies, soaked for
    about 2 hours, then chopped
4 candlenuts or macadamia nuts,
    crushed
1 teaspoon ground coriander
1 teaspoon paprika
1 teaspoon ground cumin
6 laksa or Asian mint leaves
1 teaspoon turmeric
1 tablespoon blachan (Asian
    shrimp paste)

First make the laksa paste. Put all the ingredients into a mortar and pound with a pestle for 10–15 minutes, until a thick, fragrant, amalgamated paste is formed. Alternatively, blend in a food processor, adding the ingredients gradually.

Cook the rice vermicelli for 5–6 minutes in boiling water, then drain. Cut the beancurd puffs in half diagonally and set aside.

Heat a wok, then add the oil. When hot, add the laksa paste and fry for about 5 minutes, until fragrant. Add the stock, sugar and salt and bring to the boil. Reduce the heat and add the coconut milk, stirring constantly until it is hot. Add the chicken, fish balls and prawns and simmer gently for 2–3 minutes.

Put the drained rice vermicelli and fresh egg noodles into a large bowl, pour boiling water over them, then drain and rinse. Rinse the beansprouts with boiling water, then drain.

Divide the noodles and beancurd between four deep soup bowls. Using tongs, distribute the chicken, fish balls and prawns between the bowls, then top with hot soup. Arrange the cucumber and beansprouts on top, scatter with mint and coriander and serve at once.

Serve individual bowls of laksa lemak as a simple lunch, or as part of a Malaysian feast, along with chicken curry, roti bread, spinach fried with chilli and blachan (page 150), and achar, or pickled vegetables.

WON TON NOODLE SOUP

Dumpling soup with noodles

SERVES 4

150 g/5 oz uncooked prawns, finely chopped

150 g/5 oz minced pork

2 tablespoons finely chopped pork or bacon fat

4 dried shiitake mushrooms, soaked in warm water for
    1–2 hours, then drained and finely chopped

4 water chestnuts, finely chopped

2 spring onions, finely chopped

1 small egg white

salt and pepper

200 g/7 oz fresh thin egg noodles

1 packet fresh won ton wrappers

1 heaped teaspoon cornflour blended with
    1 tablespoon cold water

1.5 litres/2½ pints homemade chicken stock
    (page 372)

2 slices of fresh ginger

125 g/4 oz choi sum (flowering cabbage),
    roughly sliced

2 spring onions, sliced

To make the dumplings, put the prawns, pork, pork fat, mushrooms, water chestnuts, spring onions, egg white, salt and pepper in a bowl and mix with your hands until totally amalgamated. Chill in the refrigerator for 1–2 hours.

Put the noodles in a bowl, pour boiling water over them and leave for 1–2 minutes or until they soften. Rinse under cold water, drain and set aside.

Lay a won ton wrapper on the work surface. Place up to a teaspoon of filling in the centre. Dip your finger into the cornflour paste and run it around the edges. Fold over to form a triangle, pressing the edges together. Now bring the two outer corners together to meet and overlap in the middle, and seal with a little paste. Allow four or five won tons per person.

Put the stock into a wide saucepan, add the ginger and bring to a gentle simmer. Blanch the Chinese cabbage in boiling water for 1 minute, then drain and add to the stock. Rinse the noodles in boiling water, drain, then divide between four warmed deep soup bowls.

Place the won tons in a saucepan of boiling water and simmer until they float to the surface. Drain and distribute between the bowls. Discard the ginger and pour the hot stock over the won tons. Sprinkle with sliced spring onions.

This is the perfect lunch in a bowl, but could also be made part of a shared Cantonese meal, by adding a plate of steamed Chinese sausage (lup cheong), and crisp pork and mushroom spring rolls. Finish with fresh lychees or sliced oranges.

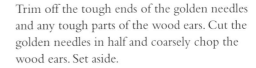

PEKING HOT AND SOUR SOUP

SERVES 4

1 tablespoon dried golden needles, soaked and
   drained (page 378)

3–4 dried wood ears, soaked and drained (page 379)

85 g/3 oz lean pork, shredded

1 teaspoon rice wine or dry sherry

3 tablespoons cornflour

1 litre/1¾ pints chicken stock

1 tablespoon light soy sauce

85 g/3 oz soft tofu (beancurd), shredded

1 egg, beaten

2 tablespoons cider vinegar

¼ teaspoon ground white pepper

1½ teaspoons sesame seed oil

½ teaspoon salt, or to taste

1 spring onion, very thinly sliced

Trim off the tough ends of the golden needles
and any tough parts of the wood ears. Cut the
golden needles in half and coarsely chop the
wood ears. Set aside.

Put the pork in a small bowl with the rice
wine and 1 teaspoon of the cornflour. Set aside.
Dissolve the remaining cornflour in 125 ml/
4 fl oz cold water and set aside.

Put the chicken stock and soy sauce in a
saucepan and bring to the boil. When the stock
is boiling, stir in the pork and cook until it
separates, about 30 seconds. Then stir in the
golden needles and wood ears. Allow the stock
to come back to the boil and cook for 1 minute.
Add the beancurd and, as soon as the stock
comes back to the boil, stir the cornflour
mixture and add it to the soup, stirring
constantly until the soup thickens.

Still stirring constantly, pour the beaten egg into
the hot soup in a steady stream. Remove from
the heat and immediately stir in the vinegar,
pepper and sesame seed oil. Add salt to taste and
garnish with spring onion. Serve hot.

*This hearty soup makes a perfect cold-weather snack
or light lunch when served with triangles of homestyle
spring onion pancakes (page 48). Alternatively, serve
as the soup course in a multi-course meal.*

PHO GA
Chicken noodle soup

SERVES 4

1 whole chicken, preferably with head and feet
1 kg/2¼ lb chicken bones
2 onions, 1 quartered, 1 sliced paper-thin
1 teaspoon salt
5 cm/2 inch piece of fresh ginger, sliced
1 cinnamon stick
1 star anise
3 cardamom pods
2 teaspoons sugar
3 tablespoons fried shallots
3 tablespoons fish sauce
400 g/14 oz fresh rice sheet noodles (page 378)
4 spring onions, finely sliced
8 sprigs of coriander

To serve
generous handful of beansprouts
sprigs of mint
sprigs of holy basil (sweet Asian basil)
sprigs of coriander
1 fresh red chilli, finely chopped
1 lemon or lime, cut into wedges

Put the whole chicken and the bones into a large saucepan with the quartered onion, the salt, ginger, cinnamon, star anise, cardamom and 3 litres/2½ pints water. Bring to the boil. Skim off any froth that rises to the surface, then lower the heat and simmer for 1½ hours. Remove the chicken and set aside.

Add the sugar, 2 tablespoons of the fried shallots and the fish sauce to the stock and cook for a further hour. Strain through a fine sieve.

Slice the chicken thigh and breast meat into fine slices.

If not pre-cut, cut the rice noodles into 1 cm/ ½ inch strips, like tagliatelle. Place in a bowl and pour boiling water over them to cover, gently shaking the strips apart with a pair of chopsticks. Drain, then divide the noodles between four deep soup bowls. Layer the chicken meat neatly on top along with a few paper-thin onion slices, and spoon some hot soup into each bowl. Scatter the remaining fried shallots and the coriander on top.

Serve with an accompanying platter of bean-sprouts, fresh herbs, chopped chilli and lemon or lime wedges, for each person to add according to their taste.

In Vietnam, this is a self-sufficient breakfast in a bowl. You can turn it into a satisfying lunch or dinner by adding a plate of Vietnamese spring rolls (page 57) with a sweet chilli dipping sauce.

NABEYAKI UDON

Udon noodles in broth with tempura

SERVES 2

1 chicken thigh, boned and cut into bite-sized pieces
2½ tablespoons Japanese soy sauce
4 teaspoons mirin
150 g/5 oz dried udon noodles
750 ml/1¼ pints dashi (page 372)
2 teaspoons sugar
pinch of salt
2 dried shiitake mushrooms, soaked in warm water
    for 1–2 hours
½ Japanese fishcake (kamaboko), finely sliced
½ tablespoon dried wakame seaweed
vegetable oil for deep-frying
2 large uncooked prawns, peeled, tails left on
about 1 tablespoon plain flour
1 large egg
2 spring onions, cut into 6 cm/2½ inch lengths

Tempura batter
1 egg yolk
250 ml/8 fl oz iced water
125 g/4 oz plain flour, sifted

Put the chicken in a small bowl with 1 teaspoon of the soy sauce and 1 teaspoon of the mirin and leave to marinate for 30 minutes.

Bring a large saucepan of water to the boil and add the noodles. When the water returns to the boil, add 250 ml/8 fl oz cold water. Repeat three times, until the noodles are cooked and tender. Drain, rinse under cold water and set aside.

In a casserole, combine the dashi, sugar, salt and the remaining soy sauce and mirin, and bring to the boil. Add the mushrooms, fishcake slices and chicken and simmer gently for 15 minutes. Meanwhile, soak the wakame in cold water for 10 minutes. Drain and set aside.

For the tempura batter: put the egg yolk in a bowl. Add the iced water and mix with chopsticks. Add the flour and mix lightly; don't overmix, or the batter will be heavy.

Heat the oil in a wok until it begins to smoke. Dredge the prawns in flour, dip each one into the tempura batter and drop into the hot oil. Deep-fry for about 2 minutes, until the batter is lightly golden and crisp.

Rinse the noodles in boiling water, add to the soup and bring to the boil. Add the egg, spring onions and wakame, then cover the pot for about 1 minute, until the egg white is just cooked. Put the prawns on top and bring to the table. Break the egg with chopsticks and stir through.

Traditionally, nabeyaki udon is served with one egg per person, as a meal in a bowl. This version is for two to share. Turn it into a meal by starting with sushi or sashimi. Finish with green tea ice cream and fruit.

STARTERS

Strange to see how a
good dinner and feasting
reconciles everyone.

SAMUEL PEPYS

HOMESTYLE SPRING ONION PANCAKES

In a bowl, mix together the eggs, flour, spring onions, bacon, stock and salt to make a thin batter.

Heat 2 teaspoons of the oil in a hot frying pan (25 cm/10 inches in diameter) over medium heat. Tip the pan so that the oil spreads across the bottom of the pan, then pour in a quarter of the batter and spread, using a spatula, until it covers the bottom of the pan.

Cook until the edges are slightly brown, then turn the pancake over and lightly brown the other side. Repeat with the remaining oil and batter, to make four pancakes. Cut into wedges and serve hot.

Cut the cooked pancakes into triangles, roll them up and secure with a cocktail stick for a delicious hors d'oeuvre. My mother used to make these for us as a nutritious after-school snack.

SERVES 4–8

2 eggs, beaten
175 g/6 oz flour
4 spring onions (green and white parts), thinly sliced
2 rashers of bacon, finely chopped
250 ml/8 fl oz chicken stock
½ teaspoon salt
3 tablespoons groundnut or corn oil

WHITE BEAN PÂTÉ
with horseradish

SERVES 4

2 x 400 g/14 oz cans of butter beans,
    drained and rinsed
4 teaspoons creamed horseradish
5 tablespoons olive oil
grated zest and juice of 1 lime
salt and pepper
175 g/6 oz broad beans, cooked and peeled
2 tablespoons flat-leaf parsley leaves (left whole)

Put three-quarters of the butter beans in a food processor with the horseradish, 4 tablespoons of the olive oil, the lime zest and plenty of salt and pepper. Blend until smooth and creamy, adding a little warm water if necessary.

Toss the remaining butter beans and the broad beans with the lime juice, parsley leaves and the remaining olive oil. Season to taste.

Pile the creamy pâté into a shallow serving dish and scatter over the bean relish. Grind over plenty of black pepper and serve with warm crusty bread or chill until required.

For a main course I might serve hot paprika chicken with fruity salsa.

MEZZE PLATE

SERVES 4

175 g/6 oz goats' cheese, chilled
virgin olive oil for drizzling
salt and pepper
4 large sprigs of mint
pitta bread

Aubergine caviar
1 aubergine
2 tablespoons virgin olive oil
1 garlic clove, crushed
juice of ½ lemon
1 thin slice of bread,
    plunged into cold water
    and well squeezed out

Lentil salad
400 g/14 oz can of green lentils,
    drained and rinsed
225 g/8 oz cherry tomatoes,
    halved
½ bunch of spring onions,
    finely chopped
2 tablespoons balsamic vinegar
3 tablespoons virgin olive oil

First make the aubergine caviar. Preheat the oven to 200°C/400°F/ Gas Mark 6. Prick the aubergine all over with a fork and bake in the oven for 40 minutes or until soft. Cut the aubergine in half lengthways and scoop out the pulp. Put the pulp into a food processor or liquidizer together with the remaining caviar ingredients and purée until smooth. Season to taste and set aside.

Combine all the lentil salad ingredients in a bowl and season well.

Cut the chilled goats' cheese into four slices.

To serve, spoon a generous heap of lentil salad and aubergine caviar on to four large dinner plates. Top each plate with a round of goats' cheese and drizzle with olive oil and freshly ground black pepper. Garnish with fresh mint and serve with a wedge of warm pitta bread.

The flavours are evocative of the eastern Mediterranean. Continue the meal with barbecued or grilled fish or chicken, marinated with oil and herbs if you like, followed by fresh fruit served on crushed ice.

TINY SPINACH SOUFFLÉS

MAKES 8 SMALL SOUFFLÉS

25 g/1 oz butter or margarine, melted
2 tablespoons finely grated Parmesan cheese
500 g/1 lb 2 oz fresh spinach
2 eggs, separated, plus 2 egg whites
5 tablespoons grated Gruyère cheese
freshly grated nutmeg
salt and pepper

Béchamel sauce
25 g/1 oz butter
2 tablespoons flour
150 ml/5 fl oz milk

Preheat the oven to 180°C/350°F/Gas Mark 4. Brush the melted butter evenly inside 8 small soufflé dishes (9 cm/3½ inches diameter). Taking each dish in turn, sprinkle in some of the grated Parmesan, then roll the dish around until the inside is evenly coated. This will prevent the soufflé from sticking to the sides, and give it a delicate cheesy crust.

For the béchamel sauce, put the butter, flour and milk into a small, heavy-bottomed saucepan and beat continuously with a wire whisk over medium heat until the sauce thickens. Bring to the boil, now stirring with a wooden spoon, and simmer gently for 5–6 minutes to allow the flour to cook. Season to taste.

Wash the spinach thoroughly and cook it in just the water clinging to the leaves, until tender. Drain thoroughly by pressing it into a sieve. Chop it finely and add to the béchamel sauce. Remove from the heat, add the two egg yolks, stir in the Gruyère and season to taste with nutmeg, salt and pepper.

Put the four egg whites into a bowl and whisk until stiff. Gently fold into the sauce. Divide the mixture between the prepared soufflé dishes. Stand them in a tray of hot water and bake for 20–23 minutes, until well risen but still creamy in the centre. Serve at once.

Serve these classic French soufflés with garlic bread as a light supper for three or four people. Or serve them as a starter before penne with red and yellow pepper sauce (page 109), plus a stir-fry or a green salad. A lime sorbet would provide the perfect finale.

MUSHROOM AND PESTO TARTLETS

Preheat the oven to 220°C/425°F/Gas Mark 7. Grease four 15 cm/6 inch diameter flan tins with removable bases.

On a lightly floured surface, roll out the pastry to about 5 mm/¼ inch thick and cut into rounds about 1 cm/½ inch larger than the tins. Line the flan tins with the pastry, trim the edges and brush with beaten egg yolk. Spread a thin layer of pesto over the bottom of each pastry base.

Arrange the sliced mushrooms over the pastry, overlapping them and slanting them up around the edges. Brush liberally with olive oil, then sprinkle with the herbs and grind on some black pepper. Bake for 20–25 minutes, until the pastry is well risen and cooked through. Carefully remove the tartlets from the tins and eat as soon as possible, while they are fresh and crisp.

Serve as a first course for a supper party, followed by polenta with sun-dried tomatoes (page 159) and a green salad, and finish with a classic lemon meringue pie. Or, for lunch, serve with a mixed leaf salad and warm homemade bread.

SERVES 4

500 g/1 lb 2 oz puff pastry

1 egg yolk, beaten

6–8 teaspoons pesto (page 374)

8 brown mushrooms, thinly sliced

4 tablespoons virgin olive oil

2 tablespoons chopped fresh mixed herbs,
    or 1 tablespoon dried mixed herbs

salt and pepper

TWICE-BAKED GRUYÈRE SOUFFLÉS

SERVES 4

8 tablespoons dry grated Parmesan cheese
225 g/8 oz skimmed milk soft cheese
4 eggs, separated, plus 1 egg white
150 g/5 oz Gruyère cheese, grated
salt and pepper

Preheat the oven to 180°C/350°F/Gas Mark 4. Generously grease eight ramekins or tea cups, then sprinkle the insides with 4 tablespoons of the Parmesan.

Put the soft cheese into a bowl and mash it until smooth, then gradually mix in the egg yolks and half the grated Gruyère cheese. Using a clean, grease-free whisk, whisk the egg whites until they form firm peaks. Stir a heaped tablespoon of the beaten whites into the egg yolk mixture to loosen it, then gently fold in the rest of the egg whites.

Spoon the mixture into the ramekins or cups: it can come level with the top, but don't pile it up any higher. Stand them in a roasting tin, pour boiling water around them so that it comes half-way up the sides of the ramekins, then bake for 15 minutes, until the soufflés are risen and set.

Remove them from the oven and leave them to cool; they'll sink a bit. Then loosen the edges and turn them out; it's easiest to turn them out on to your hand. Transfer them to an ovenproof serving dish. Sprinkle each one first with the remaining Gruyère cheese, then with the rest of the Parmesan. They can now wait until you are ready to bake them.

To serve, preheat the oven to 220°C/425°F/Gas Mark 7. Bake the soufflés for 15–20 minutes, until they are puffed up and golden brown. Serve at once.

Serve these as a starter before a simple salad meal. Alternatively, for a main course, serve them with a fresh tomato sauce or tomato and basil salad and steamed green beans; follow with fresh fruit salad and thick yogurt.

DEEP-FRIED CAMEMBERT

with apricot sauce

SERVES 4

2 whole Camembert (250 g/9 oz each), not too ripe
2 eggs, beaten
125 g/4 oz dried breadcrumbs
225 g/8 oz apricot jam
juice of ½ lemon
vegetable oil for deep-frying
salad leaves for serving

If the Camembert is not the kind which has already been cut into sections, cut each cheese into six equal portions. Put the beaten eggs into a bowl, and the breadcrumbs in another. Dip the pieces of Camembert into the egg, then into the crumbs, to coat them evenly. Repeat the process so that they are really well coated. Chill them in the refrigerator for at least 30 minutes.

Put the apricot jam into a saucepan with the lemon juice and melt it over a very gentle heat.

To serve, heat the oil for deep-frying. To test that it is at the right temperature, dip the end of a wooden chopstick or wooden spoon into it: the oil should bubble immediately. Carefully lower some of the pieces of Camembert into the hot oil and fry for 4–5 minutes, until they are crisp and golden brown. Remove them with a slotted spoon and drain on crumpled kitchen paper. Keep them warm while you fry the rest, then serve immediately, with the apricot sauce and a salad garnish.

Serve as a first course before a vegetable or grain-based meal (such as risotto), or as a meal in itself, accompanied with a leafy green salad with a light dressing. Finish the meal with a refreshing pudding, for example a compote of fruits of the forest: strawberries, raspberries, redcurrants and blueberries.

CHA GIO

Vietnamese spring rolls

MAKES 25–30 ROLLS

200 g/7 oz sugar
25–30 dried rice papers
    (page 379)
peanut oil for frying

Filling
6 dried shiitake mushrooms,
    soaked in boiling water for
    30 minutes, finely chopped
25 g/1 oz cellophane (bean
    thread) noodles, soaked in hot
    water for 30 minutes, cut into
    2.5 cm/1 inch lengths
1 large chicken breast (about
    275 g/10 oz), chopped
275 g/10 oz uncooked prawns,
    shelled and coarsely chopped
125 g/4 oz minced pork
85 g/3 oz beansprouts, chopped
2–3 carrots, grated
1 onion, finely chopped
2–3 garlic cloves, finely chopped
4 tablespoons fish sauce
2 teaspoons sugar
½ teaspoon salt
pepper
3 eggs

To serve
plenty of soft-leaved lettuce,
    fresh coriander and mint
double quantity of chilli dipping
    sauce (page 375)

To make the filling, put the chopped mushrooms and noodles in a large bowl. Add all the remaining ingredients and mix thoroughly with your hands.

To assemble the rolls, fill a large bowl with 2 litres/3½ pints hot water and dissolve the sugar in it. Work with one sheet of rice paper at a time, keeping the remaining sheets covered with a barely damp cloth. Immerse the rice paper in the hot water, then quickly remove and lay it flat on a damp tea towel.

Fold up the bottom third of the rice paper. Place 4 tablespoons of filling in the centre of the folded-over portion. Shape the filling into a log about 15 cm/6 inches long. Fold in the right and left sides of the rice paper over the mixture. Roll up the rice paper from bottom to top to enclose the filling. Place the filled rolls, seam side down, in a single layer on a baking sheet. (These can be prepared ahead, covered and refrigerated.)

Preheat the oven to 120°C/250°F/Gas Mark ½. If possible, use two large frying pans to fry the rolls. Pour about 5 cm/2 inches of oil into each pan and heat to 165°C/330°F (well below smoking point). Add some rolls to each pan (do not crowd or they will stick together) and fry for 10–12 minutes, turning often, until crisp and browned. Drain on paper towels. Keep warm in the oven while you fry the remaining rolls.

To serve, cut each roll in half with a serrated knife. Wrap in a lettuce leaf, along with some coriander and mint, and dip into the chilli dipping sauce.

Serve as an appetizer, or as buffet food for a special occasion.

MARINATED VODKA SALMON

SERVES 4

225 g/8 oz salmon fillet in one piece, cut on a slant
   lengthways into very thin slices
salt and pepper
1 shallot, finely chopped
juice of 1 lemon
3 tablespoons vodka
2 tablespoons extra virgin olive oil
½ bunch of dill tips

Place the salmon slices on a large serving plate and season well.

In a bowl, mix together the shallot, lemon juice and vodka. Pour over the salmon and leave to marinate for 30 minutes.

To serve, drizzle the olive oil over the salmon and sprinkle with the dill tips. Serve at once with crispbreads or melba toasts.

Continue the meal with venison ragout and a purée of root vegetables, such as potato and celeriac.

PRAWNS, PESTO AND CORIANDER

SERVES 4

12 large uncooked prawns
3 tablespoons olive oil
4 tablespoons pesto (page 374)
small bunch of fresh coriander,
     finely chopped
salt and pepper

Shell and devein the prawns, leaving the tails on.

Heat a wok or large pan, then add the oil. When the oil is hot and begins to smoke, add the prawns, pesto and coriander and stir-fry for 30 seconds. Lower the heat and stir-fry for 2–3 minutes. Season to taste with salt and pepper. Serve immediately.

This makes a fabulous starter or a lunch dish served with rice or a green salad. Follow it with a fresh fruit salad, or cheese, grapes and strawberries.

OTAK OTAK

Grilled fish in banana leaf

MAKES 12

500 g/1 lb 2 oz fish fillet
3 dried red chillies, soaked
   and drained (page 378)
5 candlenuts or macadamia nuts
1 onion, grated
1 tablespoon blachan
   (dried shrimp paste)
1 teaspoon turmeric
1 egg, beaten
2 tablespoons coconut milk
1 tablespoon palm sugar
   or white sugar
1 teaspoon salt
4 banana leaves or 12 dried lotus
   leaves, soaked until pliable
vegetable oil for brushing

Using a fork, scrape the fish into fine flakes and place in a bowl, or briefly blend to a paste in a food processor. Add 4 tablespoons water, a tablespoon at a time, beating with a wooden spoon until it feels light and fluffy.

Pound or grind the drained chillies, nuts, onion, blachan and turmeric together to make a paste. Mix the paste with the fish, then add the egg and beat well. Add the coconut milk, sugar and salt.

Cut the banana leaves into 15 cm/6 inch squares and dip into boiling water for 2 minutes to soften them. Drain and pat dry. Place 2 tablespoons of the fish mixture in the centre of each square and roll up to form open-ended tubes. Fasten each end with a strong cocktail stick.

Heat the grill until very hot. Brush the banana leaves lightly with oil and grill for about 5 minutes on each side, until the leaves are slightly charred and the filling is firm when pressed.

Serve as an appetizer followed by a Malaysian curry, or as part of a shared meal with coconut rice (page 375), curries and sambals. Finish with thin crepes (kueh dadar) with a sweet coconut filling.

THAI SPICED CRAB AND POTATO CROQUETTES

SERVES

450 g/1 lb Desiree potatoes,
    very finely diced
50 g/2 oz butter
85 g/3 oz shallots, sliced
2 garlic cloves, crushed
4 eggs
2 tablespoons soy sauce
2 tablespoons Thai fish sauce
small bunch of coriander,
    chopped
½ teaspoon grated fresh ginger
juice of 2 limes
1–3 tablespoons sweet
    chilli sauce
salt and pepper
225 g/8 oz fresh white crabmeat
50 ml/2 fl oz milk
125 g/4 oz Japanese
    or dried breadcrumbs
85 g/3 oz plain flour
vegetable oil for deep-frying

Place the diced potatoes in a saucepan of cold salted water, bring to the boil, then turn down the heat and simmer until tender. Drain and return to the warm pan to dry thoroughly.

Meanwhile, melt the butter in a saucepan, add the shallots and garlic and cook over a low heat until soft but not browned.

Put the potatoes in a large bowl. Beat two of the eggs and add to the bowl, with the shallots and garlic, soy sauce, fish sauce, coriander, ginger, lime juice, chilli sauce and seasoning to taste. Mix together well, then add the crabmeat and mix in lightly but evenly. Chill in the refrigerator for 3–4 hours.

Beat the remaining eggs and milk together in a bowl and spread the breadcrumbs on a plate. Divide the potato mixture into twelve croquettes and coat each in flour. Dip the croquettes into the egg mixture to coat evenly, then coat in the breadcrumbs.

Heat the oil for deep-frying to 180–190°C/350–375°F or until a cube of bread browns in 30 seconds. Fry the croquettes until golden brown, drain on paper towels and serve hot, with a spicy tomato salsa.

Continue the Thai theme with a main course of salmon with coconut noodles, lemongrass and lime leaves, and a dessert of poached lychees.

CRAB TARTS
with ginger pistou

SERVES 4

325 g/12 oz shortcrust pastry
8 cm/3 inch piece of fresh ginger, chopped
3 tablespoons flat-leaf parsley, plus extra to garnish
1 tablespoon sunflower oil
325 g/12 oz white crabmeat (fresh or frozen)
2 egg yolks
4 tablespoons crème fraîche
salt and pepper

Oriental vinaigrette
3 tablespoons medium sherry
2 teaspoons finely chopped lemongrass
1 kaffir lime leaf (optional)
2 tablespoons dark soy sauce
1 garlic clove, finely chopped
1 green chilli, seeded and finely chopped
1 sprig of basil
juice of ½ lime
2 tablespoons fish sauce
3 tablespoons sunflower oil

Preheat the oven to 200°C/400°F/Gas Mark 6. Roll out the pastry and use to line four tartlet tins, 10 cm/4 inches in diameter. Bake blind, then reduce the oven temperature to 180°C/350°F/Gas Mark 4.

In a small food processor, blend the ginger, parsley and oil together until they form a paste. Spread on to the base of the tartlets. Flake the crab and place on top of the paste.

In a bowl, mix together the egg yolks and crème fraîche and season with black pepper. Spoon this mixture into the tarts and return to the oven for about 15 minutes or until just set.

For the vinaigrette, put the sherry, lemongrass, lime leaf, soy sauce, garlic, chilli and basil in a small saucepan and simmer gently for 2 minutes. Combine the lime juice, fish sauce and sunflower oil in a bowl and stir in the lemongrass mixture. Lift out the lime leaf and basil and season to taste.

To serve, place each tart in the centre of a large plate, scatter parsley leaves around the tart and spoon the warm dressing over the leaves. Serve at once.

Follow with more spicy Oriental flavours, such as stir-fried Sichuan beef.

TIAN OF CRAB AND GUACAMOLE

SERVES 4

100 ml/3½ fl oz groundnut or sunflower oil
1 stalk of lemongrass, peeled and chopped
2 egg yolks
salt and pepper
200 g/7 oz white crabmeat
½ Granny Smith apple, peeled and finely chopped
selection of salad leaves
1 tablespoon vinaigrette (page 373)

Guacamole

1 ripe avocado
2 teaspoons fresh lime juice
1 small spring onion, finely chopped
1 tomato, skinned, seeded and chopped
1 tablespoon chopped fresh coriander or parsley
pinch of ground cumin

Put the oil in a small saucepan, add the lemongrass and 50 ml/2 fl oz water and simmer for 5 minutes. Leave until cool, then strain the scented oil and water into a jug. Discard the lemongrass.

Whisk the egg yolks with a good pinch each of salt and pepper, then gradually trickle in the scented oil and water, whisking well until you have a thick mayonnaise. Alternatively, make the mayonnaise in a liquidizer or food processor. Set aside in the refrigerator.

Flake the crabmeat and mix with the apple and 1 tablespoon of the mayonnaise. Season well.

When nearly ready to serve, toss the salad leaves with the vinaigrette. Set aside while you make the guacamole. Peel, halve and stone the avocado, then mash the flesh with a fork to a chunky purée. Mix in the lime juice, spring onion, tomato, herbs, cumin and salt and pepper to taste. Spoon a quarter of the guacamole into a plain scone cutter in the centre of each of four dinner plates, then press the crab salad on top and lift off the cutter.

Arrange the dressed salad leaves around the edge. Stir the mayonnaise until it is smooth, then trail in a ribbon around the salad. Serve immediately.

Follow this pretty first course with noisettes of lamb and a gratin dauphinoise. Pudding could be a rich vanilla ice cream into which you have stirred some chopped prunes and Armagnac.

MEDITERRANEAN SQUID, SCALLOP AND CRAB SALAD

SERVES 4

5 tablespoons olive oil

5 shallots, chopped

4 tomatoes, skinned, seeded
  and chopped

150 ml/5 fl oz white wine

5–6 fresh basil leaves, chopped,
  plus extra to garnish

salt and pepper

vegetable oil for frying

6 small squid, cleaned and sliced

48 small 'queen' scallops

125 g/4 oz white crabmeat

1 small courgette

Heat the oil in a frying pan, add the shallots and sauté until soft. Add the tomatoes and white wine and simmer until all the liquid has evaporated. Add the chopped basil and season to taste with salt and pepper.

Heat the vegetable oil in a deep frying pan until very hot. Dip the squid and scallops into the hot oil a few at a time to seize them, but do not overcook. Lift out with a slotted spoon and drain on paper towels, then add to the tomato sauce. Add the crabmeat and chill.

Cut the courgette lengthways into ribbons, using a potato peeler. Reheat the oil and fry the courgette strips for a second or two; drain on paper towels.

Serve the seafood salad surrounded by courgette ribbons.

Follow with garlicky veal cutlets and mashed potatoes.

VERMOUTH MUSSELS
on fennel steaks

SERVES 4

900 g/2 lb fresh mussels
2 fennel bulbs, trimmed and thickly sliced
olive oil for brushing
salt and pepper
50 g/2 oz butter
150 ml/5 fl oz dry vermouth
1 garlic clove, crushed
1 bunch of flat-leaf parsley, roughly chopped

Clean the mussels by scrubbing well and rinsing in several changes of cold water. Pull away the 'beards' or seaweed-like threads and discard any mussels that are cracked or that do not close when tapped.

Steam the fennel for 10 minutes or until just tender. Dry well on paper towels. Brush generously with olive oil and season well. Heat a chargrill pan or heavy frying pan and fry the fennel for 8–10 minutes on each side until very brown.

Melt the butter in a large saucepan. Add the mussels, vermouth, garlic and half the parsley. Season well. Bring to a simmer, cover the pan with a tight-fitting lid and leave to steam over medium heat for 4–5 minutes or until the mussels' shells have opened. (Discard any mussels that remain closed.)

Arrange the fennel steaks on four serving plates and spoon the mussels with all their juices over the top. Scatter with the remaining parsley and serve at once.

Follow this with lamb meatballs with a mint and coriander sauce, then a raspberry pie served with crème fraîche.

SALAMI RAVIGOTTE

SERVES 4

225 g/8 oz Italian salami
2 tablespoons Greek black olives,
    pitted and roughly chopped
2 tablespoons baby caper berries
2 tablespoons virgin olive oil
1 shallot, very finely chopped
1 tablespoon fresh thyme leaves
juice of ½ lemon
pepper

Roasted tomatoes
25 g/1 oz butter, melted
1 plump garlic clove, crushed
½ teaspoon sugar
4 plum tomatoes, halved horizontally

Preheat the oven to 200°C/400°F/Gas Mark 6.

Arrange the salami on one large platter or four individual serving plates.

In a bowl combine the olives, capers, olive oil, shallot and thyme. Season with the lemon juice and black pepper. Set aside.

For the roasted tomatoes, combine the melted butter, garlic and sugar. Place the tomato halves on a baking sheet. Spoon the garlic butter over the tomatoes and place in the oven for 15–20 minutes, until softened and lightly charred, but still holding their shape.

To serve, spoon the olive mixture over the salami and serve at once with the warm tomatoes.

After this vibrant first course, I might serve a spinach and ricotta tart and a dessert of fresh dates with sweet white wine.

PAN-FRIED CHICKEN LIVERS

with caramelized red onions

SERVES 4

450 g/1 lb chicken livers, trimmed
300 ml/10 fl oz milk
2 red onions, halved and cut into wedges
3 tablespoons olive oil
25 g/1 oz butter
3 tablespoons brandy
½ baguette
1 bunch of watercress, washed

Place the chicken livers and milk in a bowl and leave to soak for 30 minutes.

Brush the onion wedges with olive oil and place under a low grill for about 15 minutes or until softened and lightly charred.

Drain the chicken livers and pat dry on paper towels. In a frying pan, heat the oil and butter until lightly foaming. Add the livers and fry for 3–4 minutes or until just cooked. Remove the pan from the heat and add the brandy.

Meanwhile, slice the baguette on a slant, allowing two slices per person. Lightly toast the slices and arrange on four plates.

To serve, top the baguette slices with the chicken livers and spoon over any pan juices. Garnish with watercress and wedges of grilled red onion.

A simple starter to prepare before a main course of roast guinea fowl with port gravy.

POTATO AND FOIE GRAS MILLE FEUILLES

SERVES 4

25 g/1 oz butter
2 tablespoons olive oil
175 g/6 oz shallots, sliced
1 teaspoon red wine vinegar
325 g/12 oz Maris Piper potatoes, finely grated
salt and pepper
4 tablespoons vegetable oil
400 g/14 oz fresh foie gras or chicken livers
225 g/8 oz mixed lettuce leaves
15 g/½ oz fresh black truffle, sliced (optional)

Garlic cream dressing
2 teaspoons brown sugar
3 teaspoons Dijon mustard
6 garlic cloves, crushed
85 ml/3 fl oz sherry vinegar
200 ml/7 fl oz olive oil
200 ml/7 fl oz peanut oil
85 ml/3 fl oz double cream
salt and pepper

Heat the butter and olive oil in a frying pan, add the shallots and cook until soft and browned. Add the vinegar and cook for a further 5 minutes.

Season the grated potatoes with salt and pepper. Place a 10 cm/4 inch diameter metal pastry cutter in a large frying pan. Heat the pan and trickle a little of the vegetable oil into the pastry cutter. Add some of the grated potato, to form a very thin layer. When the potato begins to colour, turn it over and cook lightly on the other side until crisp. Repeat this process to make 12 potato layers.

For the garlic cream dressing, put the sugar, mustard, garlic and vinegar in a mixing bowl and mix well until the sugar has dissolved. While beating vigorously, gently pour in the oils a little at a time until fully incorporated and emulsified. Finally whisk in the cream and beat well until smooth. Season to taste.

Slice the foie gras into eight pieces and sauté quickly over a high heat. Season lightly and remove from the pan.

To assemble the dish, place a potato layer on each plate, top with a teaspoon of shallots and then a piece of foie gras. Repeat, then top with a final layer of potato. Surround with lettuce leaves and truffle slices, then drizzle over the dressing.

A decadent starter to precede any dish, from a simple piece of seared salmon fillet to roast pigeon (ideally from Bresse) with fresh ceps.

BAKED NEW POTATOES
with smoked salmon, crème fraîche and caviar

SERVES 4

12 Jersey Royal or Roseval
    potatoes
225 g/8 oz sea salt
85 g/3 oz smoked salmon,
    cut into fine strips
85 g/3 oz crème fraîche
juice of ½ lemon
small bunch of chives,
    finely chopped
salt and pepper
85 g/3 oz caviar (optional)
sprigs of chervil

Preheat the oven to 200°C/400°F/Gas Mark 6.

Prick each potato two or three times with a fork, then wrap in foil. Spread the sea salt in an ovenproof dish, which should be just large enough to hold the potatoes in a single layer. Sit the wrapped potatoes on the salt, place in the oven and bake for about 45–55 minutes or until cooked through.

In a bowl, mix together the smoked salmon, crème fraîche, lemon juice and chives. Season to taste.

When the potatoes are cooked, remove from the dish and cut a cross in the top of each one. Mix the sea salt with 2–3 tablespoons water and divide this between four plates, as a base for the potatoes. Open up the potatoes and spoon in the smoked salmon mixture. Serve at once, topped with caviar and a sprig of chervil.

Serve as a starter or perhaps a light supper dish, followed by roast chicken with lemon and rosemary.

HONEYED DUCK

with papaya salsa

SERVES 4

1 tablespoon soy sauce
2 duck breasts, skin on
1 tablespoon clear honey
4 sprigs of basil

Papaya salsa
2 small papayas, peeled and diced
1 orange pepper, diced
½ bunch of spring onions, finely sliced
2 tablespoons olive oil
zest and juice 1 of orange
juice of ½ lime
salt and pepper

In a bowl, combine all the salsa ingredients together and set aside to allow the flavours to develop.

Preheat the grill to its highest setting.

Sprinkle the soy sauce over the duck skin and rub it in. Season with black pepper, then spread the skin with the honey. Reduce the grill to a medium heat and grill the breasts for 8–10 minutes or until the skin is browned and the duck is still slightly pink.

To serve, carve the duck breasts into thin slices and arrange on individual serving plates. Add a mound of fresh salsa and top with a sprig of basil.

Follow with a main course of salmon steaks with gingered lentils.

SMOOTH CHICKEN LIVER PÂTÉ
with Armagnac and sultanas

SERVES 4

40 g/1½ oz sultanas
3 tablespoons port
2 tablespoons Armagnac
350 g/13 oz chicken livers, trimmed
100 g/3½ oz unsalted butter, softened
85 ml/3 fl oz double cream, warmed
¼ teaspoon ground allspice
1 teaspoon salt
½ teaspoon pepper
50 g/2 oz butter, melted

Put the sultanas in a small bowl, warm the port and Armagnac together and pour over the sultanas. Leave to soak for 30 minutes.

Meanwhile, poach the livers in simmering salted water for a couple of minutes, until just bouncy and tight but not firm (lift one out with a slotted spoon to test); overcooking will result in grey pâté. Drain and tip into a food processor or liquidizer. Add the sultana soaking liquid, the softened butter, cream, allspice, salt and pepper and blend briefly, until smooth. Fold in the sultanas, then pour into a shallow dish and smooth the surface with a spatula. Cover with cling film and put into the refrigerator to chill for 30 minutes.

Remove the cling film and carefully spoon over the melted butter to seal. Return to the refrigerator for at least 6 hours or overnight. Eat within 48 hours, with hot toast.

Follow this rich first course with either a simple roast chicken cooked with tarragon or a handsome piece of baked cod with olive oil and fresh herbs. Serve with green beans and new potatoes.

SATAY AYAM

Chicken satay

**SERVES 8 AS A STARTER,
4 AS A MAIN COURSE**

500 g/1 lb 2 oz chicken thigh
    meat
6 shallots or 1 onion,
    finely chopped
1 garlic clove, crushed
1 tablespoon grated fresh ginger
1 stalk of lemongrass,
    peeled and sliced
1 tablespoon brown sugar
    or palm sugar
½ teaspoon salt
1 teaspoon turmeric
1 teaspoon ground cumin
1 teaspoon ground coriander
200 ml/7 fl oz coconut milk

To serve
peanut sauce or
    sweet chilli sauce

Sambal satay (peanut sauce)
1 tablespoon tamarind pulp
    (page 379)
200 g/7 oz roasted peanuts
4 dried red chillies, soaked and
    drained (page 378)
4 shallots, roughly chopped
2 garlic cloves, crushed
4 candlenuts or macadamia nuts
1 stalk of lemongrass,
    peeled and sliced
2 tablespoons vegetable oil
250 ml/8 fl oz coconut milk
2 tablespoons palm or
    brown sugar
1 teaspoon salt

Soak 20–24 bamboo skewers in cold water for 4–5 hours to prevent them from burning.

Cut the chicken into thin strips about 5 cm/2 inches long and 2 cm/¾ inch wide.

Grind, pound or blend the shallots or onion, garlic, ginger and lemongrass together, then add the sugar, salt, turmeric, cumin, coriander and coconut milk and mix until smooth. Marinate the chicken pieces in the coconut mixture for at least 2 hours or overnight.

For the peanut sauce, soak the tamarind in 2 tablespoons boiling water for 10 minutes, then squeeze and knead until dissolved. Strain the tamarind water and set aside. Pound the peanuts in a mortar or whizz in a food processor until finely ground. Pound, grind or blend the drained chillies, shallots, garlic, nuts and lemongrass together to make a paste. Heat the oil in a wok or heavy-bottomed saucepan and fry the chilli paste for 3 minutes. Add the coconut milk and bring to the boil, stirring constantly. Add the tamarind water, ground peanuts, sugar and salt to taste and cook for 5 minutes. If too thick, thin with up to 250 ml/8 fl oz water.

Thread two or three strips of chicken on to each bamboo skewer, being sure to cover the pointed end. Heat a lightly oiled grill until very hot: satay is at its best cooked outside over glowing charcoal, the coals fanned to create even more smoke to flavour the meat.

Grill the satay on both sides until golden, brushing with the marinade while grilling. Serve hot, with peanut sauce or sweet chilli sauce for dipping.

Serve as an appetizer or a main course, accompanied by plates of chilled cucumber and steamed rice. Finish the meal with fresh, ripe mangoes or a refreshing mango and yogurt lassi.

DUCK 'HAM' AND BLACK FIG SALAD

SERVES 4

1–2 magrets of duck
3 tablespoons brandy
salt and pepper
8 figs

Put the duck breasts in a bowl, add the brandy and turn the breasts until well moistened. Sprinkle with crushed sea salt and grind on some black pepper. Cover and refrigerate for 24–36 hours.

Place the duck breasts on a wire rack and leave in a cold oven with the fan operating for 3 hours or until a dry skin has formed on the meat. Alternatively, you could leave them on a rack in a cool, well-ventilated larder, blowing a cold hair-drier on them from time to time. Wrap them individually in muslin and hang them in a cool but not chilled place to dry for 10–14 days. The thicker the duck breast, the more moisture it will retain once it is dried, but there will be some shrinkage.

To serve, cut the figs across three times to make a flower shape, and sprinkle with salt and pepper. Slice the duck 'hams' very thinly and serve like Parma ham.

Serve as a first course, followed by osso bucco Milanaise.

GA LUI

Skewered five-spice chicken

MAKES 48 SKEWERS

8 boned and skinned chicken breasts (about 900 g/
    2 lb), trimmed and halved

Marinade

1 shallot, chopped

3 large garlic cloves, chopped

1 thick stalk of lemongrass, peeled and thinly sliced

2 tablespoons sugar

½ teaspoon chilli paste

1 tablespoon fish sauce

1 tablespoon soy sauce

1 tablespoon sesame seed oil

2 tablespoons peanut or vegetable oil

1 teaspoon five-spice powder

To serve

chilli dipping sauce (page 375)

Place all the ingred[...]
liquidizer or food p[...] blend until
finely puréed. Transfer to a large mixing bowl.

Cut each of the chicken breasts lengthways into
four strips. Lightly pound the strips to 1 cm/
½ inch thick, using a meat mallet or the flat side
of a cleaver. Cut the strips in half and add them
to the marinade. Toss well to coat all the strips
thoroughly, then cover and leave to marinate at
room temperature for 1 hour, or overnight in
the refrigerator.

Soak 48 bamboo skewers in salted hot water for
30 minutes.

Prepare the barbecue or preheat the grill. Thread
a slice of chicken on to each skewer.

Grill the skewers, turning once, until the chicken
is browned on both sides and cooked through,
about 3−4 minutes. Serve immediately, passing
the chilli dipping sauce separately.

*Serve as an appetizer, or as a main course as part of a
family meal. Accompany with steamed rice, a sautéed
vegetable such as green beans, and a bowl of soup.*

MAHARAJAH SHEEK KEBAB

Mince kebabs

SERVES 4 AS A STARTER

600 g/1¼ lb lean beef, lamb, pork or venison,
   or skinless chicken, turkey or duck breast
4–6 garlic cloves, chopped
2 tablespoons dried onion flakes
1 tablespoon garam masala
2 teaspoons bottled mild curry paste
1–3 fresh green chillies, seeded and chopped
   (optional)
2 tablespoons chopped fresh coriander leaves
1 tablespoon chopped fresh mint leaves
1 teaspoon salt

Preheat the oven to 190°C/375°F/Gas Mark 5.

Chop the meat into cubes, removing all fat
and gristle. Place the meat and all the other
ingredients in a food processor and pulse-grind
until the mixture becomes relatively smooth.

Divide the mixture into four large or eight small
pieces, then shape each piece into a sausage. If
you wish, form the sausage shapes on skewers.

Place on a baking sheet and bake for 10–12
minutes. Serve hot or cold.

*Serve with fresh, crisp baguettes, lime wedges and
a salad of shredded spinach, rocket, radicchio,
spring onion and celeriac, tossed with a dressing of 4
tablespoons olive oil mixed with 6 tablespoons Greek-
style yogurt and ½ teaspoon each of chilli and mango
powder, with some chopped garlic and fresh chives.*

MOO SHI PORK

SERVES 3–4, OR 5–6 AS PART OF A MULTI-COURSE MEAL

150 g /5 oz lean pork, shredded

2 teaspoons rice wine

2 tablespoons light soy sauce

1 teaspoon cornflour

25 g/1 oz dried golden needles, soaked and drained
(page 378)

3–4 dried wood ears soaked and drained
(page 379)

3 tablespoons groundnut or corn oil

4 eggs, beaten

1 slice of fresh ginger

2 spring onions (green and white parts), thinly sliced

150 g /5 oz bamboo shoots, shredded

½ teaspoon salt

To serve

9–12 Mandarin pancakes (page 378), steamed

hoisin sauce

Mix the pork with the rice wine, soy sauce and cornflour. Set aside.

Trim off the tough ends of the golden needles and any tough parts of the wood ears. Cut the golden needles in half and coarsely chop the wood ears. Set aside.

Heat 2 tablespoons of the oil in a wok over medium-high heat. When the oil is hot, add the eggs and cook for about 2 minutes, stirring constantly, until scrambled finely. Remove and set aside.

Pour the remaining oil into the wok over high heat. Add the ginger and stir a few times until it sizzles. Stir the pork mixture and add it to the wok, stirring a few times to separate the shreds, then add the spring onions, bamboo shoots, wood ears, golden needles and salt. Continue stirring over high heat until the vegetables are heated through and the pork is thoroughly cooked, about 2–3 minutes. Return the eggs to the wok and mix well. Serve hot, with steamed pancakes and hoisin sauce.

This classic Peking dish is a fabulous appetizer or a meal in itself. Instead of the pancakes, it could be served with steamed or boiled rice.

SALADS

The urge to entertain,
to open our doors to our friends
and to give them
the best fare we can provide
is deep and good.

DESMOND BRIGGS

FLOWER POWER

SERVES 4–6

a selection of edible flowers (chive, lavender,
   thyme, borage, strawberry, viola, nasturtium,
   fennel, marigold)
a selection of leaves (fennel, tarragon, chervil,
   nasturtium, flat-leaf parsley)
200 g/7 oz mixed baby salad leaves

Dressing
2 tablespoons clear honey
4 tablespoons grapeseed oil
2 tablespoons white wine vinegar
chopped fresh tarragon or chervil
salt and pepper

Mix together all the ingredients for the mustard-free vinaigrette and season to taste.

Divide up the flower heads of chive, lavender and thyme into individual florets. Borage, strawberry and viola can be left whole, the others torn into petals.

Arrange the leaves and flowers in a bowl and serve the dressing separately.

Serve as an accompaniment to any light summer meal such as poached salmon with sorrel sauce.

FRISÉE AUX LARDONS

Salad of curly endive with hot bacon dressing

SERVES 4 AS A FIRST COURSE, 2 AS A MAIN COURSE

a large head (about 450 g/1 lb) curly endive
    or escarole
1 tablespoon vegetable oil
175 g/6 oz thickly sliced lean smoked bacon, diced
2 garlic cloves, thinly sliced
5 tablespoons red wine vinegar
freshly ground black pepper

Discard the tough outer green leaves from the curly endive or escarole and pull apart the central white leaves. Wash, dry well and put them in a salad bowl.

Just before serving, heat the oil in a frying pan, add the bacon and fry, stirring often. When the bacon is well browned and the fat is rendered, lower the heat and discard some fat if you have more than 3–4 tablespoons. Add the garlic and cook until the garlic is soft and fragrant but not browned, about 30 seconds. Pour the hot fat, bacon and garlic over the leaves and toss thoroughly so they wilt slightly.

Return the pan to the heat, add the vinegar and boil for a few seconds, until reduced by half, stirring to dissolve the pan juices. Pour them over the salad and toss again. Add pepper to taste and spoon the salad on to warmed individual plates or bowls. Serve at once.

Fried croûtons, walnuts or a poached egg are optional additions.

This salad is the classic start to a winter meal. For a main course, look no further than coq au vin, boeuf bourguignon or blanquette de veau, with fresh noodles or boiled rice. I would add a traditional dessert such as floating island, crème caramel or chocolate mousse to finish a nostalgic menu which is right back in style.

ROQUEFORT, PEAR AND WALNUT SALAD

SERVES 4

2 sweet ripe pears such
　　as Comice
juice of ½ lemon
85 g/3 oz washed and
　　prepared watercress
200 g/7 oz Roquefort cheese
12 walnuts, cracked and
　　shells removed

Peel, quarter and core the pears, then cut them into long thin slices and sprinkle with the lemon juice. Arrange the slices of pear on a serving platter or on four individual plates, together with the watercress. Slice the cheese or break it into pieces and add to the plates, along with the walnuts. Serve at once.

Alternatively, you can put all the ingredients into a salad bowl – a glass one is nice – and toss them together lightly.

Serve as a first course before a meal of grilled fish or, for vegetarians, puréed white beans with grilled red and yellow peppers, new potatoes and green salad.

GAZPACHO SALAD

SERVES 4–6

4 ripe plum tomatoes, diced
175 g/6 oz red seedless grapes, halved
¼ cucumber, finely chopped
1 red pepper, finely chopped
juice of 1 lemon
2 teaspoons chilli sauce or to taste
salt and pepper

To serve
225 g/8 oz curd cheese
1 tablespoon plain yogurt
2 tablespoons fresh basil leaves
granary toast

In a bowl, combine all the salad ingredients together, season well and set aside.

Beat the curd cheese with the yogurt and season with black pepper. Spread the cheese mixture over the base of four serving plates. Spoon the gazpacho salad over the cheese, scatter with the basil leaves and serve with crisp granary toast.

Keep to the Spanish theme with a main course of paella or any hot shellfish dish.

SALADS

PEAR AND PEAR SALAD

SERVES 4

1 large or 2 small ripe avocados, sliced
mixed baby salad leaves
4 tablespoons olive oil
175 g/6 oz smoked bacon, diced
1 tablespoon white wine vinegar
2 teaspoons wholegrain mustard
1 large or 2 small ripe dessert pears, cored and sliced
salt and pepper

Arrange the avocado slices and some salad leaves on four large serving plates.

In a large frying pan, heat the olive oil. Add the bacon and fry until crisp. Add the vinegar, mustard and pear slices to the pan, season to taste and briefly heat through. Spoon the bacon and pears over the salad leaves and avocado and serve at once.

Wild mushroom risotto would be the perfect main course after this starter. Finish with some Brie or Roquefort cheese.

AVOCADO, BASIL, FETA AND TOMATO SALAD

SERVES 6

4 tomatoes, skinned, seeded and diced
8–10 basil leaves, shredded
100 g/3½ oz feta cheese, diced
2–3 avocados

Dressing
½ tablespoon Dijon mustard
1 tablespoon red wine vinegar
4 tablespoons olive oil
pinch or two of sugar
salt and pepper

Mix the ingredients for the dressing together and season to taste.

Season the tomatoes lightly. Mix the tomatoes with the basil and feta and chill.

When you are nearly ready to serve, cut the avocados in half, remove the stones and peel, then slice or dice the flesh. Coat them with the dressing and then gently fold into the tomato mixture with as much of the dressing as necessary to coat well. Chill for up to 30 minutes – no longer or the avocado will blacken.

This makes a delicious light lunch, accompanied by crusty bread and a glass of white wine, followed with fresh fruit.

CUCUMBER AND CHICKEN SHREDS
in spicy peanut sauce

SERVES 4 AS PART OF A MULTI-COURSE MEAL

2 cucumbers (about 450 g/1 lb)
4 tablespoons smooth peanut butter
4 tablespoons chicken stock
1 tablespoon light soy sauce
¼ teaspoon Sichuan peppercorns,
    toasted and ground
1 tablespoon sesame seed oil
1 teaspoon dried chilli flakes, or to taste
125 g/4 oz cooked chicken, shredded
salt
50 g/2 oz dry-roasted unsalted peanuts,
    coarsely chopped

Partially peel the cucumbers, leaving alternate strips of green skin for colour and texture. Cut the cucumbers in half lengthways, then scoop out and discard the seeds. Cut the cucumbers on the diagonal into thin slices.

In a small bowl, combine the peanut butter, stock, soy sauce, Sichuan pepper, sesame seed oil and chilli flakes. Mix to a smooth, thin paste.

When ready to serve, toss the cucumber slices and shredded chicken together with the peanut dressing and add salt to taste. Sprinkle with the chopped peanuts.

Perfect by itself as a light lunch salad, with slices of crusty bread.

NOM GIA

Beansprouts and crabmeat salad

SERVES 6 AS A STARTER OR ABOUT 40 AS A BUFFET DISH

1 large garlic clove,
   finely chopped
2 fresh red chillies,
   finely chopped
1 tablespoon sugar
1 tablespoon fresh lime juice
1 tablespoon rice vinegar
   or distilled white vinegar
3 tablespoons fish sauce
2 tablespoons peanut
   or vegetable oil
1 carrot, shredded
1 small cucumber, peeled,
   halved lengthways, seeded
   and thinly sliced
1 teaspoon salt
450 g/1 lb fresh beansprouts
325 g/12 oz fresh or canned
   crabmeat, well picked over
4 tablespoons coarsely chopped
   fresh coriander leaves
2 tablespoons coarsely ground
   roasted peanuts
2 tablespoons coarsely ground
   toasted sesame seeds

Whisk together the garlic, chillies, sugar, lime juice, vinegar, fish sauce and oil in a small mixing bowl. Set aside.

Toss the carrot and cucumber in a colander with the salt, and leave to stand for 15 minutes. Rinse under cold running water and squeeze dry with your hands (it is very important that the vegetables are completely dry to ensure that they remain crunchy).

Place the carrot and cucumber in a large bowl and add the remaining ingredients. Pour the dressing over the salad and toss until well combined.

This salad is excellent for parties. Serve with prawn crackers (page 379), so that bite-sized portions of the salad can be picked up on the crackers and eaten with the hands. Follow with sticky rice and chicken (page 221) or beef curry (page 254).

SAFFRON POTATOES
with orange segments and pickled walnuts

SERVES 4–6

large pinch of saffron strands
300 g/11 oz waxy new potatoes
2–3 sweet pickled walnuts, sliced
½ bunch spring onions, sliced on the diagonal
1 orange, segmented without pith or skin
1 tablespoon hazelnut oil
baby salad leaves
2 small heads of chicory, quartered
2 tablespoons white of leek, finely sliced

Dressing
½ tablespoon Dijon mustard
1 tablespoon white wine vinegar
6 tablespoons groundnut or grapeseed oil
salt and pepper

Mix the ingredients for the dressing together and season to taste.

Simmer the saffron strands in 300 ml/10 fl oz water to infuse. Scrape the skins from the potatoes and parboil them in plenty of boiling salted water. Drain and finish cooking them in the saffron water (leaving the strands in) until it is all absorbed. While the potatoes are still warm, mix them with the dressing and leave to cool. Chill overnight if possible.

To serve, slice the potatoes into rounds, add the walnuts, spring onions, orange segments and hazelnut oil. Pile on to a plate and surround with salad leaves and chicory. Scatter the leek rings over the salad.

Serve with cold roast beef and follow with a raspberry roulade or pavlova.

SALADE CAUCHOISE

Potato and ham salad

SERVES 4

300 g/11 oz new potatoes
1 garlic clove, crushed
85 g/3 oz ham, cut into strips
1 fennel bulb or
   2–3 sticks of celery, chopped
150 ml/5 fl oz double cream
½ lemon
½ bunch of spring onions, sliced
3 black olives, chopped

Dressing

½ tablespoon Dijon mustard
1 tablespoon white wine vinegar
6 tablespoons grapeseed oil
salt and pepper

Mix the ingredients for the dressing together and season to taste.

Boil the potatoes (with or without their skins) until just tender, then drain well. While the potatoes are still warm, mix them with the dressing and leave to cool.

Cut the potatoes into chunks and add the garlic, ham and fennel or celery.

Add the cream and some salt and pepper and mix well. Add a squeeze of lemon juice and mix very lightly, otherwise the cream will separate. Mix the spring onions with the olives and scatter over the salad.

Serve as an accompaniment to a duck terrine, or with cold roast pork with crackling. Follow with a hot apple charlotte and custard.

SALAD OF SCALLOPS

with truffle vinaigrette

SERVES 4

12 new potatoes
selection of salad leaves
2 tablespoons simple vinaigrette (page 373)
olive oil for frying
12 large fresh scallops, cleaned, corals discarded

Truffle vinaigrette
4 egg yolks
salt and pepper
250 ml/9 fl oz groundnut or sunflower oil
2 tablespoons truffle oil
2 tablespoons truffle essence (optional)
4 teaspoons white wine vinegar
2 teaspoons finely chopped fresh truffle

Boil the potatoes until just tender, about 12 minutes. Leave to cool slightly, then peel and slice. Set aside.

To make the truffle vinaigrette, blend the yolks, salt and pepper in a liquidizer or food processor until thick and pale. With the machine still running, slowly trickle in the groundnut oil until you have a creamy sauce. Trickle in the truffle oil, truffle essence, if using, and vinegar. If the texture is too thick, adjust with a little hot water. Transfer to a jug and stir in the chopped truffles.

Toss the salad leaves with the simple vinaigrette. Place small mounds of the leaves in the centre of four dinner plates.

Heat a little olive in a frying pan and fry the potato slices, turning once or twice, until browned. Remove and keep warm.

Wipe out the pan with paper towels. Add a little more oil and heat until very hot, just below smoking point. Add the scallops and fry for about 2 minutes on each side, until just caramelized. Do not overcook: they should feel slightly springy. Season well.

Arrange the potatoes and scallops around the salad leaves, then trickle over the truffle vinaigrette. Serve immediately.

A main course of plain roast chicken, green beans and a light creamy sauce would be good after the scallop salad. For dessert, make a crème brûlée flavoured with orange zest and serve with sliced strawberries.

FRESH TUNA SALAD

with white radish and balsamic vinaigrette

SERVES 4

300 g/11 oz loin of fresh tuna, in one piece
juice of 1 lime
grated zest of 1 small orange and 1 lemon
1 teaspoon coriander seeds, lightly crushed
salt and pepper
1 large white radish (also sold as mooli or daikon)
2 tablespoons simple vinaigrette (page 373)
1 teaspoon lemon juice
selection of salad leaves

Balsamic vinaigrette
5 tablespoons olive oil
1 teaspoon Dijon mustard
1 tablespoon balsamic vinegar

Place the tuna loin in a food bag with the lime juice, orange and lemon zest, coriander seeds and ½ teaspoon salt. Rub well together, then leave to marinate in the refrigerator for 2 hours, turning the bag occasionally.

Remove the tuna, rinse in cold water and pat dry. Wrap in cling film to form a tight roll, then freeze for about 15 minutes to firm the flesh slightly.

Meanwhile, peel the white radish and slice very thinly, preferably on a mandolin. Toss the slices with the simple vinaigrette, lemon juice and salt.

Make the balsamic vinaigrette by whisking all the ingredients together. Season to taste.

Place small mounds of salad leaves in the centre of four dinner plates and arrange the dressed radish slices in a circle around the leaves.

Remove the tuna from the freezer, unwrap and cut into wafer-thin slices, using a very sharp long knife. Lay the tuna slices over the radish.

Whisk the balsamic vinaigrette and swirl in a ribbon around the tuna. Serve immediately.

This makes a good starter, to be followed by a main course of tagliatelle with a wild mushroom sauce flavoured with a trickle of truffle oil. For dessert, serve a selection of red berry fruits sprinkled with sugar and lightly browned under a hot grill accompanied by a Champagne sabayon sauce.

SEARED GARLIC, LEMON AND CHILLI CHICKEN WITH PARMESAN

SERVES 4 AS A STARTER

2 large boneless chicken breasts, skinned
coarsely grated zest of 1 lemon
2 teaspoons chilli oil
2 teaspoons olive oil
1 garlic clove, very finely chopped
1 red chilli, seeded and very finely chopped
salt and pepper
2 tablespoons sunflower oil
juice of ½ lemon
25 g/1 oz Parmesan cheese, shaved

Tomato and chive dressing
6 tablespoons olive oil
2 tablespoons fresh lemon juice
2 plum tomatoes, skinned, seeded and finely diced
1 tablespoon chopped fresh chives

Salad of fresh herbs
50 g/2 oz sugar snap peas, each cut into 3 or 4 pieces
small bunch each of fresh flat-leaf parsley, tarragon,
   chives and rocket

Remove the little fillet from the underside of each chicken breast. Cut the breasts into very thin slices and cut each fillet into three. You should end up with 25–30 pieces of chicken. Mix the lemon zest, chilli oil, olive oil, garlic, red chilli and some salt and pepper in a bowl. Stir in the chicken and marinate for 3–6 hours.

For the dressing, whisk together the oil, lemon juice and some seasoning. Spoon out 2 teaspoons of the mixture and set aside. Stir the diced tomatoes and chives into the remainder.

Heat a frying pan until very hot. Add the sunflower oil and the chicken (in batches if necessary) and stir-fry over high heat for a few minutes until browned. Sprinkle over the lemon juice and some seasoning, shake the pan over high heat for a second or two, then set aside.

To serve, toss the sugar snap peas and the mixed fresh herbs with the reserved dressing to coat the leaves lightly. Pile into the centre of four large plates. Place the chicken around the edge of the salad and spoon over the tomato and chive dressing. Scatter the Parmesan shavings over the chicken and serve immediately.

After this vibrant starter, serve steamed fillet of cod with spinach, chive mashed potatoes and a rich butter sauce, and a passion fruit cream dessert.

SALAD OF GREEN LENTILS
with quails' eggs

SERVES 4–6

olive oil for frying
2 slices of white bread, cut into cubes
8 slices of smoked streaky bacon
350 g/13 oz carrots, boiled in their skins
200 g/7 oz Puy lentils, cooked until just tender
5–6 fresh sage leaves, chopped
6 quails' eggs, hard-boiled, shelled and halved

Dressing
1 teaspoon Dijon mustard
1 tablespoon red wine vinegar
6 tablespoons olive oil
large pinch of sugar
salt and pepper

Mix the ingredients for the dressing together and season to taste.

Heat the olive oil in a frying pan, add the cubes of bread and fry until golden, then drain on paper towels.

Grill the bacon until dry and crisp, then crumble. Peel the carrots and finely dice. Put the lentils, sage, bacon and carrots in a bowl and mix with the dressing.

When you are nearly ready to serve, add the croûtons and decorate with the quails' eggs.

This is a substantial starter, or serve as an accompaniment to grilled gammon with french beans.

PASTA AND NOODLES

I like all simple things, boiled eggs, oysters
and caviare, truite au bleu, grilled salmon,
roast lamb (the saddle by preference),
cold grouse, treacle tart and rice pudding.
But of all simple things, the only one
I can eat day in and day out, not only
without disgust but with the eagerness of
an appetite unimpaired by excess, is macaroni.

SOMERSET MAUGHAM
FROM *THE HAIRLESS MEXICAN*

COOKING PASTA

It is easy to cook pasta, but it can be spoiled by carelessness. Pasta needs to be cooked in a large saucepan and a lot of water – about 1 litre/1¾ pints for 100 g/3½ oz pasta. Bring the water to the boil and then add salt – about 1½ tablespoons for 4 litres/7 pints water, which is the quantity needed for 300–450 g/11 oz–1 lb pasta. Slide all the pasta into the boiling water, stir with a wooden fork or spoon to separate the pasta shapes, and cover so that the water returns to the boil as soon as possible. Remove the lid and adjust the heat so that the water boils briskly, but does not boil over. The pasta is ready when it is *al dente*, which means that it offers some resistance to the bite. It is unnecessary to add cold water to pasta after cooking it. The timing of cooking varies according to shapes; all fresh pasta cooks more quickly than dried pasta.

DRAINING PASTA

Pasta should be drained as soon as it is *al dente*. However, if the pasta is going to be cooked further, by baking or frying, or if it is going to be served cold, drain it when slightly undercooked.

It is important to drain pasta properly. Use a colander that is large enough to contain all the pasta. Tip the pasta in, give the colander two or three sharp shakes and immediately turn the pasta into a heated bowl or dish, into the frying pan with the sauce or back into the saucepan in which it has cooked. Penne, gnocchi or any shapes that are hollow need more draining because water may be trapped in the hollows. However, pasta should never be overdrained, as it needs to be slippery for coating with the sauce.

Many Italians do not use a colander for long pasta. The strands are lifted out of the pan with two long forks and kept in the air for only a few seconds for the excess water to run off. All pasta must be dressed as soon as it is ready. A few tablespoons of the water in which the pasta has cooked are added for some types of thick sauces, such as pesto or carbonara.

PASTA SALAD
with truffle oil, Parmesan and trompettes de la mort

SERVES 4

50 g/2 oz fresh or 7 g/¼ oz dried trompettes
  de la mort (horn of plenty mushrooms)
½ lemon
2 tablespoons truffle oil
1–2 tablespoons grapeseed oil
salt and pepper
150 g/5 oz dried farfalle
15 g/½ oz Parmesan cheese, shaved in curls

If using dried mushrooms, soak in cold water for 1–2 hours, then drain and check that no sand or dirt remains. Place in a saucepan with as little water as possible, acidulated with a small squeeze of lemon juice. Bring to the boil, then simmer until tender. Drain, reserving the cooking liquid. Return the liquid to the pan and boil to reduce to a couple of teaspoons. Add the truffle oil.

If using fresh mushrooms, trim the stalks and clean with a brush. Rinse them only if they are dirty, then cut into pieces if they are large. Sauté in a little grapeseed oil, adding salt and pepper. When cooked, add the truffle oil.

Cook the pasta in plenty of boiling salted water until just tender but still firm to the bite (*al dente*). Drain, coat with a little grapeseed oil, then leave to cool but do not chill.

Mix the mushrooms with the pasta, season well and garnish with curls of Parmesan.

Serve as a first course, followed by breadcrumbed escalopes of veal with asparagus.

PAPPARDELLE CON FUNGHI

Pappardelle with mushrooms

SERVES 4

200 g/7 oz fresh mixed wild mushrooms
    (e.g. porcini/ceps, chanterelles) or 175 g/6 oz
    brown cap mushrooms and 15 g/½ oz dried porcini
4 tablespoons extra virgin olive oil
1 onion, finely chopped
2 garlic cloves, chopped
125 ml/4 fl oz chicken stock
1 glass of dry white wine or dry vermouth
225 g/8 oz dried pappardelle
1 teaspoon balsamic vinegar
2 tablespoons finely chopped flat-leaf parsley
salt and pepper

To serve
freshly grated Parmesan cheese

Brush any soil from the mushrooms and wipe with a damp cloth. Finely slice the porcini or brown caps, keep small chanterelles whole and cut larger ones in half. If using dried mushrooms, rinse them under a running tap, then soak in warm water for 20 minutes. Remove from the soaking liquid, reserving the liquid, and roughly chop. Carefully strain the liquid, leaving behind any gritty deposits.

Heat the olive oil in a wide saucepan, add the onion and sauté for 5 minutes. Add the garlic and sauté for a further 2 minutes; do not let the garlic colour. Add the porcini or brown cap mushrooms and sauté for 5 minutes.

If using only fresh mushrooms, add the more delicate mushrooms and cook for a further 3 minutes. Add the stock and wine, bring to the boil, then simmer to reduce to a light coating consistency.

Alternatively, add the soaked dried mushrooms, soaking liquid, stock, wine and 100 ml/3½ fl oz water to the sautéed brown caps. Simmer, covered, for 20 minutes or until the dried mushrooms are tender.

To serve, cook the pasta (page 103). Sprinkle the balsamic vinegar over the mushrooms. Heat through for a couple of minutes, then add the parsley and season to taste. Toss with the cooked, drained pasta and serve with Parmesan.

Follow with grilled spatchcocked quail that has been marinated with garlic, lemon zest, chilli and herbs, or roast guinea fowl.

FLAT MUSHROOMS ON LINGUINE

SERVES 4

4 large flat mushrooms, wiped
    and stalks removed
40 g/1½ oz butter, melted
salt and pepper
175 g/6 oz fresh linguine
    or fine spaghetti
1 tablespoon walnut oil
2 tablespoons roughly chopped
    flat-leaf parsley

Roquefort sauce
125 g/4 oz Roquefort cheese
3 tablespoons fromage frais
juice of ½ orange
½ tablespoon wholegrain mustard

Preheat the grill to its highest setting.

Place the mushrooms, gills side down, on a chopping board and slice through each mushroom, but do not separate the slices. Using a fish slice or palette knife, carefully transfer the mushrooms on to a baking sheet. Using the palm of your hand, gently flatten each mushroom to fan the slices. Spoon over the melted butter and season well. Grill the mushrooms for 6–8 minutes or until tender and golden brown.

Meanwhile, cook the pasta (page 103). In a small bowl, blend the Roquefort, fromage frais, orange juice and mustard until smooth. Season to taste.

Drain the pasta well and toss with the walnut oil and parsley. Using a large spoon and fork, twist the pasta into four portions on individual plates. Top each pile of pasta with a fanned mushroom and a generous spoonful of the Roquefort sauce. Serve at once.

This would be a good prelude to a supper of chicken roasted with lemons and thyme, accompanied by a crisp green herby salad.

LINGUINE PRIMAVERA

Linguine with spring vegetables

Heat the olive oil in a saucepan, add the garlic and sauté for 1 minute. Discard the garlic.

Cook the pasta (page 103). Steam the carrots for 2 minutes. Add the beans and steam for a further 2 minutes. Add the courgettes and cook for 1 minute.

Mix the pesto with the garlic-infused oil, a generous squeeze of lemon juice, salt and pepper. Add the hot vegetables and stir to coat. Add the cooked, drained pasta and toss well. Serve with Parmesan.

Follow with fresh prawns sautéed in olive oil with garlic and parsley.

SERVES 4

3 tablespoons extra virgin olive oil

1 garlic clove, chopped

150 g/5 oz dried linguine

3 carrots, shredded

125 g/4 oz fine green beans, topped and tailed, halved lengthways if thick

3 courgettes, shredded

1 tablespoon pesto (page 374)

½ lemon

salt and pepper

To serve

freshly grated Parmesan cheese

PENNE WITH RED AND YELLOW PEPPER SAUCE

SERVES 4

2 large red peppers, quartered, stalks removed,
    seeded
2 large yellow peppers, quartered, stalks removed,
    seeded
200 ml/7 fl oz crème fraîche
500 g/1 lb 2 oz dried penne
1 tablespoon finely chopped fresh coriander

To serve
freshly grated Parmesan cheese

First, skin the peppers. You can either place them under a hot grill, skin-side up, until the skin blisters, or microwave on full power for 4–5 minutes. Leave until cool enough to handle, then peel off and discard the skins.

Purée the pepper flesh in a liquidizer or food processor and mix into the crème fraîche. This sauce needs no seasoning.

Cook the pasta (page 103), drain thoroughly and toss with the sauce. Serve in a warmed dish, with coriander sprinkled on top. Hand round the grated Parmesan in a small bowl.

This pasta dish from Sicily is at its best with warm ciabatta bread and a tossed green salad, followed by a fresh peach tart, or coffee ice cream.

CASARECCIA AL POMODORO

Casareccia with tomato sauce

SERVES 4

1.5 kg/3 lb good-flavoured vine-
ripened tomatoes
6 tablespoons extra virgin
olive oil
225 g/8 oz dried casareccia
or penne rigate
salt and pepper

To serve
Parmesan cheese

Halve the tomatoes, scoop out the seeds, cut away and discard any tough cores and chop the flesh finely.

Heat half the olive oil in a heavy-bottomed saucepan. Add the tomatoes and simmer for 30 minutes, shaking the pan occasionally to release the moisture from the tomatoes. Add the remaining oil from time to time.

Meanwhile, cook the pasta (page 103). The sauce is ready when the oil separates from the tomato pulp. Season to taste, add the cooked, drained pasta and toss well. Serve with shavings of Parmesan.

To serve as a light lunch or supper, begin with a selection of Italian salami.

FETTUCELLE CON BOTTARGA

Fettucelle with bottarga and rocket

SERVES 4

225 g/8 oz dried fettucelle
4 tablespoons extra virgin olive oil
125 g/4 oz fresh rocket (arugula)
2 tablespoons grated bottarga, plus extra, to serve

To serve
freshly ground black pepper
lemon halves
freshly grated Parmesan cheese

Cook the pasta (page 103).

Heat the olive oil in a saucepan, add the rocket and toss for 1 minute or until wilted. Add to the cooked, drained pasta, sprinkle with 2 tablespoons of bottarga and toss well. Season with black pepper and serve with lemon halves, Parmesan, and extra bottarga at the table.

Follow with grilled fresh tuna that has been briefly marinated with lemon, garlic, a little chilli, fresh herbs and olive oil, accompanied by a tomato salad.

SPAGHETTINI CON AGLIO E OLIO

Spaghettini with garlic, oil and chilli

SERVES 4

4 tablespoons extra virgin olive oil
12 garlic cloves, thinly sliced
4 dried red chillies, seeds removed, chopped
225 g/8 oz dried spaghettini
salt and pepper

Heat the olive oil over a gentle heat, add the garlic and cook gently until tender and lightly coloured. Add the chillies and cook for a further minute. Remove from the heat and leave to stand while you cook the pasta (page 103).

Add the cooked, drained pasta to the garlic-infused oil. Toss well and season with salt and freshly ground black pepper. This should not be served with Parmesan.

Follow with chargrilled squid and mixed grilled vegetables.

TAGLIARDI CON CARCIOFINI

Tagliardi with baby artichokes and pancetta

SERVES 4

12 baby artichokes
1 lemon
4 tablespoons extra virgin
    olive oil
2 onions, sliced
2 slices of pancetta, about
    1 cm/½ inch thick,
    cut into lardons
2 glasses of dry white wine
225 g/8 oz dried tagliardi
salt and pepper

To serve
freshly grated Parmesan cheese

Break off any short stalks from the artichokes and then pull away the tough outer leaves until the tender yellow leaves are visible. Trim the bases and cut off the top 1–2.5 cm/½–1 inch of the leaves. Quarter or cut into six, depending on size, and toss into a large bowl of cold water, to which you have added the juice of the lemon.

Heat the olive oil in a large sauté pan, add the onions and pancetta and sauté for 5 minutes. Add the artichokes and cook, stirring occasionally, for about 20 minutes, until the artichokes are golden and tender. Add the wine and cook over a high heat to reduce to a syrupy glaze.

Meanwhile, cook the pasta (page 103). Add the cooked, drained pasta to the artichokes and toss well. Season to taste and serve with Parmesan.

Follow with roast lamb cooked with fresh rosemary or thyme, with whole, unpeeled garlic cloves added to the roasting dish for the final 40 minutes.

SPAGHETTI COI PEPERONI ARROSTITI

Spaghetti with grilled peppers

SERVES 4

4 large yellow or red peppers
400 g/14 oz spaghetti
2 garlic cloves, very finely sliced
100 ml/3½ fl oz olive oil
1 small dried chilli, seeded and crumbled
salt
3 tablespoons chopped fresh flat-leaf parsley

Place the peppers under a hot grill or on a wire rack directly over a gas flame. Cook, turning constantly, until the skin is black and charred all over. Peel off the burnt skin with a small sharp knife and then wipe the peppers with paper towels. Do not rinse the peppers under the tap, or the water will wash away the lovely juices. Cut the grilled peppers lengthways into strips.

Cook the spaghetti (page 103). While the spaghetti is cooking, put the garlic and oil in a large frying pan and cook over medium-high heat for 30 seconds. Add the peppers and the chilli, reduce the heat and cook gently for 4 minutes, stirring occasionally. Add salt to taste.

When the pasta is ready, drain but do not over-drain and tip it into the frying pan. Sprinkle with the parsley and fry for a further minute, tossing constantly. Serve at once.

A typical southern Italian first course that can precede baked hake (page 199), accompanied only by a salad, such as french bean and tomato salad. Finish with stewed fruits or a fruit salad. The grilled peppers also make a very good antipasto. Dress them with extra virgin olive oil, capers and anchovy fillets.

PASTA AND NOODLES

ORECCHIETTE COI CECI

Orecchiette with chickpeas

With the root end intact, cut the leek lengthways into very thin slices, no thicker than 5 mm/ ¼ inch, and then cut each slice thinly lengthways to form thin strands. Then cut off the root end so that the strands separate. Wash and dry these strands thoroughly.

Heat 1 tablespoon of the oil in a large frying pan. Add the leek strands and stir-fry for 3 minutes. They should be crisp but not brown. Remove from the pan with a slotted spoon and set aside.

Cook the pasta (page 103). While the pasta is cooking, heat the remaining oil in the frying pan. Add the parsley, garlic and chilli and sauté for 1 minute. Mix in the chickpeas, a grinding of black pepper and salt to taste and stir-fry for 2 minutes.

When the pasta is ready, drain immediately and transfer to the frying pan. Stir-fry together for 1 minute, then pour into a warmed bowl. Scatter the leek strands over the top and serve at once.

A rustic first course that can precede a dish of grilled sardines or grilled sausages, both accompanied by a green salad. A menu more suitable for lunch than for dinner. The finale should be a platter of cheese — to include a wedge of Parmigiano-Reggiano — and a bowl of fruit.

SERVES 4

1 leek, white and pale green part only
6 tablespoons extra virgin olive oil
350 g/13 oz orecchiette or fusilli
salt and pepper
3 tablespoons chopped fresh flat-leaf parsley
1 garlic clove, chopped
½ fresh red chilli, seeded and chopped
400 g/14 oz can of chickpeas, drained

TAGLIATELLE CON SALMONE E CAVIAR

Tagliatelle with fresh salmon, caviar and truffle

SERVES 4

125 g/4 oz dried tagliatelle
175 g/6 oz fresh salmon fillet
2–3 tablespoons extra virgin olive oil
sea salt and freshly ground black pepper
25 g/1 oz caviar
few slices of white or black truffle (optional),
    or substitute 1–2 teaspoons truffle oil for some
    of the olive oil

Cook the pasta (page 103).

Skin and thinly slice the salmon. Drain the pasta, add the salmon and stir to cook in the heat. Add the olive oil, salt and pepper and toss well.

Serve at once on individual plates, topped with a teaspoonful of caviar and a couple of thin shavings from the truffle. This should not be served with Parmesan.

A very luxurious, elegant starter, which could be followed with grilled asparagus accompanied by boiled quails' eggs and prosciutto.

TAGLIARDI CON TOTANI E CIPOLLA

Tagliardi with baby squid and spring onions

SERVES 4

12 baby squid
8 large spring onions, trimmed
3–4 tablespoons extra virgin olive oil
225 g/8 oz dried spinach tagliardi
3 garlic cloves, chopped
4 tomatoes, seeded and finely chopped
1 tablespoon chopped fresh parsley
1 small red chilli, seeded, ribs removed and
    finely chopped
salt and pepper

To serve
lemon halves

Pull the squid tentacles away from the bodies and cut off the tentacles just below the eyes. Feel around the body tube for the transparent backbone and remove. Rub the purple skin from the tubes, then cut the tubes into rings.

Brush the spring onions with olive oil and grill or griddle for 2–3 minutes on each side until golden, tender and slightly charred. Cut each one into three pieces.

Cook the pasta (page 103). Meanwhile, heat 2 tablespoons of the oil in a sauté pan, add the garlic and sauté for 2 minutes. Add the squid and cook over a high heat for 3 minutes. Add the tomatoes, spring onions, parsley and chilli and stir to combine. Toss with the cooked, drained pasta, season with salt and freshly ground black pepper and serve with lemon halves. This should not be served with Parmesan.

Precede or follow with a platter of grilled aubergines and mixed peppers.

ZARU SOBA

Chilled soba noodles with dipping sauce

SERVES 4

350 g/13 oz dried buckwheat noodles (soba)
500 ml/16 fl oz dashi (page 372)
4 tablespoons Japanese soy sauce
4 tablespoons mirin
½ teaspoon sugar
1 sheet dried nori seaweed
1 teaspoon wasabi powder, mixed to a paste
   with a little water
3 spring onions, finely sliced

Bring a large saucepan of water to the boil and add the noodles. When the water returns to the boil, add 250 ml/8 fl oz cold water. Repeat the process, then continue to boil until the noodles are just past *al dente* (firm, but cooked through). Drain the noodles and plunge them into cold water, washing them with your hands to remove all the starch. Drain and chill.

Put the dashi, soy sauce, mirin and sugar in a saucepan, bring to the boil, stirring frequently, then cool and chill in the refrigerator.

When ready to serve, divide the noodles between four shallow bowls or slatted bamboo boxes. Lightly toast the nori over a gas flame or under a hot grill until crisp, then cut with scissors into long, thin strips and arrange over the noodles.

Divide the chilled sauce between four small serving bowls. Each diner picks up some noodles with chopsticks and dips them into the sauce, adding wasabi and spring onions to taste.

Serve on a warm summer's day as part of a simple Japanese meal, along with a dish of vinegared crab, clams in butter sauce, grilled aubergine and salted mackerel. Finish with a platter of carved fresh fruit.

TAGLIATELLE CON SARDE IN SAOR

Tagliatelle with marinated sardines

SERVES 6

4 tablespoons extra virgin olive oil

3 onions, thinly sliced

2 bay leaves

3 tablespoons white wine vinegar

1 teaspoon black peppercorns

1 tablespoon raisins, plumped for 15 minutes
    in hot water

8 fresh sardines, scaled, cleaned, heads removed

plain flour for dredging

salt and pepper

275 g/10 oz dried tagliatelle

To serve

lemon halves

Heat 3 tablespoons of the olive oil in a saucepan over a low heat and gently cook the onions with the bay leaves until tender and starting to colour, about 20 minutes. Add the vinegar, peppercorns and raisins and stir to mix.

Rinse the sardines well under running water, cleaning out any blood from near the bone. Dry thoroughly on paper towels. Heat the remaining oil in a frying pan. Dredge the sardines in seasoned flour and fry a few at a time for 2 minutes on each side until golden. Drain on paper towels.

Put half the onion mixture into a dish large enough to hold the sardines in a single layer. Season with salt and pepper. Top with the sardines and the remaining onion mixture. Cover and leave to marinate in a cool place (not the refrigerator) for 10 hours, turning after 5 hours.

Cook the pasta (page 103) and fillet the sardines, keeping the tails intact. Heat the onion mixture through gently, add the sardines and the cooked pasta and toss for 1 minute. Season with freshly ground black pepper and serve with lemon halves.

I would be tempted to follow this robust dish with a selection of steamed or chargrilled vegetables tossed with olive oil and lemon juice and flakes of fresh Parmesan. Perhaps new potatoes (Jersey royals if in season), fresh peas, broad beans, baby artichokes or quartered artichoke bottoms.

DUCK CONFIT
with lentil and herb fettuccine

SERVES 4

4 large duck legs
1 whole head of garlic,
    cut in half horizontally
salt and pepper
leaves from 4 sprigs of thyme
4 dried bay leaves, crumbled
duck fat or sunflower oil to cover
225 g/8 oz dried fettuccine pasta

Lentil and herb sauce

25 g/1 oz unsalted butter
4 shallots or 1 small onion,
    very finely chopped
6 button mushrooms, sliced
½ garlic clove, crushed
1 bay leaf
1 sprig of thyme
4 white peppercorns, crushed
250 ml/8 fl oz dry white wine
450 ml/15 fl oz chicken stock
85 ml/3 fl oz double cream
50 g/2 oz dried Puy lentils
1 tablespoon each of chopped
    fresh chives, parsley
    and tarragon

To serve

sunflower oil for deep-frying
4 thin slices of Parma ham

The day before, prepare the duck confit. Lay the duck legs in a small roasting tin, rub the garlic over the skin, then sprinkle with plenty of salt and pepper and rub it in well. Tuck the garlic in among the legs and sprinkle over the thyme and bay leaves. Cover with cling film and leave in the refrigerator overnight. The next day, rub the aromatics off the duck and pack into a large saucepan. Cover with duck fat or sunflower oil and bring up to a very gentle simmer. Cook over a very low heat for 2–2½ hours or until very tender.

For the sauce, melt the butter in a saucepan. Add the shallots, mushrooms, garlic, bay leaf, thyme and peppercorns. Fry until golden, then add the wine and boil until reduced to a couple of tablespoons. Add the stock and boil until reduced by two-thirds. Add the cream, bring back to the boil and then strain into a clean saucepan. Check the seasoning and set aside. Simmer the lentils in lightly salted boiling water for about 15 minutes or until tender. Drain and set aside.

Preheat the oven to 220°C/425°F/Gas Mark 7. Lay the duck legs on a rack set over a roasting tin and roast at the top of the oven, turning once or twice, until the skin is crisp and golden. Leave to cool slightly, then remove the meat from the bones and flake it.

For the deep-fried Parma ham, heat about 5–8 cm/2–3 inches of sunflower oil in a deep pan to 190°C/375°F, or until a cube of bread browns in 30 seconds. Deep-fry the Parma ham, two slices at a time, for about 30 seconds, until crisp. Using a slotted spoon, lift out and drain on paper towels.

Cook the pasta (page 103). Reheat the sauce and stir in the lentils and the herbs. Drain the pasta and return to the pan. Add the sauce and the duck and toss together over a low heat. Divide between four warmed bowls and top with deep-fried Parma ham.

Almost a meal in itself, serve a light first course such as a gâteau of roast vegetables with goats' cheese and rocket salad and finish with rich but cool and silky chocolate pots.

HOKKIEN MEE

Fried noodles with pork and prawns

SERVES 4

400 g/14 oz fresh egg noodles (Hokkien noodles)
2 dried red chillies, soaked in water to cover for
    about 2 hours
200 g/7 oz squid, cleaned
200 g/7 oz uncooked prawns in their shells
3 tablespoons peanut oil
250 ml/8 fl oz chicken stock
3 garlic cloves, crushed
200 g/7 oz Chinese roast pork (char sieu)
    or leftover roast pork, finely sliced
½ bunch of choi sum (flowering cabbage), chopped
200 g/7 oz beansprouts, rinsed in cold water
1 tablespoon dark soy sauce
2 tablespoons light soy sauce
2 spring onions, finely sliced

Put the noodles in a bowl, pour boiling water over them and leave to stand for about 30 seconds, then drain and rinse under cold water. Drain the chillies and chop. Cut the squid into small squares and lightly score one side in a criss-cross pattern. Shell the prawns, retaining the heads and shells.

Heat 1 tablespoon of the oil in a wok and fry the prawn heads and shells for 1 minute. Add the stock and simmer for 5 minutes. Strain out the shells, return the stock to the wok and add the prawns. Simmer gently until they just turn white (about 1 minute). Remove the prawns with a slotted spoon and set aside. Pour the stock into a jug and set aside.

Heat the remaining oil in the wok. Add the garlic and cook for 2–3 minutes, until the garlic turns golden, then discard the garlic. Add the squid, pork and cabbage and stir-fry over high heat for 2 minutes. Add the prawns and bean-sprouts and stir-fry for 1 minute. Add the noodles and stir-fry for 1–2 minutes, tossing constantly, then add the stock, soy sauces and spring onions and cook until everything is hot. Serve at once.

Create a Singapore-style feast by starting with beef rib soup (bah kut teh). Serve Hokkien mee along with deep-fried chicken (enche kebin) and rojak, a refreshing fruit and vegetable salad.

PAD THAI

Stir-fried noodles

SERVES 4

150 g/5 oz thin dried rice stick noodles*

1½ tablespoons tamarind pulp

1½ tablespoons palm sugar or brown sugar

3 tablespoons vegetable oil

3 garlic cloves, finely chopped

3 tablespoons dried shrimp, chopped

1 tablespoon salted radish, chopped

1 teaspoon dried chilli flakes

2 tablespoons fish sauce

150 g/5 oz beansprouts, rinsed

2 eggs, lightly beaten

2 tablespoons cubed firm tofu (beancurd)

20 garlic chives, cut into 5 cm/2 inch lengths

4 tablespoons roasted peanuts, lightly crushed

2–3 coriander sprigs

* known as sen lek in Thailand, banh pho in Vietnam

Soak the noodles in a saucepan of hot water for about 10 minutes, then bring to the boil and cook for about 2 minutes or until the noodles are tender. Strain, rinse in cold water, drain and set aside.

Combine the tamarind, sugar and 3 tablespoons boiling water in a bowl and stir until the sugar dissolves. Leave to stand for about 10 minutes, then strain off the liquid and set aside.

Heat a wok, then add 2 tablespoons of the oil. When hot, add the garlic, dried shrimp, salted radish and chilli and fry for 2 minutes, until the garlic just turns golden. Add the drained noodles and toss continually for 2–3 minutes. Add the tamarind liquid and fish sauce, and all but a handful of beansprouts.

Add the remaining tablespoon of oil to the wok. Move the noodles to one side of the wok and pour the eggs into the space created, scrambling them roughly. When the eggs start to set, cover with noodles and toss through. Add the tofu, garlic chives and the last handful of beansprouts. Tip out on to a warmed serving platter and scatter the crushed peanuts and coriander sprigs on top.

In Thailand, this is often accompanied by little dishes of more crushed peanuts, dried chillies and sugar to add at the table. Serve as part of a Thai meal with a hot and sour prawn soup (tom yam goong), Thai fishcakes with a sweet chilli dipping sauce, and a refreshing chilli and cucumber salad.

DAN DAN NOODLES

Chilled spicy noodles

SERVES 4

1 small piece of fresh ginger, sliced into matchsticks

1 teaspoon vegetable oil

3 teaspoons sugar

500 g/1 lb 2 oz fresh flat Chinese wheat noodles

3 teaspoons peanut oil

2 teaspoons sesame oil

generous handful of beansprouts

1 tablespoon sesame seeds

3 tablespoons sesame paste, tahini or peanut butter

2–3 teaspoons Sichuan chilli oil (page 375)

2 tablespoons light soy sauce

1 tablespoon Chinese black vinegar or rice vinegar

½ teaspoon Sichuan pepper or black peppercorns, crushed

2 spring onions, finely chopped

Put the ginger in a small bowl with the vegetable oil and 1 teaspoon of the sugar and leave to marinate for 1 hour.

Put the noodles in a saucepan of boiling water and cook for 2–3 minutes, until tender. Rinse in cold water, drain and shake dry. Add 1 teaspoon each of the peanut oil and sesame oil, and toss to prevent the noodles from sticking.

Pour boiling water over the beansprouts, drain, rinse and shake dry.

Toast the sesame seeds in a dry pan until they just start to turn brown. Crush lightly.

Mix the remaining peanut oil and sesame oil with the sesame paste, chilli oil, 3 tablespoons water and the toasted sesame seeds. Add the soy sauce, vinegar, pepper and the remaining sugar. Pour the sauce over the cold noodles and top with the beansprouts, marinated ginger and spring onions.

Serve as part of a Sichuan banquet with dry-fried shredded chilli beef, tea-smoked duck and Mandarin pancakes. Finish with sweet walnuts, fresh mandarins or lychees.

HOR FUN WITH BEEF

Fried rice noodles with beef

SERVES 4

5 tablespoons peanut oil

200 g/7 oz lean beef, thinly sliced

1 tablespoon light soy sauce

1 teaspoon cornflour blended with 1 tablespoon
    cold water

600 g/1¼ lb fresh rice sheet noodles*

1 teaspoon sugar

2 tablespoons dark soy sauce

2 slices of fresh ginger, shredded

generous handful of beansprouts, rinsed

2 spring onions, finely chopped

* known as hor fun or he fen in China, pho in Vietnam
and kueh teow in Malaysia

Heat the oil in a wok. When hot, leave over the heat for 2 minutes, then leave to cool. (This 'cooked' oil is necessary for an authentic flavour.)

Mix 2 tablespoons of the oil with the beef, the light soy sauce and the cornflour mixture and leave to marinate for 30 minutes.

If the rice sheets are not pre-cut, cut them into 2 cm/¾ inch strips, like tagliatelle. Place in a bowl and pour boiling water over them to cover, gently shaking the strips apart with a pair of chopsticks. Immediately drain and rinse under cold running water and set aside.

Mix the sugar with the dark soy sauce and set aside.

Heat a wok, then add the remaining oil. When hot, add the ginger and cook for 1 minute. Add the beef mixture and stir-fry until it changes colour, about 1 minute. Add the beansprouts and stir-fry for 1 minute. Lift out and set aside.

Add the drained noodles to the wok, together with the sugar and soy sauce mixture, and stir well for 2 minutes. Return the beef to the wok and stir-fry until everything is hot, sprinkle the spring onions on top and serve at once.

A favourite lunch or supper dish, this also works as part of a Cantonese dinner. Serve with prawns steamed in their shells, and steamed Chinese vegetables with shiitake mushrooms. Finish with a traditional Cantonese sweet walnut soup.

MEE KROB
Crisp fried noodles

SERVES 4

2 tablespoons palm sugar
  or brown sugar
2 tablespoons fish sauce
2 tablespoons fresh lime or
  lemon juice
1 tablespoon rice vinegar
175 g/6 oz dried rice vermicelli
vegetable oil for deep-frying
2 garlic cloves, finely chopped
6 shallots, finely chopped
225 g/8 oz minced pork
  or chicken
200 g/7 oz uncooked prawns,
  finely chopped
125 g/4 oz firm tofu (beancurd),
  diced
2 fresh red chillies, sliced
2 eggs, lightly beaten
100 g/3½ oz beansprouts, rinsed
generous handful of
  coriander leaves
3 spring onions (green parts),
  finely chopped

Put the sugar, fish sauce, lime juice and vinegar into a saucepan and bring to the boil, stirring constantly. Allow to bubble for 3–4 minutes, until the liquid reduces in volume by one-third and starts to turn dark and sticky. Keep warm.

Put the uncooked noodles in a large bowl and break into short lengths. Heat the oil in a wok until it begins to smoke, then add a handful of noodles at a time to the oil. Immediately they puff up, use a large slotted spoon to flip them over for 1 second, then, before they begin to turn brown, remove and drain on paper towels. Keep the noodles warm in a low oven.

Pour off all but 2 tablespoons of the oil and fry the garlic and shallots until they start to colour. Add the pork or chicken, prawns, beancurd and one of the chillies and stir-fry for about 3 minutes.

Add the eggs a little at a time, stirring constantly, until cooked. Add the vinegar liquid and beansprouts and toss well until steaming hot.

Arrange the crisp fried noodles on a large platter and spoon the mixture in the centre. Pile a few crisp noodles on top and scatter with coriander, spring onions and the remaining chilli. Serve immediately, as the noodles will soften after about 10 minutes.

Create a full-flavoured Thai dinner by serving alongside a green chicken curry, a platter of fresh raw vegetables with a chilli dip, and som tum, a refreshing green papaya salad. Finish with sticky rice and mango drizzled with coconut cream.

CHAP CHAE

Stir-fried noodles with beef and vegetables

SERVES 4–6

2 tablespoons dried wood ears or 6 dried shiitake
    mushrooms, soaked in warm water for 2 hours
1 tablespoon sesame seeds
400 g/14 oz good quality beef,
    cut into thick matchsticks
4 garlic cloves, crushed
2 spring onions, thinly sliced
2 teaspoons sugar
5 tablespoons dark soy sauce
1 tablespoon sesame oil
250 g/9 oz cellophane (bean thread) noodles
5 tablespoons vegetable oil
2 eggs, lightly beaten
½ carrot, cut into matchsticks
1 onion, sliced lengthways into slivers
generous handful of beansprouts, rinsed
½ head of Chinese leaves (Peking cabbage)
    or Savoy cabbage, shredded
½ cucumber, cut into matchsticks
salt

Drain the wood ears or mushrooms and cut into
fine strips. Toast the sesame seeds in a dry pan
until they just start to turn golden.

Put the beef in a bowl with the sesame seeds,
garlic, spring onions, 1 teaspoon of the sugar,
2 tablespoons of the soy sauce and 1 teaspoon of
the sesame oil, and leave to marinate for 1 hour.

Soak the noodles in hot water for about 15
minutes or until soft. Rinse in cold water,
drain and cut into 10 cm/4 inch lengths.

Heat a wok, then add 1 tablespoon of the
vegetable oil, swirling the wok to coat the entire
surface. Pour in the eggs and swirl around the
wok to form a thin omelette. When the omelette
has just set, remove it from the wok. Roll into
a cylinder, cut into thin strips and set aside.

Add 2 tablespoons of the vegetable oil to the
wok and heat through. Add the carrot and onion
and stir-fry until they soften, then add the beansprouts and cabbage and stir-fry for a further
2 minutes. Add the cucumber and toss through,
then tip out on to a plate and keep warm.

Heat the remaining 2 tablespoons of oil in the
wok, add the beef mixture and the mushroom
strips and stir-fry for 2 minutes. Add the
noodles, the remaining soy sauce, sesame oil,
sugar and a pinch of salt. Return the vegetables
to the wok, heat through and serve scattered
with omelette strips.

This is a simple family meal. When entertaining,
begin with Korean oxtail soup then serve chap chae,
with preserved cabbage (kim chee) and chicken cooked
with ginseng.

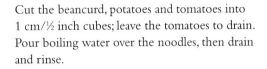
MEE GORENG

Hokkien noodles with potato and tomato

SERVES 4

2 squares of dried beancurd cake (page 378) or
    4–6 pieces of fried beancurd
2 cooked potatoes
2 firm tomatoes
500 g/1 lb 2 oz fresh egg noodles
2 tablespoons vegetable oil
3 garlic cloves, pounded
1 onion, chopped
125 g/4 oz fresh beansprouts
2 tablespoons tomato sauce or ketchup
1 tablespoon chilli sauce, or to taste
2 tablespoons light soy sauce
½ teaspoon salt
½ teaspoon sugar
10 small uncooked prawns or shrimps, shelled
1 egg, beaten
2 spring onions, sliced

To garnish
2 tablespoons crisply fried shallots
½ small iceberg lettuce, finely shredded
1 lime or lemon, quartered

Cut the beancurd, potatoes and tomatoes into
1 cm/½ inch cubes; leave the tomatoes to drain.
Pour boiling water over the noodles, then drain
and rinse.

Heat a wok until hot, then add the oil. When the
oil is hot, add the garlic and onion and fry until
the onion is soft. Add the drained noodles and
stir-fry for 2 minutes over high heat.

Add the beansprouts, potatoes, tomatoes, beancurd, tomato sauce, chilli sauce, soy sauce, salt,
sugar and prawns and stir-fry over high heat
until the prawns are cooked.

Tilt the wok, push the noodles to one side, and
pour in the egg. Cover the egg with noodles and
leave to set for 30 seconds over medium heat,
then toss well. Add the spring onions, and serve
topped with fried shallots, shredded lettuce and
lime quarters.

*Start the meal with rojak, a Malaysian fruit and
vegetable salad, and finish with ice kachang, a
refreshing dessert of shaved ice and sweet things,
such as sweetcorn kernels, peanuts and red azuki
beans with palm sugar syrup and evaporated milk.*

CHUNGKING NOODLES

Transparent noodles with pork

SERVES 2–4

200 g/7 oz minced pork
2 tablespoons light soy sauce
1 tablespoon sugar
1 teaspoon cornflour
1 teaspoon soybean and chilli paste, or chilli sauce
100 g/3½ oz cellophane (bean thread) noodles
3 tablespoons vegetable oil
1 small fresh red chilli
2 spring onions, finely chopped
125 ml/4 fl oz chicken stock or water
1 tablespoon dark soy sauce
2 spring onions, thinly sliced

Mix the minced pork with the light soy sauce, sugar, cornflour and soybean and chilli paste or sauce. Leave to marinate for about 30 minutes.

Soak the noodles in hot water for 10 minutes or until soft, then drain.

Heat a wok and add the oil. When hot, add the chilli and chopped spring onions, then the pork and its marinade, stirring well. When the meat starts to brown, add the drained noodles and stir well.

Add the chicken stock or water and dark soy sauce and continue to cook until the noodles absorb all the liquid. Turn out on to a warm serving platter and surround with sliced spring onions.

Serve as part of a Western Chinese meal, with hot and sour soup, sweet-and-sour spare ribs and braised aubergine.

PEKING MEAT SAUCE NOODLES

SERVES 6 (MAKES 600 ML/1 PINT MEAT SAUCE)

225 g/8 oz minced pork
2 teaspoons rice wine
2 teaspoons cornflour
2 tablespoons hoisin sauce
1 tablespoon dark soy sauce
1 tablespoon sugar
8 tablespoons bean paste or Japanese miso
250 ml/8 fl oz water
1 tablespoon groundnut or corn oil
2 garlic cloves, finely chopped
1 onion, finely chopped
2 spring onions (green and white parts), thinly sliced
450 g/1 lb dried egg noodles or thin spaghetti

Garnishes
6–8 radishes, shredded
1 cucumber, peeled, seeded and shredded
200 g/7 oz beansprouts, parboiled for 15 seconds
    and drained
325 g/12 oz spinach, parboiled for 15 seconds,
    squeezed dry and finely chopped

Mix the pork with the rice wine and cornflour. Set aside. In another bowl, mix the hoisin sauce, soy sauce, sugar, bean paste and water. Set aside.

Heat the oil in a wok over high heat. When the oil is hot, add the pork mixture and stir until the meat becomes opaque and separates, about 2 minutes. Add the garlic and onion and continue stirring for another minute. Then add the spring onions and stir for another minute, until the spring onions are wilted.

Add the bean paste mixture and stir thoroughly into the meat; the sauce will be thin. Reduce the heat to low and simmer for 3–4 minutes.

Bring 5 litres/9 pints of water to a boil in a large saucepan. Add the noodles or spaghetti and boil until it is a little more tender than *al dente*. Drain and rinse in hot water. Divide the noodles between six individual bowls. Transfer the meat sauce to a serving bowl and place on the table. Set the vegetable garnishes, each in their own bowls, on the table. Allow your guests to add their own sauce and garnishes.

A satisfying lunch or simple dinner, serve it with a crisp green salad, or with crunchy green vegetables such as mangetout.

CHAR KUEH TEOW
Fried rice noodles with pork and prawns

SERVES 4–6

500 g/1 lb 2 oz fresh rice
noodles (kueh teow)
125 g/4 oz fresh beansprouts
200 g/7 oz fresh squid tubes,
cleaned
2 tablespoons peanut oil
2 garlic cloves, crushed
3 dried red chillies, soaked,
drained and pounded
(page 378)
200 g/7 oz Chinese roast pork
(char sieu), finely sliced,
or leftover roast pork,
or Chinese sausages
(lup cheong), finely sliced
on the diagonal
12 small prawns, deveined and
shelled
1 tablespoon dark or mushroom
soy sauce
2 tablespoons light soy sauce
2 tablespoons oyster sauce
salt and pepper
2 eggs, lightly beaten
2 tablespoons finely chopped
spring onions (green parts)

Cut the noodles into 2 cm/¾ inch wide strips and place in a heat-proof bowl. Pour boiling water on top and gently pull the noodles apart with chopsticks. Drain and rinse in cold water. Put the beansprouts in another bowl, pour boiling water over them, then drain and rinse in cold water.

Cut the squid tubes lengthways and use the tip of the knife to lightly score a crisscross pattern on the surface, without cutting right through. Cut into 5 cm/2 inch squares.

Heat a wok until hot, then add the oil. When the oil is hot, add the garlic and fry for 1 minute, stirring. Add the pounded chillies and fry for 1 minute, stirring. Add the pork, prawns and squid and stir-fry over high heat for 2 minutes. Add dark and light soy sauces, oyster sauce, salt, pepper and beansprouts and stir-fry for 2 minutes. Add the noodles and cook over high heat for 3 minutes, tossing to coat the noodles in the sauce.

Make a well in the centre of the noodles and pour in the beaten eggs. Stir the eggs as they start to scramble, then cover with noodles and toss to combine. Add the spring onions and serve immediately.

Serve as a shared main course, with some steamed tofu (beancurd) in peanut sauce (page 77), and finish with pulut hitam, a sweet black rice dessert.

VEGETABLES, RICE, COUSCOUS

Let the sky rain potatoes.

WILLIAM SHAKESPEARE
FROM *THE MERRY WIVES OF WINDSOR*

FAMILY-STYLE FRIED RICE

SERVES 3–5

450 g/1 lb cold cooked long-grain white rice
2 large eggs
1 teaspoon rice wine or dry sherry
3–4 spring onions, thinly sliced
1 teaspoon salt, or to taste
4 tablespoons groundnut or corn oil
6 tablespoons frozen peas
50–85 g/2–3 oz ham, chopped

Place the rice in a large bowl and use your fingers to break up any lumps. Break the eggs over the rice and add the rice wine, spring onions and salt. Mix together with a wooden spoon or your hands, until well blended.

Heat the oil in a wok over high heat. When the oil is hot, add the rice mixture and stir constantly for about 5 minutes, then add the peas and ham and continue stirring for another 5 minutes or until the rice is loose, fluffy and completely heated through. Taste and add more salt if desired. Serve hot.

Often served as a lunch or snack in China, fried rice goes well with grilled meat or seafood, in place of potatoes.

NAVRATTAN PULLAO

Nine vegetables 'jewelled' rice

SERVES 4

4 tablespoons ghee

20–30 saffron strands

1 large onion, finely sliced

450 g/1 lb cooked rice

2 carrots, diced

¼ small red cabbage, diced

50 g/2 oz small green beans, diced

24 asparagus tips

3 tablespoons peas

3 tablespoons cooked sweetcorn

3 tablespoons cooked red kidney beans

3 tablespoons cooked chickpeas

6 radishes, quartered

2–3 tablespoons chopped fresh coriander leaves

salt

Spices

1½ teaspoons fennel seeds

3–4 green cardamoms, crushed

5–6 cloves, crushed

2–3 pieces of cassia bark

½ teaspoon black cumin seeds

Heat the ghee in a wok or karahi until hot, but well below smoking point. Add all the spices and stir-fry briskly for about 30 seconds. Add the saffron, stir briskly, then add the onion and mix well. Stir-fry briskly for a further 30 seconds. Keeping the heat high at first, stir-fry until the onion caramelizes; this will take 10–15 minutes and the heat should be lowered progressively during this time.

Meanwhile, reheat the rice and all the vegetables, ensuring they are all piping hot.

To serve, mix everything together, adding the fresh coriander and salt to taste. Serve at once.

This pillau is an ideal accompaniment to any curry, or it can be served as a meal in its own right.

SPICED COUSCOUS

SERVES 6

3 tablespoons olive oil
½ tablespoon turmeric
½ tablespoon ground cumin
½ tablespoon ground ginger
4 whole cloves
½ stick of cinnamon
1 bay leaf
1 garlic clove, sliced
165 ml/5½ fl oz (measured in a jug) couscous
250 ml/8 fl oz hot chicken stock
salt and pepper
½ cucumber, peeled and finely diced
1 tablespoon chopped fresh mint
150 g/5 oz ready-to-eat dried apricots, chopped
100 g/3½ oz almonds, toasted and halved
50 g/2 oz pine kernels, toasted
100 g/3½ oz pecan nuts, roughly chopped
85 g/3 oz raisins
2 teaspoons clear honey

Dressing
1 tablespoon white wine vinegar
4 tablespoons olive oil
1 tablespoon clear honey

Mix the dressing ingredients together until smooth.

Heat the olive oil in a large frying pan, add the spices, bay leaf and garlic and fry together until the garlic is lightly browned, then mix in the couscous. Pour over the hot stock and stir over a low heat until the mixture swells and cooks, about 2 minutes. Remove from the heat, season to taste and keep stirring, off the heat, for a further 2 minutes, to free the grains. Stir in the dressing and leave to cool.

Remove the cloves if you can find them, and the cinnamon stick if you like.

Add the cucumber, mint, apricots, nuts, raisins and honey to taste.

Serve as an accompaniment to, or first course before, roast guinea fowl or chicken. Finish the meal with a piece of halva.

COUSCOUS WITH SPICY LEEKS AND TOMATOES

Cut the leeks into 2 cm/¾ inch lengths. Heat the oil in a saucepan, add the leeks and toss to coat in the oil, then add the lemon juice. Cover with a lid and cook over a low heat until the leeks 'wilt', about 15–20 minutes, stirring occasionally.

Add the tomatoes, garlic, paprika and cumin and simmer together for a further 5–6 minutes, then season to taste with a little salt.

Bring some water to the boil in a saucepan, pour in the couscous and bring back to the boil, stirring constantly. Remove from the heat, cover with a lid, and leave to steam for 5–6 minutes or until tender. Drain, then add a little olive oil and fluff up with a fork to prevent the grains from sticking together.

Pile the couscous on to a serving dish and spoon the leeks around the edge. Sprinkle with parsley and serve at once.

Couscous, a traditional Moroccan dish, makes a colour-ful meal preceded by watercress soup (page 12). For a Sunday lunch with friends, I also served mushroom and pesto tartlets (page 53), and we ended the meal with oranges in syrup, sprinkled with cinnamon.

SERVES 4–6

675 g/1½ lb leeks, trimmed

2 tablespoons olive oil

3 teaspoons fresh lemon juice

600 g/1¼ lb canned chopped tomatoes, with juice

1 garlic clove, finely chopped

2 teaspoons each of paprika and cumin

a little salt

175 g/6 oz couscous

1–2 teaspoons olive oil

1 tablespoon chopped fresh parsley

BARBECUED CORN ON THE COB
with cucumber relish

SERVES 4

4 corn on the cob

Cucumber relish
1 cucumber
450 g/1 lb green tomatoes
2 onions
1 red pepper
salt
600 ml/1 pint white vinegar
225 g/8 oz brown sugar
225 g/8 oz white sugar
1 tablespoon plain flour
1 tablespoon curry powder
1 teaspoon mustard powder

First make the cucumber relish. Slice the cucumber in half length-ways, scoop out the seeds and cut off the ends. Finely chop the cucumber, tomatoes, onions and red pepper. Place in a colander, sprinkle with salt and leave overnight.

The next day, pour off any liquid that has drained out and put the vegetables into a preserving pan together with the vinegar and both sugars. Boil for 1 hour.

Mix the flour, curry powder and mustard with a splash of vinegar to make a paste. Stir into the pan and simmer for 30 minutes.

There are two ways of barbecuing the corn cobs. You could trim off the husks and silks, then boil the cobs in salted water for 15 minutes; drain, refresh in cold water and brown them on the barbecue for about 5 minutes. Alternatively, you could pull down the husks, trim off the silks and soak the cobs in water for about 5 minutes. Then pull the husks back up and twist to seal. Grill on a hot barbecue for 15–20 minutes.

Serve the corn hot from the grill, accompanied by the cucumber relish.

This is a great dish to serve with spit-roasted or barbecued chicken with lemon and herbs, and then perhaps enjoy a white chocolate mousse.

MIXED GRILLED VEGETABLE SALAD

SERVES 6–8

½ each of red, green and yellow pepper, seeds
    removed, cut into six
1 courgette, cut into thick rounds
½ aubergine, sliced into rounds
4 tablespoons olive oil
¼ small celeriac, cut into batons
10 button mushrooms, quartered
salt and pepper
2 tablespoons balsamic vinegar

Marinade
150 ml/5 fl oz olive oil
1 sprig of rosemary
1 sprig of thyme
1 garlic clove, chopped
1 shallot, chopped
2 tablespoons sherry vinegar

Place all the marinade ingredients in a saucepan and heat through.

Heat a chargrilling pan, add the peppers, allow to blacken a little, then remove and set aside. Brown the courgette and aubergine rounds in the same way. Add to the peppers.

Heat the olive oil in a large frying pan, add the celeriac and mushrooms and cook briefly to soften a little. Add the peppers, courgette and aubergine, stir in the marinade and season to taste. Pour into a bowl, add the balsamic vinegar and leave to marinate overnight in the refrigerator.

To serve, remove the rosemary and thyme sprigs and drain off excess oil.

Serve as an accompaniment to grilled lamb cutlets.

CAPONATINA

Aubergines in a sweet and sour sauce

SERVES 4

675 g/1½ lb aubergines, cut into 2.5 cm/1 inch cubes

salt and pepper

vegetable oil for frying

1 head of celery

85 ml/3 fl oz extra virgin olive oil

1 onion, sliced

225 g/8 oz canned plum tomatoes, drained,
    or fresh ripe tomatoes, skinned and seeded

1 tablespoon sugar

100 ml/3½ fl oz red wine vinegar

50 g/2 oz capers

50 g/2 oz large green olives, stoned and quartered

Sprinkle the aubergine cubes with salt and place them in a colander to drain. Put a weight on top and leave to stand for at least 30 minutes. Rinse the aubergines, then dry well on paper towels.

Heat 2.5 cm/1 inch of vegetable oil in a frying pan. When the oil is hot, add a layer of aubergines and fry until golden brown on all sides. Drain on paper towels. Repeat until all the aubergines are cooked.

Remove the outer sticks of the celery and reserve for another dish or to make stock. Remove any threads from the inner sticks. Wash, dry and cut into 2.5 cm/1 inch matchsticks. Fry the celery in the same frying pan as the aubergines, until golden and crisp. Drain on paper towels.

Pour the olive oil into a clean frying pan and add the onion. Cook gently for about 2 minutes, until soft and just coloured. Pass the tomatoes through the fine holes of a food mill and add to the onion together with the sugar, salt and pepper and cook over moderately high heat, stirring frequently, for 15 minutes. Then add the vinegar, capers, olives, aubergines and celery and cook over very low heat for a further 20 minutes, stirring occasionally. Taste and adjust the seasoning. Pour the caponatina into a serving dish and leave to cool. Serve at room temperature.

Caponatina is served with bread as an antipasto. It could be followed by the loin of pork braised in milk (page 292), or by red mullet in prosciutto (page 196) or any other dish not too delicately flavoured. To end the dinner I suggest a fresh-tasting pudding based on fruit, such as a fruit tart.

FINOCCHI STUFATI
Stewed fennel

SERVES 4

3 large fennel bulbs or 4 smaller ones
5 tablespoons extra virgin olive oil
about 150 ml/5 fl oz vegetable stock
salt and pepper

Trim the fennel, cutting off the stalks and paring away any brown parts. Keep the green fronds for decoration. Cut the fennel lengthways into quarters and then into wedges about 1 cm/ ½ inch thick, keeping some of the central core attached to each wedge to prevent them from breaking up during cooking. Place the fennel in a colander and wash. Dry thoroughly.

Heat the oil in a large sauté pan into which the fennel will fit in a single layer. When the oil is hot, add the fennel and sauté for about 7–8 minutes, stirring occasionally with a fork rather than a spoon, until the wedges are browned at the edge. Pour in enough stock to cover the bottom of the pan and season with a little salt. Cover the pan and cook gently for about 20 minutes, until the fennel is tender, not crunchy. You might have to add a little more stock during cooking. When the fennel is ready there should be just a few spoonfuls of liquid left.

If there is still a lot of liquid, transfer the fennel to a warmed serving dish and boil the liquid over high heat until syrupy. Add a generous grinding of pepper and then taste and adjust the salt. Sprinkle the fennel with the reserved snipped fronds.

A delicious accompaniment to roast or grilled fish, or to a dish of simply cooked poultry or meat such as steaks. This is a typical Italian method of cooking vegetables. Some vegetables, such as courgettes, do not need any added liquid; others, like french beans, may be blanched first.

VEGETARIAN STIR-FRY

SERVES 4

2 tablespoons groundnut oil

2 garlic cloves, crushed

2 teaspoons grated fresh ginger

125 g/4 oz fresh asparagus tips

125 g/4 oz green beans, sliced, or small broad beans

125 g/4 oz mangetout, tips removed

125 g/4 oz courgettes, thinly sliced diagonally

1 red or orange pepper, deseeded and cut into strips

125 g/4 oz button mushrooms, sliced

3 spring onions, finely sliced

12 pitted black olives, cut in halves

1 tablespoon light soy sauce

1 tablespoon chopped fresh basil

1 tablespoon chopped fresh parsley

50 g/2 oz pine nuts, toasted

salt and pepper

2 teaspoons sesame or basil oil

Heat a wok or large pan, then add the oil. When the oil is hot and begins to smoke, add the garlic and ginger and stir for 30 seconds. Add the asparagus and beans and stir-fry for 2 minutes. Add the mangetout and courgettes and stir-fry for 1 minute. Add the pepper and mushrooms and stir-fry for a further 2 minutes, or until the vegetables are tender but still crisp.

Add the spring onions and olives and stir-fry for 1 minute. Stir in the soy sauce, herbs and half the pine nuts. Season to taste with salt and pepper, add the sesame or basil oil and stir for 30 seconds. Sprinkle with the remaining pine nuts and serve immediately.

This is a meal in itself, but is also great as an accompaniment to roast chicken or grilled chicken breast. Follow with an apple or rhubarb crumble.

LA VRAIE RATATOUILLE
Real ratatouille

SERVES 4–6

2 small aubergines,
    about 400 g/14 oz
3 small courgettes,
    about 400 g/14 oz
salt and pepper
150 ml/5 fl oz olive oil
2 onions, sliced
2 red peppers, cored,
    seeded and sliced
2 green peppers, cored,
    seeded and sliced
800 g/1¾ lb plum tomatoes,
    skinned, seeded and chopped
4 garlic cloves, chopped
1 tablespoon coriander seeds
1 teaspoon fennel seeds
4–5 sprigs of thyme
2–3 sprigs of rosemary
2 bay leaves

Note: ratatouille should be made
at least a day ahead so the
flavours have time to develop.

Trim the ends of the aubergines and courgettes without peeling them. Cut the aubergines into 2 cm/¾ inch cubes. Halve the courgettes lengthways and then cut them into 1 cm/½ inch slices.

Put the aubergines and courgettes into a colander, sprinkle generously with salt and toss to mix. Leave for 30 minutes to draw out the juices. Rinse well and drain on paper towels.

Heat 2–3 tablespoons of the oil in a heavy casserole, add the onions and fry until soft, 3–5 minutes. Add the aubergines and courgettes, peppers, tomatoes, garlic, coriander and fennel seeds, salt, pepper and remaining oil and heat, stirring, until very hot. Tie the thyme, rosemary and bay leaves into two or three bundles with string and add to the casserole. Cover and cook over low heat for 30–40 minutes, until the vegetables are very tender and any liquid is reduced and concentrated. Stir often, particularly towards the end of cooking, and if necessary remove the lid so that the liquid evaporates.

Discard the herb bundles, taste the ratatouille and adjust the seasoning. Let it cool and store overnight in the refrigerator. For maximum flavour, serve at room temperature and check the seasoning just before serving.

Ratatouille is wonderfully versatile. It can act as a first course or an accompaniment to roast chicken, lamb, beef or even grilled fish. I've served it over spaghetti with great success, topped with a sprinkling of Parmesan cheese. Dessert can be minimal – perhaps some chilled slices of melon, or strawberries or raspberries sprinkled with a little sugar and balsamic vinegar to draw out their juice.

BLACHAN KANG KONG

Chilli-fried spinach

SERVES 4

500 g/1 lb 2 oz fresh water spinach (kang kong in
    Malaysian, ong choy in Chinese) or regular spinach
2 dried red chillies, soaked and drained
2 garlic cloves, crushed
2 candlenuts or macadamia nuts
6 shallots or 1 small onion, chopped
2 teaspoons blachan (dried shrimp paste)
1 tablespoon dried shrimps, ground
1 tablespoon vegetable oil
½ teaspoon salt
½ teaspoon sugar

Wash the spinach and shake dry.

Grind, pound or blend the drained chillies,
garlic, nuts, shallots or onion, blachan and dried
shrimps together to make a paste.

Heat the oil in a wok or frying pan and fry the
paste for about 5 minutes, stirring, until fragrant.
Add the spinach and toss to coat in the paste.
As soon as the leaves start to wilt, add the salt
and sugar, and keep tossing until the stems soften
and leaves have wilted.

*Serve as a side dish to a fiery Malaysian curry,
seafood sambal or fried noodles. Follow with a tropical
fruit salad drizzled with coconut milk and palm sugar
syrup.*

SPINACH, BACON AND MUSHROOMS

Wash the spinach and drain well. Chop into large pieces.

Heat a wok or large pan, then add the oil. When the oil is hot and begins to smoke, add the garlic and stir for 30 seconds. Add the bacon and stir-fry for 2 minutes, or until the bacon is nearly crisp. Add the mushrooms and stir-fry for 1 minute. Add the spinach and stir-fry for 3 minutes, or until the spinach has wilted. Add the pine nuts and stir-fry for a further 2 minutes. Serve immediately.

Serve as a vegetable side dish, along with new potatoes, to accompany grilled steak, pork or veal escalopes. Follow with a compote of peaches and plums.

SERVES 4

450 g/1 lb spinach or Swiss chard
1 tablespoon groundnut oil
2 garlic cloves, sliced
2 rashers of lean bacon, chopped into strips
125 g/4 oz button mushrooms, sliced
2 tablespoons pine nuts, toasted

VEGETARIAN DISHES

He may live without books -
what is knowledge but grieving?
He may live without hope -
what is hope but deceiving?
He may live without love -
what is passion but pining?
But civilised man cannot live
without dining.

OWEN MEREDITH, EARL OF LYTTON

MAHARANI DAL
The Queen's lentils

SERVES 4

225 g/8 oz black lentils (urid dal)
50 g/2 oz split red lentils (masoor dal)
4 tablespoons ghee
12 garlic cloves, finely chopped
2.5 cm/1 inch cube of fresh ginger, finely chopped
2 onions, finely chopped
50 ml/2 fl oz double cream
2 tablespoons chopped fresh coriander leaves
salt

Whole spices
2 teaspoons coriander seeds
1 teaspoon cumin seeds
2–3 brown cardamoms
2–3 pieces of cassia bark
3–4 bay leaves

Ground spices
1 teaspoon ground coriander
½ teaspoon ground cumin
½ teaspoon turmeric
½ teaspoon chilli powder
¼ teaspoon asafoetida
¼ teaspoon mango powder

Check the lentils and remove any grit or impurities. Rinse them several times, then soak in plenty of cold water for about 4 hours.

Drain and rinse the lentils, then measure an amount of water twice the volume of the drained lentils. Put the water in a 2.3 litre/4 pint saucepan and bring to the boil. Add the lentils and the whole spices and simmer for about 45 minutes, stirring occasionally, until the water is absorbed and the lentils are tender.

Meanwhile, heat the ghee in a wok or karahi until hot, but well below smoking point. Add the garlic and ginger and stir-fry briskly for about 30 seconds. Add the ground spices, stir briskly, then add the onions and stir-fry until the onions caramelize, gradually lowering the heat; this will take between 10 and 15 minutes.

Add the stir-fried mixture to the lentils, together with the cream, coriander and salt to taste. Mash lightly, then serve.

This dal accompanies any curry and rice combination, or makes a nutritious meal with plain rice and pickles.

POTATO DUMPLINGS

with wilted spinach and Parmesan

SERVES 4

900 g/2 lb Catriona potatoes
3 egg yolks
150 g/5 oz plain flour
salt and pepper
250 ml/8 fl oz double cream
225 g/8 oz baby leaf spinach
175 g/6 oz Parmesan cheese, grated

Preheat the oven to 200°C/400°F/Gas Mark 6.

Bake the potatoes in their skins until the flesh is soft and tender, about 1–1½ hours.

Scoop out the potato flesh into a bowl and mash while still hot. Add the egg yolks and flour, season to taste and beat to a smooth dough. Divide the mixture into 2.5 cm/1 inch diameter balls and lay on a floured tray. Chill until ready to cook.

Bring a wide saucepan of water to the boil, add salt and reduce the heat to a gentle simmer. Lower in the dumplings and simmer for 8–12 minutes. Test one to check that they are cooked through, then drain and place in a serving dish. Preheat the grill.

Pour the cream into a saucepan and boil to reduce by half. Add the spinach and half the Parmesan. Heat through for 2 minutes, just long enough to wilt the spinach, then pour over the dumplings and sprinkle with the remaining Parmesan. Place under the hot grill for 3 minutes, until golden and bubbling. Serve hot.

As this is an Italian-influenced dish, start with tomato and basil bruschetta. After the dumplings, finish with pannacotta or zabaglione and biscotti. Don't forget the Pinot Grigio.

POLENTA PASTICCIATA IN BIANCO

Baked polenta with cheeses

SERVES 6

300 g/11 oz polenta
   (coarse maize flour)
2 teaspoons salt
150 g/5 oz gorgonzola,
   cut into small pieces
125 g/4 oz fontina,
   cut into small pieces
125 g/4 oz taleggio,
   cut into small pieces
70 g/2½ oz Parmesan,
   freshly grated
½ teaspoon freshly grated
   nutmeg
2–3 pinches of cayenne pepper

Béchamel sauce
750 ml/1¼ pints full-fat milk
85 g/3 oz unsalted butter
70 g/2½ oz plain flour

First make the polenta: fill a large saucepan with 1.7 litres/3 pints water. Bring to a simmer and add the salt. Remove from the heat and add the polenta, letting it fall into the water through the fingers of your clenched fist while with the other hand you beat with a large wooden spoon or a balloon whisk. When all the polenta has been added, return the pan to the heat and cook at a lively boil for 40 minutes. Whisk constantly at first and then as often as you can between one short rest and the next. It is also possible to add the polenta to hot water instead of boiling water. You can then add it more quickly because there is no risk of lumps forming. Leave to cool, which will take at least 2 hours.

When cold, cut the polenta into slices no more than 1 cm/½ inch thick. Preheat the oven to 200°C/400°F/Gas Mark 6.

Make the béchamel sauce. Heat the milk to simmering point. Melt the butter in a saucepan and blend in the flour. Cook for 30 seconds or so and then draw off the heat and begin gradually to add the milk. When all the milk has been incorporated, put the pan back on the heat and bring to a simmer, stirring constantly. Continue cooking the sauce for about 10 minutes, either in a bain-marie (put the saucepan inside a larger saucepan of gently simmering water) or using a heat dispersing mat. Add the cheeses and stir until dissolved. Add the nutmeg and cayenne pepper, taste and add a little salt if needed.

Butter a large shallow oven dish into which the polenta will fit in three or, maximum, four layers. Spread 3–4 tablespoons of the cheese sauce over the bottom and cover with a layer of polenta slices. Continue with these layers, finishing with plenty of cheese sauce. Bake for about 15 minutes, or about 25 minutes if the dish was cold, having been prepared totally in advance. The top should show patches of golden crust. Serve hot.

This is a winter dish, quite rich, which can be a first course, followed, in an informal dinner, by a light second course based on vegetables. Alternatively it can be a main course in a vegetarian meal, when a platter of roast vegetables or a vegetable mousse would be a good opening.

LAHORI ACHARI ALOO

Potatoes in a pickle sauce

SERVES 4 AS A SIDE DISH

450 g/1 lb small new potatoes
2 tablespoons vegetable oil
4–6 garlic cloves, very finely chopped
3–4 spring onions, finely chopped
1 tablespoon tomato purée
2 tablespoons natural yogurt
1 teaspoon chilli powder
4 tablespoons cooked peas
1 tablespoon fresh mint leaves
salt

Spices
1 teaspoon ground coriander
1 teaspoon ground cumin
1 teaspoon chilli powder
½ teaspoon mango powder
½ teaspoon garam masala
½ teaspoon turmeric

Boil the potatoes in their skins.

While they are cooking, heat the oil in a wok or karahi until hot but well below smoking point. Add all the spices and stir-fry briskly for about 30 seconds, then add the garlic and stir-fry for 3–4 minutes.

Add the spring onions, tomato purée, yogurt, chilli powder, peas, mint and salt to taste, then add the potatoes, and serve as soon as everything is mixed.

Serve hot or cold as a simple starter, accompanied by yogurt dip and chapatti. Follow with any curry, rice and vegetable dish. Alternatively, stuff inside naan bread for a snack meal.

POLENTA WITH SUN-DRIED TOMATOES AND MOZZARELLA

Bring the stock to the boil with the herbs, then trickle in the polenta, stirring all the time. Turn the heat down and simmer gently for several minutes, until the polenta is cooked through. Season to taste with cayenne, salt and pepper, and then stir in the butter or margarine. Pour into a rectangular, buttered heatproof dish and smooth the top. Leave to cool.

To serve, heat the grill. Spread the crushed sun-dried tomatoes over the cooled polenta, and cut it into four squares. Top each square with finely sliced red onion and cover with mozzarella. Place under the grill for 2−3 minutes, until the cheese melts. Serve immediately.

Serve this Italian dish for supper with some new potatoes and a mixed leaf salad, followed by tiramisu. I also serve it cut into tiny squares, as a nibble to go with drinks before a meal.

SERVES 4

600 ml/1 pint vegetable stock
good pinch of dried herbs
125 g/4 oz part-cooked 'instant' polenta
1−2 teaspoons cayenne pepper
salt and pepper
25 g/1 oz butter or margarine
2 tablespoons crushed sun-dried tomatoes
½ red onion, very thinly sliced
125 g/4 oz mozzarella cheese, thinly sliced

CHIMICHANGAS WITH SALSA

SERVES 3–4

8 wheat tortillas, 15 cm/
   6 inches diameter
125 g/4 oz hummus
50 g/2 oz Cheddar cheese,
   grated
3 tablespoons chilli sauce
olive oil for frying

Salsa
4 canned tomatoes
¼ red onion, roughly chopped
1 fresh chilli, sliced
small bunch of parsley, chopped

First make the salsa: put all the ingredients into a liquidizer or food processor and blend briefly.

If the tortillas are a little hard, you will need to soften them so that they will not break when you wrap them around the filling. You can do this by wrapping them in a clean tea towel and then placing them in a colander over a saucepan of boiling water for 20–30 seconds. Alternatively, soften them in the microwave for a few seconds.

Put 1 tablespoon of the hummus in the centre of each tortilla, and top with grated cheese and 1 teaspoon of the chilli sauce. Wrap up into a neat parcel, secure with a toothpick or cocktail stick and fry in hot oil until golden all over. Eat at once, accompanied by the salsa.

In Mexico, chimichangas are traditionally served with salsa, a bowl of soured cream and a simple salad of crisp lettuce, tomatoes and avocado. You could follow them with bananas flambéed in rum, served with chocolate ice cream.

BUTTERNUT SQUASH GRATIN

First make the béchamel sauce. Put the butter, flour and milk into a heavy-bottomed saucepan and beat continuously with a wire whisk over a medium heat until the sauce thickens. Bring to the boil, now stirring with a wooden spoon, and simmer gently for 5–6 minutes to allow the flour to cook. Season to taste with nutmeg, salt and pepper.

Preheat the oven to 160°C/325°F/Gas Mark 3.

Peel the squash and cut into quarters, then scoop out the seeds and cut the flesh into very thin slices. Put them into a large bowl and mix with the béchamel sauce. Season with chilli powder, plenty of freshly ground black pepper, and a little salt if necessary. Put into an ovenproof dish and sprinkle with the cheese. Bake for 45 minutes and serve hot.

This dish, which I first ate in New York City, is wonderful with warm crusty bread, a mixed salad and a glass of Chardonnay. If it's cold outside, serve with a bowl of steaming rice to mop up the juices.

SERVES 4

1 butternut squash, about 1 kg/2¼ lb
1–2 teaspoons chilli powder
salt and pepper
50 g/2 oz Cheddar cheese, grated

Béchamel sauce
40 g/1½ oz butter or margarine
40 g/1½ oz plain flour
450 ml/¾ pint milk
freshly grated nutmeg
salt and pepper

DAU PHU XAO XA

Stir-fried beancurd with lemongrass and chillies

SERVES 4

675 g/1½ lb firm beancurd (tofu)

peanut oil for frying

12 dried shiitake mushrooms, soaked in boiling water
   for 30 minutes, stems trimmed, and drained,
   reserving 175 ml/6 fl oz of the soaking liquid

4 tablespoons hoisin sauce

2 tablespoons soy sauce

1 tablespoon tomato purée, plus 1 teaspoon

2 fresh red chillies, finely chopped

2 leeks, white part only, thinly sliced and well rinsed

2 thick stalks of fresh lemongrass,
   peeled and finely chopped

1 red pepper, seeded and cut into
   2.5 cm/1 inch squares

1 green pepper, seeded and cut into
   2.5 cm/1 inch squares

pepper

Cut the beancurd into 2.5 cm/1 inch cubes and drain between double layers of paper towels.

Heat 2.5 cm/1 inch of oil in a large frying pan over moderately high heat. Carefully add the beancurd and fry, without crowding, until crisp and browned on all sides, about 8 minutes. Remove the beancurd with a slotted spoon and drain on paper towels.

Put the reserved mushroom soaking liquid, hoisin sauce, soy sauce, tomato purée and chillies in a bowl and stir to mix well.

Pour off all but 2 tablespoons of the oil from the frying pan. Add the leeks and lemongrass and stir-fry over moderately high heat until tender, about 1 minute. Add the peppers and mushroom caps, and stir-fry for a further 1 minute.

Stir in the sauce and the fried beancurd, then bring to the boil. Cook until the sauce thickens slightly, about 2 minutes, stirring frequently. Transfer to a serving dish, sprinkle with freshly ground black pepper and serve immediately.

Substantial enough as a main course, this stir-fry also makes a great side dish. Serve with plenty of steamed rice. If you like, start with a light vegetable broth.

STIR-FRIED MANGETOUT AND MUSHROOMS

SERVES 2

1 tablespoon olive oil

3 spring onions, sliced

175 g/6 oz mangetout

1 large garlic clove, sliced

1 teaspoon grated fresh ginger

125 g/4 oz mushrooms, sliced

1–2 teaspoons chilli sauce

1 scant tablespoon light soy sauce

1 tablespoon sesame oil

Heat a wok or saucepan, add the oil, then add the spring onions and stir-fry briskly for 1 minute. Add the mangetout and cook for a further 2 minutes, then add the garlic and ginger. Add the mushrooms and stir-fry for about 1 minute, then add the chilli sauce, soy sauce and sesame oil. Stir well, remove from the heat and cover with a lid. Leave to steam lightly for 3–4 minutes, then serve at once while the mangetout is still crisp and bright green.

This stir-fry is perfect for a light meal, served with boiled noodles or fried rice, and followed by ripe mango slices garnished with fresh mint.

AUBERGINE, MOZZARELLA AND TOMATO LAYER

Heat 1 tablespoon of the olive oil in a saucepan, add the onion and garlic, cover and cook gently for 10 minutes.

Add the tomatoes, breaking them up with a spoon, then leave to simmer, uncovered, for about 20 minutes, until the sauce is very thick. Season to taste.

Preheat the grill and set the oven to 200°C/ 400°F/Gas Mark 6. Remove the stem from the aubergine, then cut the aubergine horizontally three times to make four slices. Brush the slices with the remaining oil, then put them under the hot grill until they are lightly browned on both sides. Cut the mozzarella cheese into thin slices.

On a baking sheet, reassemble the aubergine, sandwiching each layer with tomato sauce, grated Parmesan cheese and slices of mozzarella. Press it together gently but firmly, then bake in the oven for 20 minutes, or until the cheese has melted. Some liquid will probably ooze out from the sauce but this doesn't matter; and if the aubergine lurches a bit to one side, just gently push it together again. Cut in half to serve.

Serve as a vegetarian main course with cooked green beans and a leafy salad, perhaps including some fresh basil. Start the meal with carrot and coriander soup, and finish with fresh dates and yogurt.

SERVES 2

3 tablespoons olive oil
1 onion, chopped
1 garlic clove, crushed
400 g/14 oz can of tomatoes
salt and pepper
1 aubergine
125 g/4 oz mozzarella cheese
25 g/1 oz Parmesan cheese, grated

FRIED HALLOUMI WITH A PIQUANT DRESSING

SERVES 4

grated zest and juice of ½ lemon

1 tablespoon red wine vinegar

1 teaspoon Dijon mustard

1 garlic clove, crushed

3 tablespoons olive oil,
    plus extra for shallow-frying

2 tablespoons fresh flat-leaf
    parsley, chopped

1–2 tablespoons capers,
    rinsed and drained

salt and pepper

225 g/8 oz halloumi cheese

salad leaves for serving

First make the dressing. Put the lemon zest and juice into a small bowl with the vinegar, mustard, garlic and 3 tablespoons of olive oil and whisk together until they emulsify. Add the parsley, 1 or 2 tablespoons of capers, according to your taste, and some salt and pepper. Set aside.

Drain any water from the halloumi, then rinse the cheese under the tap to remove any excess saltiness; pat dry on kitchen paper. Cut the halloumi into slices, 7 mm/⅓ inch thick.

Heat a little olive oil in a frying pan, then fry the halloumi until golden brown – it browns quickly, so you will probably find that by the time you've put the last slice in, the first one will need turning over. When the slices are browned on both sides, take them out and drain them on kitchen paper. Serve immediately, with the dressing and some salad leaves.

Serve as a vegetarian main course with a leafy green salad or a simple tomato salad, or with steamed young vegetables. Finish the meal with a yogurt-based fruit fool, or pears poached in red wine and ginger.

FETA FRITTATA WITH SUN-DRIED TOMATOES

SERVES 4

4 eggs
salt and pepper
1 tablespoon olive oil
200 g/7 oz feta cheese, drained and cubed
6 sun-dried tomatoes, chopped
sprigs of flat-leaf parsley, torn

Preheat the grill. Beat the eggs with 1 tablespoon of cold water, with salt and pepper to taste.

Heat the olive oil in a frying pan – a 20 cm/ 8 inch one is ideal – then pour in the beaten eggs. Put the feta cheese on top of the egg mixture, then the sun-dried tomatoes, distributing them evenly. Leave to cook, undisturbed, for 3–4 minutes, until the bottom is golden brown and the top is beginning to set.

Put the frying pan under the hot grill for a further 2–3 minutes to cook the top of the frittata. Serve at once, in thick wedges, scattered with the flat-leaf parsley. It's also very good cold.

Serve with a green salad – rocket or cos lettuce continue the Mediterranean theme. Finish with strawberries, peaches or nectarines, or whatever fresh fruit is in season.

GOATS CHEESE EN CROÛTE

with cranberry sauce

SERVES 4

450 g/1 lb ready-rolled puff pastry
2 x 100 g/3½ oz goats' cheese logs
a little beaten egg or milk, to glaze

Cranberry sauce
175 g/6 oz cranberries
85 g/3 oz sugar
1 tablespoon port or fresh orange juice

Preheat the oven to 220°C/425°F/Gas Mark 7. Roll out the pastry thinly and cut out eight circles which are 2.5 cm/1 inch bigger in diameter than the goats' cheese. Cut the cheeses in half horizontally.

Place one halved goats' cheese on one of the pastry circles, cut side up – this will prevent it from oozing out during cooking. Brush the edge of the pastry lightly with cold water, put another pastry circle on top and press the edges firmly together or crimp with a fork. Repeat with the rest of the cheese and pastry.

Prick the tops to allow the steam to escape, and brush the tops lightly with beaten egg or milk. Decorate with pastry trimmings and brush again with egg or milk, then place on a baking sheet which has been brushed with water and bake for 15 minutes.

While the cheeses are cooking, make the sauce. Put the cranberries into a saucepan with 4 table-spoons water. Bring to the boil, then simmer for about 10 minutes, until the berries are tender. Add the sugar and simmer gently until it has dissolved. Remove from the heat and add the port or fresh orange juice. Serve warm, with the freshly baked goats' cheeses en croûte.

These make a lovely vegetarian Christmas dish, especially if you decorate them with pastry holly leaves and berries. Serve with stir-fried Brussels sprouts, steamed carrots and creamy mashed potatoes; start with something simple and fruity such as sliced pears and watercress, and finish with lemon or champagne sorbet.

FISH AND SHELLFISH

If you like good food,
cook it yourself.

LI LIWENG
(17th century)

THAI LOBSTER SALAD

SERVES 4

2 cooked lobsters, about 600 g/1¼ lb each
frisée, lambs' lettuce and radicchio
1–2 tablespoons light vinaigrette

Dressing
5 cm/2 inch piece of fresh ginger, sliced
200 ml/7 fl oz tinned coconut milk
grated zest of ½ lemon
½ green chilli (or to taste), sliced
1 tablespoon groundnut oil
salt and pepper

To make the dressing, finely slice a couple of pieces of the ginger into matchsticks and reserve for the garnish. Put all the ingredients in a small saucepan and simmer until thickened and the flavour has developed, about 10 minutes. Strain and leave to cool.

Cut the lobsters in half and remove the meat. Crack the claws and pick out the meat. Reserve the liver and the eggs, if there are any. Mix the liver with the cooled dressing, and use the eggs as a garnish for the claw meat. Pour the dressing over the lobster meat and chill until needed.

To serve, mix the salad leaves with the vinaigrette. Arrange the lobster meat and claw meat on a plate and surround with the salad leaves.

Serve as a main course with green salad and cold french beans. Follow with mangoes in a lime syrup.

TARTARE OF TWO SALMONS

Chop the fresh and smoked salmon quite finely, then combine with the chopped shallot, lime juice, chives, crème fraîche and salt and pepper to taste. Set aside in the refrigerator.

Cut the peeled cucumber in half lengthways. Using a teaspoon, scoop out and discard the seeds. Slice the flesh thinly into half moons. Layer the cucumber in a colander, sprinkling the layers lightly with salt. Leave for 20 minutes, then rinse and pat dry.

Bring a small saucepan of water to the boil, gently lower in the eggs and cook for 2½ minutes after the water returns to the boil. Drain and plunge into cold water. Peel and set aside. The yolks should still be very slightly soft.

To serve, make a fan of the cucumber slices in the centre of four plates. Place a scone cutter on top and press in a quarter of the salmon mixture. Lift off the scone cutter and repeat with the remaining salmon tartare. Top each salmon mound with a quail's egg and a sprig of chervil.

Serve this light summery dish with a green leafy salad and walnut bread. Start the meal with a crisp tart filled with sliced tomatoes, shredded basil and olive oil. Round off with a salad of lightly poached summer fruits accompanied by crisp shortbread biscuits.

SERVES 4

100 g/3½ oz filleted very fresh salmon
100 g/3½ oz smoked salmon
1 shallot, finely chopped
½ teaspoon fresh lime juice
1 tablespoon chopped fresh chives
1 tablespoon crème fraîche
salt and pepper
½ cucumber, peeled
4 quails' eggs
sprigs of chervil

KEBABS OF TIGER PRAWNS

with a roasted tomato and mint salsa

SERVES 4

12 uncooked tiger prawns,
 shelled
2 tablespoons olive oil
1 garlic clove, finely chopped

Roasted tomato and mint salsa
3 beefsteak tomatoes
1 garlic clove, finely chopped
juice of ½ lime
1 chilli, finely chopped,
 including its seeds
1 tablespoon finely chopped
 fresh coriander
2 tablespoons finely chopped
 fresh mint
½ teaspoon grated lime zest
½ teaspoon grated orange zest
salt and pepper

To serve
boiled new potatoes or potato
 salad

Heat the grill or barbecue. If using wooden skewers, soak them in cold water for about 30 minutes.

Slit the prawns along their backs and pull out the dark vein, opening them out butterfly style. Place them in a shallow dish with the oil and garlic and leave to marinate for 30 minutes.

To make the salsa, sear the tomatoes under a very hot grill or over a flame until their skins blacken and blister. Chop finely while they are still warm. Mix with all the other ingredients and leave to cool.

Fix the prawns on the skewers and grill until they turn pink, turning once. Serve the prawns on a bed of potatoes, with the salsa spooned around.

I often have these prawns with a green salad. Beforehand, I love a spicy gazpacho soup, and afterwards some bread and soft cheeses such as goats' cheese or feta.

WARM SEAFOOD SALAD

SERVES 4

200 g/7 oz squid tubes

200 g/7 oz uncooked prawns

200 g/7 oz scallops

2 tablespoons fish sauce

2 tablespoons groundnut oil

1 cos or iceberg lettuce,
    shredded

2 garlic cloves, crushed

handful of fresh basil,
    roughly torn

salt and pepper

1 small red chilli, deseeded
    and thinly sliced

Split open the squid tubes, remove the backbone and clean thoroughly. Lay flat and trim the wide end of any tough pieces. Pat dry with paper towels. On the upper side of each piece, make a small crisscross pattern, about 1 x 1 cm/½ x ½ inch, not cutting right through the flesh. Cut into pieces about 5 x 5 cm/2 x 2 inches. Shell and devein the prawns. Clean the scallops. Put the fish sauce in a small jug with 2 tablespoons water and mix well.

Heat a wok or large pan, then add the oil. When the oil is hot and begins to smoke, add the lettuce and stir-fry for 2 minutes. Remove with a slotted spoon and place on a serving dish in a warm place.

Add the garlic to the wok and stir for 30 seconds. Add the squid and stir-fry for 2 minutes; the pieces will fan out and begin to curl up into small tubes. Add the scallops and prawns and stir-fry for 2 minutes. Add the basil and a little salt and stir for a further 1 minute. Add the sauce mixture and stir for 1 minute, then finally stir in the chilli and some freshly ground black pepper. Serve immediately.

The seafood served on its bed of lettuce needs no accompaniment. Follow it with fresh figs and cheese, or a red plum or peach sorbet.

PRAWNS WITH MANGETOUT

SERVES 3–4, OR 5–6 AS PART OF A MULTI-COURSE MEAL

450 g/1 lb large uncooked prawns,
    shelled and deveined
¼ teaspoon grated fresh ginger
1 teaspoon rice wine or dry sherry
1 teaspoon cornflour
½ teaspoon salt
3 tablespoons groundnut or corn oil
125 g/4 oz mangetout,
    ends snapped and strings removed

Rinse the prawns in cold water, drain and place in a bowl. Stir in the ginger, rice wine, cornflour and salt and mix well. Set aside.

Heat 1 tablespoon of the oil in a wok over medium-high heat. When the oil is hot, but not smoking, add the mangetout and stir until they turn a darker green, about 1 minute. Remove the mangetout and spread out on a plate.

Pour the remaining oil into the same wok over high heat. Stir the prawn mixture and add to the wok. Stir constantly for about 1 minute, or until the prawns turn pink and opaque. Return the mangetout to the wok and stir together over high heat for about 30 seconds. Transfer to a serving dish and serve immediately.

As part of a multi-course meal with steamed rice, this light dish pairs nicely with the dark sauce of chicken with walnuts (page 220).

SAMBAL SOTONG

Chilli-fried squid

Soak the dried chillies in water for a few hours, then drain.

Cut the squid tubes lengthways and use the tip of the knife to lightly score a crisscross pattern on the surface, without cutting right through. Cut into 5 cm/2 inch squares and set aside, with the tentacles.

Soak the tamarind pulp in 125 ml/4 fl oz boiling water and leave for 5 minutes. Knead to dissolve, then strain the tamarind water and set aside.

Grind, pound or blend the lemongrass, garlic, drained chillies, blachan and onion together to make a paste.

Heat a wok until hot, then add the oil. When the oil is hot, add the chilli paste and stir-fry for 2 minutes. Add the tamarind water, salt and sugar and stir-fry for 3 minutes. Add the squid meat and tentacles and stir-fry over high heat for 3–4 minutes, until cooked but still tender.

Serve this spicy, substantial sambal with a bowl of steamed rice and a platter of stir-fried green beans, as part of a shared Malaysian meal. Follow with a sticky rice dessert drizzled with coconut milk and palm sugar.

SERVES 4

4 dried red chillies
500 g/1 lb 2 oz small squid (sotong), cleaned
2 tablespoons tamarind pulp
1 stalk of lemongrass, peeled and sliced
1 garlic clove, crushed
1 teaspoon blachan (dried shrimp paste)
1 onion, chopped
2 tablespoons peanut oil
½ teaspoon salt
2 teaspoons palm sugar or brown sugar

TOM XAO GUNG

Stir-fried prawns with honey and ginger

SERVES 4

2 tablespoons peanut oil

450 g/1 lb uncooked large
  prawns, shelled and deveined

1 large onion, halved and
  thinly sliced

6 large garlic cloves, thinly sliced

1 heaped tablespoon thinly
  shredded fresh ginger

½ red pepper, seeded and cut
  lengthways into thin strips

2 tablespoons honey

1 tablespoon fish sauce

1 tablespoon soy sauce

½ teaspoon five-spice powder

pepper

To garnish

sprigs of coriander

Heat 1 tablespoon of the oil in a large frying pan over high heat.
Add the prawns and stir-fry until they turn pink but are not cooked
through, about 1 minute. Using a slotted spoon, transfer the prawns
to a bowl.

Add the remaining oil to the same pan and heat. Add the onion,
garlic and ginger and stir-fry until browned and soft, about 3 minutes.
Add the pepper and cook for a further 1 minute. Stir in the honey,
fish sauce, soy sauce, five-spice powder and prawns. Toss to combine
all the ingredients and cook until the prawns are evenly glazed
with the sauce, about 2 minutes. Transfer to a warm platter, sprinkle
with freshly ground black pepper and garnish with coriander. Serve
at once.

*Accompany with a simple sautéed vegetable, such as green beans or sugar
snap peas, and rice. Pickled vegetables (page 375) would also make a fine
accompaniment to this dish.*

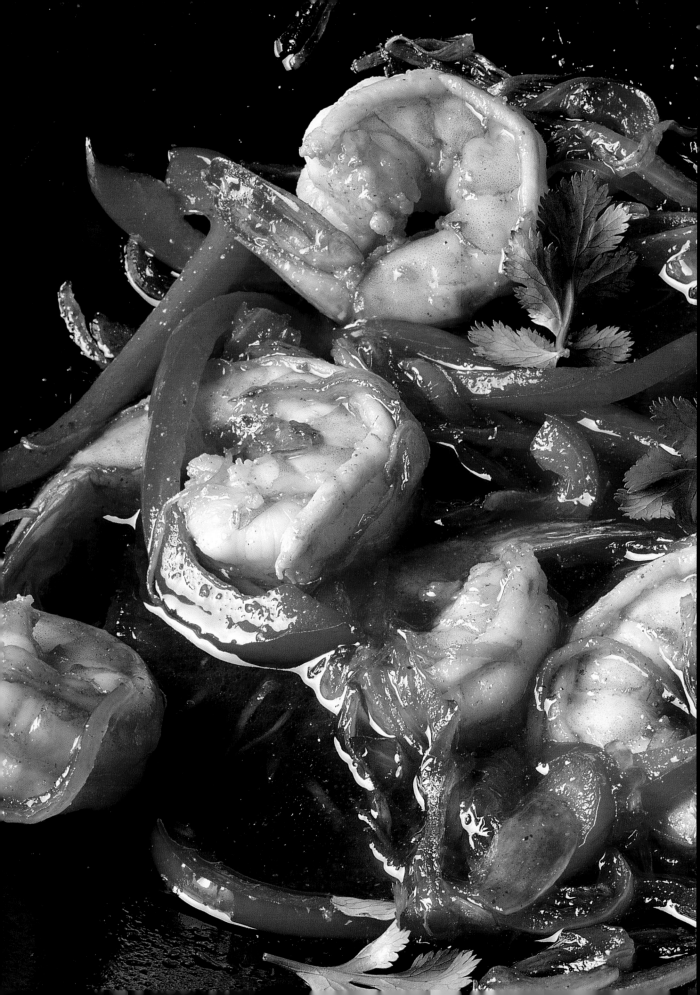

BEANCURD AND CRABMEAT

SERVES 3–4, OR 5–6 AS PART OF A MULTI-COURSE MEAL

175 g/6 oz canned crabmeat, drained
1 teaspoon rice wine
450 g/1 lb firm beancurd
3 tablespoons groundnut or corn oil
2 slices of fresh ginger
250 ml/8 fl oz chicken stock
2 tablespoons cornflour dissolved in 4 tablespoons chicken stock
1 egg white, lightly beaten
salt
2 spring onions, thinly sliced

Place the crabmeat in a small bowl and mix in the rice wine. Set aside. Drain the beancurd and cut into 2.5 cm/1 inch cubes. Set aside.

Heat the oil in a wok over medium–high heat. Add the ginger and stir until fragrant. Add the crabmeat and stock, stirring gently. Reduce the heat to medium-low, add the beancurd and simmer for about 4 minutes.

Raise the heat to high and when the mixture comes to a boil, stir in the cornflour mixture. Continue stirring until the mixture thickens and returns to the boil, then stir in the egg white, to form filmy clouds. Remove the wok from the heat and taste, adding salt if necessary. Pour into a deep serving dish and sprinkle with spring onions. Serve immediately.

Low in fat, this is excellent as a light dish as part of a multi-course meal.

CILI UDANG
Chilli prawns

SERVES 4–6

1 kg/2¼ lb uncooked prawns in their shells

3 tablespoons vegetable oil

2 garlic cloves, crushed

2 slices of fresh ginger

4 dried red chillies, soaked, drained and chopped
   (page 378)

3 tablespoons chilli sauce, or to taste

125 ml/4 fl oz tomato sauce or ketchup

375 ml/12 fl oz hot chicken stock

½ teaspoon salt

2 teaspoons sugar, or to taste

2 teaspoons cornflour blended with 2 tablespoons
   cold water

4 spring onions, chopped

2 small eggs, beaten

fresh coriander leaves

Devein the prawns by hooking out the intestinal tract with a thin bamboo skewer.

Heat the oil in a wok and fry the prawns quickly over high heat until almost cooked. Drain and set aside.

Drain off all but 1 tablespoon of the oil and reheat the wok. Add the garlic and ginger and cook for 3 minutes. Add the chopped chillies, chilli sauce, tomato sauce, stock, salt and sugar, and stir well to mix. Add the cornflour paste, bring to the boil, stirring constantly, and stir for 1 minute.

Return the prawns to the wok, together with the spring onions, and toss to coat. Slowly drizzle in the eggs, stirring all the time. Cook for a further 1–2 minutes, until you have a creamy, thick sauce. Serve immediately, scattered with coriander leaves.

Serve with plenty of coconut rice (page 375) or steamed jasmine rice to soak up the juices. Start the meal with chicken satay and peanut sauce (page 77) and finish with banana fritters (goreng pisang).

PUNJABI METHI JINGRI

Fenugreek prawn curry

SERVES 4

675 g/1½ lb uncooked large prawns or langoustines
   (scampi), weighed after removing heads and shells
4 tablespoons ghee
12 garlic cloves, thinly sliced
6–8 spring onions, chopped
½ red pepper, finely chopped
1–3 fresh red chillies, seeded and sliced
1 tablespoon tomato purée
3 tablespoons natural yogurt
2 tablespoons dried fenugreek (methi) leaves
225 g/8 oz rocket or watercress, chopped
2 tablespoons chopped fresh coriander leaves
2 teaspoons garam masala
salt

Spices

½ teaspoon each of cumin seeds, black mustard
   seeds, fennel seeds, green cardamom seeds
¼ teaspoon each of turmeric, chilli powder, mango
   powder, fenugreek seeds

Devein the prawns, rinse and pat dry.

Heat the ghee in a wok or karahi until hot, but well below smoking point. Add the cumin, black mustard, fennel and green cardamom seeds and stir-fry briskly for about 30 seconds. Add the garlic and spring onions and stir-fry for a further 30 seconds. Add the turmeric, chilli and mango powder and fenugreek seeds, stir briskly, then add the pepper, chillies, tomato purée and yogurt. When they reach a gentle simmer, add the prawns and fenugreek leaves. Stir-fry until the prawns are cooked through; this will take about 6–8 minutes. Add a little water from time to time if necessary to keep the mixture moist.

Add the rocket or watercress, coriander leaves and garam masala and stir well. Add salt to taste, and serve at once.

For a change from rice or Indian bread, try this with oven-baked chips, dusted with chilli powder and garam masala.

CHAUDRÉE DE MOULES AU FENOUIL ET SAFRAN

Cod and mussel chowder with fennel and saffron

SERVES 4

25 g/1 oz butter
325 g/12 oz fennel bulb, sliced
1 onion, chopped
salt and white pepper
800 g/1¾ lb potatoes, peeled and cut into
    2.5 cm/1 inch cubes
large pinch of saffron threads
250 ml/8 fl oz fish stock
1 bay leaf
800 g/1¾ lb mussels
500 g/1 lb 2 oz cod fillets, skinned and cut into
    2.5 cm/1 inch pieces
500 ml/16 fl oz milk
250 ml/8 fl oz double cream
2 tablespoons chopped fresh parsley

Melt the butter in a saucepan and add the fennel, onion, salt and pepper. Sauté gently, stirring occasionally, until the vegetables are translucent but not starting to brown, 7–10 minutes.

Spread the potatoes over the fennel. Mix the saffron with the fish stock and pour it over the potatoes. Add the bay leaf, cover and bring to the boil, then reduce the heat and simmer until the potatoes are just tender, 12–15 minutes.

Meanwhile, clean the mussels thoroughly and debeard.

Spread the cod over the potatoes and add the milk. Stir to mix the ingredients and spread the colour of the saffron. Add the mussels, cover tightly with the lid and simmer until the fish is just tender when flaked with a fork and the mussels have opened, 5–7 minutes. Note that the milk should simmer, not boil, or it may curdle.

Add the cream and parsley and bring just to the boil. Discard the bay leaf, taste and adjust the seasoning. Serve the chowder from the casserole, or in individual bowls.

This fish chowder is not a soup but a stew, a generous meal in itself. Serve it with sliced baguette, baked in the oven until dry so it forms croûtes for soaking in the stew. A good dessert would be figs baked in port wine or poached pears with candied ginger.

RISOTTO CON LE COZZE

Risotto with mussels

SERVES 4

200 ml/7 fl oz dry white wine

1.5 kg/3 lb mussels thoroughly scrubbed
and debearded

1 litre/1¾ pints light fish stock or vegetable stock

5 tablespoons olive oil

1 onion, very finely chopped

salt and pepper

1 stick of celery, with the leaves if possible,
finely chopped

1 garlic clove, finely chopped

350 g/13 oz Italian rice, preferably vialone nano

4 tablespoons chopped parsley, preferably flat-leaf

Put the wine in a large sauté pan, add the mussels
and cover the pan. Cook over high heat, shaking
the pan occasionally, until the mussels are open,
which will only take 3–4 minutes. Set aside a
dozen or so of the best-looking mussels in their
shells. Remove the meat from the remaining
mussels and chop coarsely. Strain the cooking
liquid through a sieve lined with muslin.

Heat the stock to simmering point and keep
it just simmering all through the cooking of
the risotto.

Heat the oil in a wide heavy saucepan, add
the onion and a pinch of salt and sauté until
soft. Add the celery and garlic and sauté for
a further minute.

Add the rice and turn it over in the oil for a
couple of minutes. Pour over the mussel liquid
and stir well. When the liquid has been absorbed,
you can begin to add the stock, a ladleful at
a time. Stir very frequently. When the rice is
cooked (after about 15–18 minutes), draw the
pan off the heat and stir in the chopped mussels.
Taste and season with plenty of freshly ground
black pepper, adding salt if necessary. Transfer to
a warmed serving dish and top with the reserved
mussels and the parsley. Serve at once.

*In Italy risotto is always served as a first course,
the reason being that it must be eaten the minute it
finishes cooking. It is also quite usual to follow a fish
first course with a fish main course. Red mullet (page
196) would be my choice. If you prefer meat or
chicken, it should be simply cooked.*

SAUMON À LA PEAU CROUSTILLANTE, COULIS DE TOMATES ET BASILIC

Crisp-skinned salmon fillet with tomato and basil coulis

SERVES 4

1–2 salmon fillets, scaled, with skin,
    about 800 g/1¾ lb
salt and pepper
2 tablespoons olive oil

Tomato and basil coulis
500 g/1 lb 2 oz tomatoes, skinned, seeded and diced
bunch of basil
1 garlic clove, finely chopped
juice of 1 lemon, or more to taste

To make the coulis: sprinkle the diced tomatoes with salt and pepper, stir gently and leave to drain in a colander for 15–30 minutes. Strip the basil leaves from the stems, reserving several sprigs for decoration. Shred the remaining leaves. Put the drained tomatoes in a bowl and stir in the garlic, lemon juice and shredded basil. Taste, adjust the seasoning and chill the coulis.

Preheat the oven to 220°C/425°F/Gas Mark 7. To prepare the salmon: run your fingers over the flesh and if you feel any bones, pull them out with tweezers. Cut the salmon into four portions and sprinkle both sides with salt and pepper. Heat the oil in a large frying pan with an ovenproof handle and add the salmon, skin side down. Fry without moving the pieces for 2–3 minutes, until the skin is crisp – when done it will shrink and loosen from the surface of the pan. Transfer the pan to the oven and bake until done to your taste: 2–4 minutes for rare, 5–8 minutes for well done. Note that cooking time depends on the thickness of the fish.

Transfer the fish to warmed serving plates, skin side up. Stir the coulis to blend, taste it again, adjusting the seasoning if necessary. Spoon the chilled coulis beside the hot fish, decorate the plates with basil sprigs and serve at once so the skin remains crisp.

Keep this salmon up to speed with an accompaniment of couscous flavoured with saffron. For dessert, I'd go for an open face fruit tart, the pastry rolled wafer-thin in the modern style.

SPICED MACKEREL FILLETS
on a plum tomato salad

SERVES 4

4 mackerel, filleted and scaled
vegetable oil for brushing
1 teaspoon each of garlic salt, onion salt,
   oregano and paprika

Plum tomato salad
125 ml/4 fl oz olive oil
1 teaspoon creamed horseradish
1 teaspoon white wine vinegar
salt and pepper
225 g/8 oz plum tomatoes
small cos or romaine lettuce

Heat the grill or barbecue.

To make the salad dressing, whisk together
the oil, horseradish, vinegar and salt and pepper
to taste.

Run your fingers over the flesh of the mackerel
to make sure no bones remain; use tweezers to
pull out any tiny bones. Cut each fillet in half.
Brush the fish with a little oil and then pass the
flesh side through the spices. Place the fish, spice
side down, on the grill. Cook for 2–3 minutes –
do not overcook – then turn and cook the
other side.

Slice the tomatoes and lay on four plates.
Shred the lettuce and toss in some of the
dressing. Put the lettuce on top of the tomatoes.
Lay the barbecued fish on top and sprinkle with
the dressing. Serve at once.

*Serve with a warm potato salad and mustard mayon-
naise, and finish with a lemon tart and clotted cream.*

BARBECUED TROUT
with spinach and bacon

SERVES 4

70 g/2½ oz unsalted butter
1 large onion, finely chopped
225 g/8 oz baby spinach,
    washed and roughly chopped
salt and pepper
4 trout, gutted and cleaned
8 rashers of smoked
    streaky bacon

Red wine sauce
1 teaspoon vegetable oil
125 g/4 oz streaky bacon,
    cut into small strips (lardons)
125 g/4 oz mushrooms, sliced
150 ml/5 fl oz red wine

Heat the grill or barbecue.

Melt 50 g/2 oz of the butter in a large saucepan, add the onion and cook over medium heat until softened, about 5 minutes. Add the spinach and cook briefly until the spinach wilts. Leave until cool enough to handle.

Season the spinach and onion mixture with salt and plenty of pepper, then use to fill the four trout. Wrap two rashers of bacon around each trout and secure with a cocktail stick. Grill the trout for 8–10 minutes, turning once, until crisp on the outside and tender in the middle.

Meanwhile, make the sauce. Heat the oil in a saucepan, add the bacon strips and cook for 5–6 minutes, then add the mushrooms and stir over medium heat for about 2 minutes. Pour in the red wine, bring to the boil, then reduce the heat and simmer for 5 minutes. At the last minute, stir in the remaining 15 g/½ oz butter to give a glossy finish. Serve the trout on warmed plates, with the red wine sauce poured around.

Why not try sautéed potatoes with the trout, and perhaps a light prawn salad to start?

KASHMIRI MACHLI

Aromatic fish curry

**SERVES 4 AS A MAIN COURSE,
8 AS A STARTER**

4 fresh mackerel,
     about 325 g/12 oz each,
     scaled and gutted

Marinade
225 g/8 oz Greek-style yogurt
1 large onion, chopped
8 garlic cloves, quartered
5 cm/2 inch cube of fresh
     ginger, chopped
1–4 fresh green chillies,
     seeded and chopped
30–40 fresh sweet basil leaves
1 tablespoon tomato purée
1 tablespoon garam masala
1 teaspoon salt

Wash the fish inside and out and pat dry. Make a few gashes in the flesh with the tip of a sharp knife.

Put all the marinade ingredients in a food processor and grind, adding enough water to make a thickish paste. Put the fish in a shallow, non-metallic dish, coat each fish with the marinade, cover and refrigerate for a minimum of 1 hour, up to a maximum of 4 hours.

To cook, preheat the grill to medium. Place the fish on the grill rack and grill for about 8 minutes. Turn and grill for a further 5–6 minutes. Serve hot.

To me this is a summertime barbecue dish, so why not serve it with a baked potato with soured cream, dusted with garam masala? Savour the fish with a glass of chilled dry rosé wine. A half portion makes a great starter, served with slices of buttered brown bread, a green salad and lemon wedges.

MONKFISH IN BLACK BEAN SAUCE

SERVES 4

450 g/1 lb monkfish, cod or hake fillets,
    cut into bite-sized pieces
4 tablespoons black bean sauce
4 tablespoons fish stock
2 tablespoons light soy sauce
5 thin slices fresh ginger
1 small red chilli, deseeded and thinly sliced
1 tablespoon groundnut oil
½ red or orange pepper, deseeded and cut into strips
125 g/4 oz mangetout, tips removed, then sliced
    in half diagonally
salt and pepper

Prepare the fish, removing all the bones. Place in a bowl with the black bean sauce and leave to marinate for 10 minutes. Put the stock, soy sauce, ginger and chilli in a small jug and mix well.

Heat a wok or large pan, then add the oil. When the oil is hot and begins to smoke, add the pepper and mangetout and stir-fry for 2 minutes. Add the sauce mixture and stir for 2–3 minutes. Using a slotted spoon, remove the pepper and mangetout and keep warm.

Lower the heat and add the fish pieces; stir carefully for 2–3 minutes, depending on the size of the fish. Season to taste with salt and pepper and serve immediately, with the vegetables. Pour any remaining sauce over the fish.

Vegetables are included in this recipe, so all that is needed is a base of rice or noodles. Have an indulgence to finish – chocolate mud cake or crème brûlée, or for the more health-conscious a selection of cheeses and fresh fruit.

IKAN GULAI

Fish curry with coconut milk

SERVES 4

500 g/1 lb 2 oz firm fish steaks e.g. cod, snapper

1½ tablespoons tamarind pulp

1 stalk of lemongrass, peeled and sliced

4 dried red chillies, soaked and drained

1 tablespoon freshly grated ginger

2 garlic cloves, crushed

8 shallots or 1 onion, chopped

2 tablespoons vegetable oil

1 tablespoon ground coriander

1 teaspoon ground cumin

1 teaspoon ground fennel

1 teaspoon turmeric

6 curry leaves

1 teaspoon salt

1 teaspoon sugar

250 ml/8 fl oz coconut milk

Remove any skin or bones from the fish and cut into bite-sized pieces.

Soak the tamarind pulp in 125 ml/4 fl oz boiling water and leave for 10 minutes. Knead to dissolve, then strain the tamarind water and set aside.

Grind, pound or blend the lemongrass, drained chillies, ginger, garlic and shallots together to make a paste.

Heat the oil in a wok or frying pan and fry the chilli paste for 5 minutes, stirring, until fragrant. Add the coriander, cumin, fennel, turmeric, curry leaves, salt and sugar, then slowly add the coconut milk, stirring. Bring to the boil, stirring constantly. Add the tamarind water and simmer, uncovered, for 10 minutes, until the sauce thickens slightly.

To serve, add the fish and simmer for 3–4 minutes, until just cooked.

Start with a spicy chicken soup or spring rolls. Serve fish curry with plenty of rice and a stir-fried green vegetable such as green beans or water spinach (page 150).

TRIGLIE ALLA MARCHIGIANA

Red mullet with prosciutto and rosemary

Lay the red mullet in a dish. Mix together the lemon juice and 2 tablespoons of the oil, add salt and pepper and spoon a little of the mixture into the cavity of each fish. Brush the rest of the lemon and oil mixture all over the fish and leave to marinate for 2 hours.

Preheat the oven to 190°C/375°F/Gas Mark 5. Brush an oven dish with a little oil.

Mix together the rosemary, garlic, breadcrumbs, a little salt and a generous amount of pepper. Coat the fish with the mixture, pressing the crumbs on to the fish with your hands. Wrap a slice of prosciutto around each fish and lay the fish in the oven dish. Drizzle with the remaining oil and bake for 15–20 minutes, basting the fish twice during cooking. Serve from the dish, handing round the lemon wedges and a little of your best extra virgin olive oil for a final blessing.

In Italy a dish of fish is served by itself, without vegetables, but with a salad to follow. Try a tomato, pepper and cucumber salad or a simple green salad. If you want to serve an accompanying vegetable I would suggest a bowl of spinach dressed with extra virgin olive oil and lemon juice. The meal can begin with gnocchi or with most pasta dishes, a risotto or a soup. If the first course is filling, the ideal dessert would be a bowl of fresh fruit or strawberries or raspberries with cream. But if the first course is a light soup I would finish with your favourite chocolate mousse or my ricotta cake (page 332).

SERVES 4

4 red mullet, cleaned but with the heads left on
juice of 1 lemon
5 tablespoons extra virgin olive oil
salt and pepper
1 tablespoon chopped fresh rosemary
1 garlic clove, chopped
4 tablespoons dried breadcrumbs
4 large slices of prosciutto, not too thinly cut

To serve
2 lemons, cut into wedges

CA CHIEN SOT CA CHUA

Pan-fried sea bass with spicy tomato sauce

SERVES 4

3 tablespoons peanut or vegetable oil

4 shallots, thinly sliced

4 large garlic cloves, thinly sliced

4 large ripe tomatoes (about 675 g/1½ lb),
    cored, seeded and coarsely chopped

2 fresh red chillies, finely chopped,
    or ½ teaspoon chilli paste

2 tablespoons fish sauce, plus 2 teaspoons

1 teaspoon sugar

2 spring onions, thinly sliced

2 tablespoons chopped fresh dill

125 g/4 oz plain flour

4 sea bass or red snapper fillets,
    about 175 g/6 oz each

pepper

Heat 2 tablespoons of the oil in a large frying pan over moderate heat. Add the shallots and garlic and stir-fry until fragrant, about 30 seconds. Add the tomatoes and chillies and stir-fry for 1 minute. Add 2 tablespoons of the fish sauce, the sugar, and 4 tablespoons water. Cover and simmer for 5 minutes, stirring occasionally.

Stir in the spring onions and dill, then remove the pan from the heat. Cover to keep the sauce warm while you cook the fish.

Sift the flour on to a large platter. Pat the fish dry and make a few diagonal slits on the skin side at the thickest part of each fillet. Rub the fillets with the remaining 2 teaspoons fish sauce and sprinkle with black pepper, then dredge in the flour, shaking off any excess. Place the fish on a platter.

Heat a large nonstick frying pan over high heat for 15 seconds, then add the remaining 1 tablespoon oil. When the oil is smoking hot, carefully add the fish, skin side down. Reduce the heat to medium-high, cover the pan and cook until the skin is crisp and golden brown, about 5 minutes. Using two wide metal spatulas, carefully turn the fish. Continue to cook, uncovered, for 1 minute, or until the fish flakes easily when tested with a fork. Transfer the fish to a large platter. Ladle the tomato sauce over the fish and serve immediately.

For a complete main course, all that is needed is a bowl of rice, a soup, and a steamed vegetable, such as asparagus or spinach. Pass chilli dipping sauce (page 375) separately.

NASELLO ALLA SIRACUSANA

Baked hake with anchovy sauce

SERVES 4

1 hake, about 900 g/2 lb
4 tablespoons olive oil
salt and pepper
2 sprigs of rosemary
½ lemon, cut into thin slices
5 salted anchovies, boned
    and rinsed, or 10 anchovy
    fillets, drained
1 garlic clove, finely chopped

To serve
boiled potatoes

Preheat the oven to 190°C/375°F/Gas Mark 5.

Wash the hake and dry well on paper towels. Brush a little oil inside the fish and season the cavity with salt and pepper. Stuff the rosemary and lemon slices inside and secure with cocktail sticks.

Heat the remaining oil in a small saucepan, add the anchovies and garlic and mash to a paste with a fork.

Lay a piece of foil, large enough to wrap the fish, on a baking sheet. Lay the hake on the foil and pour over the anchovy sauce, turning the fish over so that it is completely coated. Add a little salt and a generous amount of pepper. Seal the foil around the fish and bake for 30−35 minutes, until done.

Lay the parcel on an oval dish and open it at the table. Slice the fish into steaks and spoon around some of the cooking juices. Serve with boiled potatoes to soak up the delicious sauce.

No other vegetables are needed, possibly just a salad to follow. A minestrone or gnocchi would be a good starter. Both courses being quite substantial, the pudding could be light, an ice cream or sorbet in the summer, and a salad of caramelized oranges or fresh pineapple in the winter.

RED MULLET
with braised fennel and pesto sauce

SERVES 4

2 whole red mullets,
   about 400 g/14 oz each
salt and pepper
good pinch of saffron strands
   (optional)
8 baby fennel bulbs
   or 2 small fennel bulbs
25 g/1 oz butter
3 tablespoons olive oil
200 ml/7 fl oz fish stock
4 tablespoons pesto, preferably
   homemade (page 374)

Ask the fishmonger to fillet (but not skin) the mullets so you have four whole, neat fillets, about 100 g/3½ oz each. Score each skin side about three times. Season the fillets, crush over the saffron strands, if using, and rub into the skin. Set aside in the refrigerator while you prepare the fennel.

Trim the fennel, reserving any fronds. If not using baby fennel, cut into quarters, leaving the root intact. Heat the butter and 1 tablespoon of the oil in a deep frying pan and brown the fennel all over. Add 150 ml/5 fl oz of the fish stock, bring to the boil, season, cover and simmer gently for 15–20 minutes, until the stock has been absorbed and the fennel is tender. Keep warm in the pan.

Mix the remaining fish stock with the pesto sauce and heat gently.

Heat the remaining oil in a heavy-bottomed frying pan. When it is hot, add the fish fillets, skin side down, and fry for about 3 minutes. Season, turn carefully and cook for another 2 minutes or so.

To serve, divide the fennel between four warmed plates and arrange the mullet on top. Trickle the pesto sauce around the fish and garnish with any reserved fronds of fennel.

A salad of sliced artichoke bottoms, rocket leaves and shavings of Parmesan cheese could precede this main course. Finish the meal with a hot pistachio soufflé with scoops of rich chocolate ice cream.

BRAISED MONKFISH IN RED WINE

SERVES 4

125 g/4 oz small button onions, peeled
3 tablespoons vegetable oil
250 g/9 oz unsalted butter, cut into cubes
125 g/4 oz small button mushrooms
salt and pepper
85 g/3 oz smoked streaky bacon
675 g/1½ lb monkfish fillets,
    trimmed and cut into 12 equal pieces
50 g/2 oz shallots, finely chopped
200 ml/7 fl oz chicken stock
600 ml/1 pint red wine
4 tablespoons double cream
½ teaspoon redcurrant jelly
1 tablespoon chopped fresh parsley

Preheat the oven to 160°/325°/Gas Mark 3.

Place the button onions in a saucepan just large enough to hold them in a single layer. Add a little oil and fry over high heat until well coloured on all sides. Reduce the heat, cover with a lid and cook slowly until soft.

Heat a little butter in a saucepan, add the mushrooms and cook over high heat. Season with salt and pepper.

Grill the bacon on both sides until crisp. Cut into 1 cm/½ inch strips.

Season the fish. Heat a flameproof casserole, add a little butter, then add the fish and fry until lightly coloured on both sides. Remove the fish from the casserole, add the shallots and cook until soft. Return the fish to the casserole, add the stock and half the red wine, cover and braise in the oven for about 30 minutes, until tender.

Using a slotted spoon, remove the fish to a warmed plate, cover and keep warm.

Add the remaining wine to the casserole and boil over high heat until it reduces and thickens. Add the cream and reduce again. Remove from the heat and beat in the butter and redcurrant jelly. Add the fish, onions and mushrooms, then taste and adjust the seasoning. Serve on warmed plates, sprinkled with the crisp bacon and parsley.

Serve at any time of year, accompanied by saffron rice. Begin the meal with a salad, perhaps of marinated vegetables. Follow with a refreshing fruit dessert such as lemon sorbet.

FILLETS OF BRILL

with three mustard sauce

SERVES 4

4 fillets of brill (or halibut or cod),
    about 150 g/5 oz each, skinned
salt and pepper
4 small Little Gem lettuces
3 tablespoons olive oil
25 g/1 oz butter

Three mustard sauce

15 g/½ oz butter
3 shallots, finely sliced
200 ml/7 fl oz dry white wine
200 ml/7 fl oz Noilly Prat or dry vermouth
400 ml/14 fl oz fish stock
300 ml/10 fl oz double cream
1 teaspoon each of Dijon, Pommery and
    honey mustards

To serve (optional)

250 g/9 oz fresh peas, broad beans
    or fine green beans

Trim the fish fillets to neat shapes, season and set aside.

To make the sauce, heat the butter in a saucepan, add the shallots and cook gently for about 12 minutes or until softened. Add the wine and Noilly Prat or vermouth and boil until reduced by two-thirds. Stir in the stock and boil again until reduced by half. Add the cream and simmer for 15 minutes, until the sauce has the consistency of thin cream. Strain through a sieve, return to the pan and season to taste.

Cut the lettuces in half, leaving the root intact. Heat 1 tablespoon of the oil and the butter in a frying pan and fry the lettuces for about 5 minutes, until lightly coloured. Add about 4 tablespoons water, season and cook for a further 5 minutes, until softened. Keep warm.

In a large nonstick frying pan, heat the remaining oil and fry the fish for 3 minutes on one side. Turn over carefully and cook for a further 2 minutes.

To serve, reheat the sauce and whisk in the three mustards. Arrange two lettuce halves on each of four warmed plates. Lay the fish on top and spoon over the sauce. Lightly boiled peas, broad beans or green beans are a good accompaniment.

If you like to make your own ravioli, start this meal with homemade salmon ravioli. Alternatively, toss freshly cooked pasta in a creamy smoked salmon sauce. And for pudding, how about a French lemon tart?

GRILLED SEA BASS
with sauce antiboise

SERVES 4

2 whole sea bass, about 500 g/
    1 lb 2 oz each
1 tablespoon finely chopped
    fresh rosemary, plus extra
    sprigs to garnish
2 tablespoons olive oil
salt and pepper

Aubergine purée
1 aubergine
1 large garlic clove, crushed

Sauce antiboise
150 ml/5 fl oz olive oil
2 shallots, finely chopped
1 garlic clove, crushed
4 basil leaves
1 tablespoon fresh coriander
    leaves
1 tablespoon fresh tarragon
    leaves
325 g/12 oz fresh tomatoes,
    skinned, seeded and chopped
1 tablespoon lemon juice

Ask the fishmonger to scale and fillet (but not skin) the fish so you have four long fillets. Score the skin sides about three times, then rub in the chopped rosemary, oil and salt. Set aside in the refrigerator.

To make the aubergine purée, preheat the oven to 220°C/425°F/ Gas Mark 7. Cut the aubergine in half lengthways, slash the flesh a few times and rub with the garlic and some salt. Sandwich together, wrap in foil and bake for 50 minutes or until the skins have shrivelled and the flesh is very soft. Scoop out the flesh and chop finely. If you like, you can cook the chopped flesh in a saucepan to reduce a little for a firmer texture. Season and set aside.

To make the sauce, heat the oil in a saucepan, add the shallots and garlic and cook over a low heat for about 5 minutes, until softened. Meanwhile, shred the herbs into thin strips. Add the chopped tomatoes to the oil, together with the herbs and lemon juice. Add salt and pepper, heat until just boiling, then set aside.

When ready to serve, heat the grill until red hot. Grill the fish, skin side up, for 3 minutes. Turn carefully and cook the other side for about 2 minutes. Reheat the sauce over a low heat. Spoon the aubergine purée in the centre of four warmed plates and lay a grilled fish fillet on top. Spoon the sauce around the fish. Garnish with small sprigs of rosemary.

For a starter, serve a light chicken liver parfait or pâté, with thin slices of brioche toast. Follow with a lightly chilled rice pudding made with cream, egg yolks and vanilla, and trickled with a purée of mangoes or prunes.

COD FILLET WRAPPED IN POTATO
with bacon, onions and red wine sauce

SERVES 4

4 pieces of cod fillet, about
     175–200 g/ 6–7 oz each
salt and pepper
4 large Maris Piper potatoes,
     peeled
200 g/7 oz butter
175 g/6 oz button onions
50 g/2 oz caster sugar
2 sprigs of thyme
225 g/8 oz pancetta,
     cut into lardons

Red wine sauce
1 tablespoon olive oil
2 shallots, finely sliced
1 bottle of red wine
175 ml/6 fl oz ruby port
600 ml/1 pint veal or homemade
     chicken stock (page 372)
85 g/3 oz unsalted butter, diced
salt and pepper

Season the cod and chill in the refrigerator.

Grate the potatoes very finely, then squeeze out any excess liquid in a tea towel. Melt half the butter and brush the chilled cod with melted butter. Press the grated potato on to the fish, applying more butter as you add the potato until each fillet is totally encased in potato. Wrap tightly in cling film and chill in the refrigerator for 1 hour.

For the red wine sauce, heat the oil in a saucepan, add the shallots and cook over a low heat until soft but not browned. Add the red wine and port and boil to reduce by three-quarters. Add the stock and boil to reduce to about 200 ml/7 fl oz. Add the butter and whisk vigorously. Season to taste and set aside.

Put the button onions in a saucepan of cold water, bring to the boil for about 1 minute, then drain. Melt the remaining butter and sugar in a frying pan, add the onions, a splash of water and the thyme. Cover with a butter paper or foil and cook over a low heat until the liquid has evaporated and the onions are tender.

Preheat the oven to 200°C/400°F/Gas Mark 6.

Heat a little butter in a large frying pan, add the bacon and the fish and cook until the potato is lightly coloured all over. Place in the oven and bake for 8–10 minutes or until the potato is golden brown.

The button onions should be coated in a light caramelized glaze. If they are not, turn up the heat and gently roll them around the pan. Season to taste.

To serve, reheat the red wine sauce. Place a piece of potato-wrapped fish in the centre of each plate, pour the sauce around and garnish with the bacon and button onions.

Serve with buttered leaf spinach. Begin the meal with a starter of duck confit or terrine and finish with pear soufflé.

TRANCHE OF COD
with special parsley sauce

SERVES 4

4 cod fillets, about 125–150 g/
   4–5 oz each, skinned
about 2 tablespoons plain flour
salt and pepper
300 g/11 oz new potatoes,
   preferably Jersey Royals,
   scrubbed
25 g/1 oz butter
2 tablespoons olive oil

Parsley sauce
15 g /½ oz butter
3 shallots, finely chopped
200 ml/7 fl oz dry white wine
200 ml/7 fl oz Noilly Prat
   or dry vermouth
400 ml/14 fl oz fish stock
300 ml/10 fl oz whipping cream
about 200 g/7 oz fresh parsley

To garnish
sprigs of flat-leaf parsley

Trim the cod fillets to neat rectangles. Toss in lightly seasoned flour and set aside in the refrigerator.

To make the sauce, heat the butter in a saucepan, add the shallots and cook over a low heat for about 12 minutes or until softened. Add the wine and Noilly Prat or vermouth and boil until reduced by two-thirds. Stir in the stock and boil again until reduced by half. Add the cream and simmer for 15 minutes, until the sauce has the consistency of thin cream. Strain through a sieve, return to the pan and season to taste.

Pick the stalks from the parsley and reserve. Blanch the leaves in boiling water for 4 minutes, then drain well. Squeeze dry in a clean tea towel or thick paper towels, then purée in a liquidizer or food processor. Stir into the sauce.

Cut the potatoes in half and boil with the parsley stalks in lightly salted water until just tender. Drain well, discard the parsley stalks, and return the potatoes to the pan with the butter and seasoning.

When ready to serve, heat the oil in a frying pan and fry the cod fillets for about 3 minutes on each side, turning carefully, until just cooked, then season to taste. Gently reheat the sauce. Spoon the potatoes in the centre of four warmed plates and place the cod on top. Spoon over the sauce. Garnish with flat-leaf parsley and serve immediately.

This updated version of a traditional recipe could follow a starter of creamy leek soup, with a tarte tatin of Cox's apples for dessert.

DIAMONDS OF SOLE
with Gewürztraminer sauce

SERVES 4

4 fillets of sole (or lemon sole),
   about 100 g/3½ oz each,
   skinned
about 2 tablespoons plain flour
salt and pepper
50 g/2 oz butter
250 g/9 oz mixed wild
   mushrooms (chanterelles,
   shiitakes, ceps, pleurottes,
   blewits)
about 100 g/3½ oz baby
   spinach leaves
2 tablespoons olive oil
2 ripe, well-flavoured tomatoes,
   skinned, seeded and diced

Gewürztraminer sauce
15 g/½ oz butter
2 shallots, finely sliced
350 ml/12 fl oz Gewürztraminer
   wine
400 ml/14 fl oz fish stock
300 ml/10 fl oz double cream

To garnish
fresh chervil

To make the sauce, heat the butter in a saucepan, add the shallots and cook over a low heat for about 12 minutes or until softened. Add the wine and boil until reduced by two-thirds. Stir in the stock and boil again until reduced by half. Add the cream and simmer for about 15 minutes, until the sauce has the consistency of thin cream. Strain through a sieve, return to the pan and season to taste. Set aside.

Cut each sole fillet into about six diamond shapes and toss lightly in seasoned flour. Set aside.

Heat half the butter in a frying pan. When hot, add the mushrooms and stir-fry for about 4 minutes. Transfer to a plate, and wipe out the pan with paper towels. Add the remaining butter to the pan and when hot, return the mushrooms to the pan and sauté again, together with the spinach leaves, tossing until wilted. Season and keep warm. (The second sautéing keeps the mushrooms dry).

Heat the oil in a large nonstick frying pan. When hot, add the fish and fry for about 2 minutes on each side, until browned. Reheat the sauce.

Spoon the mushrooms and spinach in the centre of four warmed plates and arrange the fish on top. Spoon the sauce around the outside. Sprinkle the diced tomatoes around the plate and garnish with chervil.

Begin with a salad of lightly poached leeks tossed with a little vinaigrette, or a leek terrine. For dessert, fill a crisp sweet pastry case with caramelized mangoes and serve with pineapple sorbet and a little cream.

POULTRY AND GAME

Take a short view of life.
No further than dinner or tea.

REV. SYDNEY SMITH
ADVICE TO A YOUNG LADY IN LOW SPIRITS

KEBABS OF CURRIED TURKEY
with banana salsa

SERVES 4

450 g/1 lb turkey
1 teaspoon corn oil
2 tablespoons curry powder

Banana salsa
2 ripe bananas
1 teaspoon finely chopped red chilli
1 tablespoon fresh lime juice
1 tablespoon chopped fresh coriander
½ red pepper, diced

To serve
boiled rice or rice salad

Cut the turkey into 4 cm/1½ inch chunks. Mix the oil and curry powder together in a bowl, add the turkey and turn to coat in the mixture. Leave to marinate for about 30 minutes at room temperature or up to 4 hours in the refrigerator.

To make the salsa, dice the bananas and mix with all the remaining ingredients. Chill well.

Heat the grill or barbecue. If using wooden skewers, soak them in cold water for about 30 minutes.

Fix the turkey pieces on the skewers and grill for about 10 minutes or until cooked through but not dried out, turning regularly. Serve on a bed of rice, with the banana salsa on the side.

Start with smoked salmon and brown bread; fresh pineapple makes a refreshing dessert.

GLAZED DUCK SKEWERS
with Chinese greens and a soy, honey and ginger sauce

SERVES 4

4 duck breasts, 175 g/6 oz each
1 tablespoon Japanese soy sauce
1 tablespoon clear honey
juice of ½ lime
2 teaspoons Dijon mustard
1 tablespoon sunflower oil

Stir-fried Chinese greens
225 g/8 oz pak choi (Chinese cabbage)
1 tablespoon sunflower oil
few drops of sesame oil
1 garlic clove, very finely chopped
1 teaspoon Asian fish sauce
juice of ½ lime

Soy, honey and ginger sauce
2.5 cm/1 inch piece of fresh ginger
2 tablespoons Japanese soy sauce
2 tablespoons clear honey
1 tablespoon lime juice
1–2 teaspoons tomato purée
2 tablespoons dry sherry
250 ml/8 fl oz chicken stock
1 red chilli, seeded and very finely chopped

Remove the skin from the duck breasts and cut the meat into 2.5 cm/1 inch pieces. Mix together the soy sauce, honey, lime juice and mustard in a shallow dish. Add the duck and stir well to coat in the marinade. Set aside for 30 minutes.

Thread the pieces of duck on to eight 15 cm/ 6 inch bamboo skewers and set aside.

For the sauce, grate the ginger very finely and squeeze the juice into a small saucepan. Discard the remaining fibrous material. Add the remaining sauce ingredients to the pan and boil for 2–3 minutes until reduced to a thin sauce consistency. Set aside and keep warm.

For the stir-fried greens, slice the pak choi into 5 cm/2 inch pieces. Heat the sunflower and sesame oil in a wok or large saucepan, add the garlic and the pak choi and stir-fry over a high heat for 2–3 minutes, until just tender. Stir in the fish sauce and lime juice; keep warm.

Heat a ridged cast-iron griddle pan over high heat until hot. Reduce the heat, brush the pan with sunflower oil and then add the duck skewers and cook for a few minutes, turning occasionally, until the duck is browned on all sides but still moist and pink in the centre.

To serve, spoon the stir-fried greens into the centre of four warmed plates. Rest the skewers on top and spoon the sauce around the outside.

Since this dish really needs no accompaniment, you might begin with a pasta course, say fettuccine with wild mushrooms. Continue the Oriental theme with a mango pudding – if you're feeling adventurous, try mango mousse with mango sauce.

CHICKEN, MANGO AND AVOCADO

SERVES 4

450 g/1 lb chicken breast,
   cut into strips
4 tablespoons mild mango
   chutney
1 tablespoon groundnut oil
2 fresh firm ripe mangoes,
   chopped into bite-sized pieces
2 firm ripe avocados, chopped
   into bite-sized pieces
salt and pepper

Put the chicken in a large bowl with the mango chutney and leave to marinate for 10 minutes, turning several times to ensure the chicken is well coated.

Heat a wok or large pan, then add the oil. When the oil is hot and begins to smoke, add the chicken and its marinade, and stir-fry for 3–4 minutes. Remove any large pieces of chutney with a slotted spoon. Add the mango pieces and stir-fry for 1 minute, then add the avocado and stir carefully for 2 minutes, or until the mango and avocado are hot through but still firm. Season to taste with salt and pepper. Serve immediately.

An easy dish to make the most of when mangoes and avocados are in season. Serve on a bed of steamed white rice with a green salad. Serve a sweet dessert such as crème caramel or chocolate or orange mousse.

SLOW-ROAST CHICKEN THIGHS
with spicy couscous and apricot and mint sauce

SERVES 4

4 boned chicken thighs,
    about 125 g/4 oz each
salt and pepper
2 tablespoons olive oil
1 garlic clove, lightly crushed
1 tablespoon fresh lemon juice

Couscous
25 g/1 oz butter
1 teaspoon ground coriander
1 teaspoon ground cinnamon
½ teaspoon ground cumin
1 tablespoon soft brown sugar
375 ml/12 fl oz chicken stock
225 g/8 oz couscous
25 g/1 oz raisins
15 g/½ oz pine kernels, toasted
3 tablespoons olive oil
1 tablespoon fresh lemon juice
2 tablespoons chopped
    fresh mint

Apricot and mint sauce
25 g/1 oz butter
85 g/3 oz shallots, thinly sliced
1 garlic clove, crushed
1 teaspoon each of ground
    cinnamon and coriander
½ teaspoon each of ground
    cumin and turmeric
1 teaspoon light soft brown sugar
50 g/2 oz no-need-to-soak
    apricots, chopped
200 ml/7 fl oz chicken stock
1 tablespoon chopped fresh mint

For the sauce, melt the butter in a small saucepan. Add the shallots and garlic and fry gently for about 4 minutes or until soft. Add the spices and sugar and cook for 3 minutes. Add the apricots and stock, cover and simmer gently for 15 minutes. Add the chopped mint, then blend in a liquidizer or with a hand blender until smooth. If the sauce looks too thick, thin down with a little more stock. Check the seasoning and keep warm.

Season the chicken thighs well on both sides. Heat a frying pan over medium heat. Add the oil and garlic to the pan and then the chicken, skin-side down, and cook for about 20 minutes, until the skin is richly golden and very crisp. Turn the chicken over, discard the garlic and cook for another 2 minutes. Add the lemon juice and shake well to distribute it evenly. Cook for 3 minutes and then keep warm.

For the couscous, melt the butter in a large saucepan. Add the spices and fry gently for 1 minute. Add the sugar and stock and bring to the boil. Pour in the couscous in a steady stream, stir in the raisins and pine kernels and cover with a tight-fitting lid. Remove from the heat and set aside for about 6–8 minutes to allow the grains to swell up. Then uncover and fork in the olive oil, lemon juice, chopped mint and seasoning to taste.

To serve, carve each chicken thigh into six or seven pieces. Pile the couscous in the centre of four warmed plates, place the chicken on top and pour the sauce around the edge.

Begin your dinner with a celery and tomato soup and finish with a simple crème caramel or light caramel mousse.

CHICKEN WITH WALNUTS

SERVES 3–4, OR 5–6 AS PART OF A MULTI-COURSE MEAL

450 g/1 lb skinless, boneless chicken breast,
   cut into 2 cm/¾ inch cubes
2 teaspoons cornflour
2 teaspoons rice wine or dry sherry
½ teaspoon grated fresh ginger
2 tablespoons hoisin sauce
1 teaspoon sugar
2 tablespoons dark soy sauce
4 tablespoons groundnut or corn oil
2 garlic cloves, lightly crushed
85 g/3 oz shelled walnut halves, toasted
1 teaspoon sesame seed oil

Place the chicken in a bowl and add the cornflour, rice wine and ginger. Mix well and set aside.

In a small bowl, mix the hoisin sauce, sugar, soy sauce and 2 tablespoons water. Stir until smooth and set aside.

Heat the oil and garlic in a wok over high heat until the oil is hot and the garlic sizzles. Stir the chicken mixture again and add it to the wok. Stir for 1–2 minutes, until the chicken is almost done. Remove the garlic if desired.

Reduce the heat to medium and stir in the sauce mixture. Continue stirring until well blended, then add the walnuts and sesame seed oil. Give a few big stirs with a spatula, then serve immediately.

The rich and unusual flavours make this ideal as the main course of a Western-style dinner, accompanied by rice and a dish of steamed or stir-fried vegetables.

XOI GA

Sticky rice and chicken

SERVES 4–6

275 g/10 oz glutinous (sticky) rice, soaked in water
    to cover for 4 hours, or overnight

225 g/8 oz mung dhal (dried mung bean halves
    without skins), soaked in water to cover for
    4 hours, or overnight

½ teaspoon salt

2 chicken breasts (about 325 g/12 oz),
    skinned and cubed

1 large garlic clove, finely chopped

1 tablespoon fish sauce

½ teaspoon sugar

1 tablespoon vegetable oil

6 spring onions, thinly sliced

pepper

Drain the rice and beans and wash until the water runs clear. Mix the rice and beans with the salt and spread the mixture over a dampened piece of muslin in the top of a steamer. Steam above gently boiling water for 30–40 minutes, sprinkling water over the mixture frequently, until the rice is tender and the beans can be easily crushed with your fingertips.

While the rice is cooking, combine the chicken, garlic, fish sauce and sugar in a small bowl, and leave to marinate for 10 minutes.

Heat the oil in a large frying pan over high heat. Add the chicken and stir-fry until browned and tender, about 3 minutes. Add the spring onions and stir for a further 30 seconds. Mix the chicken into the rice-and-bean mixture. Sprinkle with freshly ground black pepper and serve immediately.

Beansprouts and crabmeat salad (page 92) would be a perfect accompaniment to this hearty dish (the crabmeat may be omitted if you like). Pass chilli dipping sauce (page 375) to sprinkle over the rice.

POULET EN COCOTTE AUX QUARANTE GOUSSES D'AIL

Pot roast chicken with forty garlic cloves

SERVES 4

3–4 whole heads of garlic*
1 chicken, about 1.8 kg/4 lb
salt and pepper
4–5 sprigs of thyme
25 g/1 oz butter
about 500 ml/16 fl oz chicken
   stock

*You'll need fewer cloves in winter, when garlic is drier and more pungent.

Preheat the oven to 190°C/375°F/Gas Mark 5. Separate the garlic heads into cloves, leaving them unpeeled. Season the chicken inside and out with salt and pepper, add 2–3 sprigs of thyme to the cavity and truss the bird.

Heat the butter in a casserole, add the chicken and brown over medium heat, turning so it colours evenly on all sides, 8–10 minutes. Add the garlic cloves, the remaining thyme, and enough stock to cover completely. Cover and cook in the oven until very tender, 50–60 minutes; test by piercing the thigh with a two-pronged fork. The meat will start to shrink from the drumstick bones and the garlic cloves will be very soft. Check from time to time during cooking and if the chicken seems dry, add more stock.

Transfer the chicken and half the garlic cloves to a serving dish, cover and keep warm. Work the remaining garlic with the cooking liquid through a strainer into a small saucepan, pressing well to extract all the garlic pulp and form a sauce. Bring to the boil. If necessary, simmer to reduce it until slightly thickened. Taste the sauce and adjust the seasoning. Discard the trussing strings from the chicken (but leave the garlic unpeeled for guests to squeeze out the soft pulp) and serve the sauce in a separate bowl.

This is good with roasted or glazed root vegetables – turnips, carrots, celeriac, beetroot and potatoes. Alternatively, simply toast slices of country bread to act as background to the garlic purée. In summer I would start the meal with a fresh tomato salad, in winter with a tomato soup. For dessert a batter pudding (clafoutis) of seasonal fruit such as cherries, apricots, apples or dried prunes would be an appropriate finish.

CHICKEN MOLE

SERVES 4

4 small chickens,
    about 1.1 kg/2½ lb each
1 onion, chopped
3 tablespoons olive oil
2 garlic cloves, crushed
2 tablespoons unsweetened
    cocoa powder
1 tablespoon tomato purée
2 tablespoons ground cumin
1 teaspoon ground cinnamon
1 teaspoon ground coriander
½ teaspoon cayenne pepper
85 g/3 oz roasted peanuts
500 ml/16 fl oz chicken stock
salt and pepper
125 ml/4 fl oz dry white wine
coriander leaves to garnish

Ask your butcher to split the chickens along the backs, remove the backbone and flatten them (birds prepared in this way are often referred to as butterflied or spatchcocked).

In a small saucepan, sauté the onion in 1 tablespoon of the olive oil until translucent. Add the garlic and cook for a further minute. Stir in the cocoa powder, tomato purée, spices and peanuts and mix thoroughly. Add the stock, bring to the boil and simmer, uncovered, until reduced by half: this will take at least 20 minutes.

While the sauce is cooking, season the chickens with salt and pepper, then heat the remaining olive oil in a wide saucepan or sauté pan and brown the chickens on both sides. Remove from the pan and drain on paper towels.

Pour off the oil from the pan, pour in the white wine and stir to deglaze, loosening any sediment. Return the chickens to the pan. Purée the sauce in a liquidizer or food processor and pour it over the chickens. Bring to the boil, then cover and simmer gently until the chickens are tender, about 30 minutes. Taste and adjust the seasoning and serve hot, garnished with fresh coriander.

Inspired by a traditional Mexican dish, this casserole is good in summer, served with fresh peas and rice spiced with cinnamon and cloves. Begin with some large prawns, sprinkled with crumbled feta cheese and capers, and finish with crisp filo pastry tartlets filled with exotic fruits.

PHEASANT BREAST WITH SPINACH,

potato pancake and a mushroom velouté sauce

SERVES 4

4 pheasant breasts, about
    150 g/5 oz each, skinned
salt and pepper
2 tablespoons sunflower oil
25 g/1 oz butter

**Mushroom and tarragon
velouté sauce**
300 ml/10 fl oz white wine
450 ml/15 fl oz game
    or chicken stock
150 ml/5 fl oz double cream
15 g/½ oz butter
175 g/6 oz mixed wild
    mushrooms, cleaned,
    stalks trimmed and sliced
1 tablespoon chopped fresh
    tarragon

Potato pancakes
325 g/12 oz floury potatoes,
    peeled and cut into chunks
2 tablespoons plain flour
2 tablespoons milk
2 tablespoons double cream
2 eggs, beaten
sunflower oil

Wilted spinach
1 tablespoon olive oil
1 small garlic clove, crushed
225 g/8 oz fresh spinach leaves,
    washed and large stalks
    removed
squeeze of lemon juice

For the sauce, put the white wine into a small saucepan and boil until reduced to a couple of tablespoons. Add the stock and boil until reduced by half. Add the cream, bring back to the boil, and simmer for a couple of minutes until it has acquired a good sauce consistency. Set aside.

For the potato pancakes, cook the potatoes in boiling salted water for 20 minutes or until soft. Drain well and then mash. Beat in the flour, milk, cream, eggs and seasoning to taste and then press the mixture through a sieve to remove any lumps. To cook, preheat the grill to high. Heat about 1 tablespoon of the sunflower oil in a 10 cm/4 inch blini pan. Add one quarter of the batter and cook over a high heat until the edge of the pancake begins to brown. Slide the pan on to the bottom shelf of the grill and cook for about 10 minutes, until the pancake is set and lightly browned on top. Flip over on to a baking sheet and keep warm while you make another three pancakes.

Season the pheasant breasts on both sides. Heat a large frying pan, add the oil and butter and when it is foaming, add the pheasant breasts and cook for 3–4 minutes on each side until nicely golden. Remove and keep warm.

To finish the sauce, reheat gently. Meanwhile, add the butter to the frying pan and as soon as it starts to foam, add the mushrooms and stir-fry over a high heat for 3–4 minutes until lightly browned. Stir them into the sauce together with the chopped tarragon, any juices from the pheasant and a little seasoning. Keep warm.

To cook the spinach, heat the olive oil in a large saucepan. Add the garlic, spinach and a little seasoning and stir-fry over a high heat until it has just wilted. Add the lemon juice and then drain in a colander.

To serve, place a potato pancake in the centre of four warmed plates and pile the spinach on top. Slice the pheasant breasts diagonally, rest them on top of the pancakes and spoon the mushroom sauce around the outside.

For an autumn dinner you could begin with a warm salad of seared salmon and finish with an open fruit tart – cherries or pears in an almond base.

QUAIL AND WATER CHESTNUTS

in oyster sauce

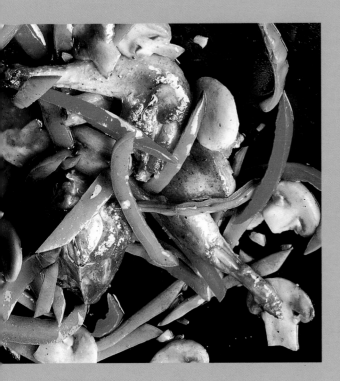

Clean the quail and pat dry. Chop each quail into 4–6 pieces; a meat cleaver is ideal for this. Rinse well and dry with paper towels. Place in a bowl and season with salt and pepper. In a small jug, combine the oyster and soy sauces, sherry, cornflour and 1 tablespoon water.

Heat a wok or large pan, then add the oil. When the oil is hot and begins to smoke, add the garlic and stir for 30 seconds. Add the quail pieces and stir-fry for 4–5 minutes, until well browned. Remove the quail with a slotted spoon and keep warm. It may be necessary to fry the quail in two batches; if so you may need to add a little more oil to the wok.

Reheat the wok and add the peppers, mange-tout, mushrooms and water chestnuts. Stir-fry for 2–3 minutes. Remove from the heat, add the cornflour mixture and stir for 2 minutes. Return the quail to the wok and stir-fry for a further 3 minutes, or until the meat is hot. Serve at once.

This is a wonderful dinner party dish and as it includes vegetables it can be served with no other accompaniments than rice or sliced boiled potatoes sprinkled with a little chopped fresh parsley or dill. It is not too rich and spicy and could be followed by strawberries in Kirsch – or Brie and figs.

SERVES 4

4 quail

salt and pepper

2 tablespoons oyster sauce

1 tablespoon light soy sauce

1 tablespoon pale dry sherry

2 teaspoons cornflour

1 tablespoon groundnut oil

1 large garlic clove, crushed

½ red pepper, cut into thin strips

½ green pepper, cut into thin strips

50 g/2 oz mangetout, trimmed and cut into thin strips

125 g/4 oz button mushrooms, thinly sliced

125 g/4 oz tinned water chestnuts, rinsed and sliced

DELHI SAG MIRCHI MUI

Chilli chicken with spinach

SERVES 4

3 tablespoons vegetable oil

½ teaspoon turmeric

½ teaspoon chilli powder

1 teaspoon white cumin seeds

1 teaspoon ground cumin

4–6 garlic cloves, finely chopped

4–6 spring onions, chopped

125 ml/4 fl oz vegetable or chicken stock or water

1 tablespoon tomato purée

675 g/1½ lb skinless, boneless chicken breast,
    cut into bite-sized pieces

1–3 fresh red chillies, seeded and cut into strips

400 g/14 oz young fresh spinach leaves,
    cut into large bite-sized pieces

2 teaspoons garam masala

4 tablespoons chopped fresh coriander leaves

salt

Heat the ⟨oil⟩ ⟨…⟩ ⟨turmeric, chilli⟩ powder a⟨nd⟩ ⟨…⟩ ⟨few⟩ seconds. Add 2–3 tablespoons water and stir well, then add the garlic and spring onions and stir-fry for about 2 minutes.

Add the stock or more water and stir in the tomato purée. As soon as the liquid begins to simmer, add the chicken pieces and the fresh chilli. Simmer for 5 minutes, stirring occasionally.

Add half the spinach and stir it in gently. When it wilts, add the remaining spinach and stir briefly. Lower the heat and simmer gently for about 5 minutes.

Add the garam masala, coriander and salt to taste. Stir-fry for a final minute, or until the chicken is cooked right through, then serve immediately.

Since this is so quick to cook, it makes a good light lunch or TV supper with plain rice or naan or pitta bread, which you can simply heat in the toaster.

...ASANT WITH SAUERKRAUT

SERVES 4

85 g/3 oz smoked streaky bacon rashers

3 tablespoons groundnut oil

1 onion, thinly sliced

450 g/1 lb sauerkraut, washed well in cold water
    and drained

100 ml/3½ fl oz dry white wine

200 ml/7 fl oz chicken stock

½ bay leaf

2 juniper berries

2 large carrots

2 oven-ready pheasants

salt and pepper

200 g/7 oz garlic sausage

Preheat the oven to 200°C/400°F/Gas Mark 6.

Put the bacon in a saucepan of cold water, bring
to the boil and simmer for 10 minutes. Drain and
refresh in cold water.

Heat a little of the oil in a flameproof casserole,
add the onion and sweat over low heat until soft
and translucent. Add the sauerkraut, wine, stock,
bay leaf, juniper berries, carrots and bacon. Bring
to the boil, cover with a lid and cook in the oven
for 1 hour, stirring frequently.

Season the pheasants inside and out with salt
and pepper. Heat the remaining oil in a roasting
tin and turn the pheasants in the hot oil. Lay
them on one side and roast in the hot oven for
5 minutes. Turn them over on to the other side
and roast for 5 minutes, then turn them on to
their backs and roast for a further 5 minutes.
Remove from the oven and leave to cool slightly.

Cut each pheasant in half and remove the
backbones. Place the pheasants in the casserole
with the sauerkraut, add the garlic sausage, cover
with the lid and return to the oven for another
30 minutes.

Remove from the oven and season the
sauerkraut to taste. Remove the rind from the
bacon and cut into slices. Remove the skin from
the garlic sausage and cut into slices. Slice the
carrots. Arrange the pheasants with the
sauerkraut, bacon and garlic sausage on four
warmed plates and garnish with the carrots.

*Serve this autumn casserole with a purée of cauliflower
and potatoes, and follow with lemon pancakes with
vanilla ice cream.*

PIGEON BREASTS WITH ROAST BARLEY,

wild mushrooms and sauce vierge

SERVES 4

8 pigeon breasts, skinned
salt and pepper
2 tablespoons sunflower oil
25 g/1 oz butter

Roast barley with wild mushrooms

3 tablespoons olive oil
175 g/6 oz pearl barley, washed and drained
1 small onion, very finely chopped
½ clove garlic, crushed
450 ml/15 fl oz chicken stock
2 tablespoons light soy sauce
150 ml/5 fl oz red wine
50 g/2 oz unsalted butter
225 g/8 oz wild mushrooms, cleaned,
   trimmed and sliced if large

Sauce vierge

200 ml/7 fl oz extra virgin olive oil
125 g/4 oz shallots, finely chopped
1 garlic clove, lightly crushed
1 sprig of thyme
1 bay leaf
2 tablespoons sherry vinegar

For the sauce vierge, put the oil, shallots, garlic, herbs, 1 teaspoon salt and 12 turns of pepper into a small pan and heat until just simmering. Cook very gently for about 20 minutes to soften the shallots, but not colour them. Remove from the heat, add the vinegar and set aside.

To cook the barley, heat a large frying pan until hot. Add the oil and barley and cook, stirring, until golden. Add the onion and garlic and cook for about 5–10 minutes until it starts to brown. Add the stock, soy sauce, wine and seasoning and simmer for about 10 minutes, until almost all the liquid has been absorbed. Meanwhile, heat another large frying pan until hot. Add 25 g/ 1 oz of the butter and the mushrooms and fry for a few minutes until lightly browned, then season. When the barley is ready, stir in the mushrooms, remove from the heat and cover loosely with foil. Pierce a few holes in the foil and set aside for about 15 minutes.

Season the pigeon breasts on both sides. Heat a large frying pan until hot, add the oil and butter and as soon as it is foaming, add the pigeon and cook for 2 minutes. Turn and cook for another minute, then remove from the heat and leave in a warm place to relax for 10 minutes.

To serve, remove the garlic, thyme and bay leaf from the sauce and gently warm through. Stir the rest of the butter into the barley, check the seasoning and then spoon onto four warmed plates. Cut each pigeon breast in half, place on the barley and spoon some sauce around the outside.

Begin your 'wild' menu with a pike mousseline, served with a tomato and chervil butter sauce. A classic lemon tart would conclude this flavoursome menu.

SEARED BREAST OF MALLARD

with savoury lentils

SERVES 4

4 mallard breasts,
    175 g/6 oz each
sea salt and white pepper
1 tablespoon sunflower oil
25 g/1 oz butter

Savoury lentils

175 g/6 oz dried Puy lentils
2 tablespoons olive oil
1 large shallot, finely chopped
1 small garlic clove, finely
    chopped
1 small carrot, finely diced
1 small parsnip, finely diced
¼ swede, finely diced
250 ml/8 fl oz chicken stock
1 teaspoon chopped fresh
    rosemary
1 teaspoon chopped fresh thyme
1 tablespoon chopped fresh
    tarragon
2 tablespoons double cream
1 tablespoon softened butter

To garnish

sunflower oil for deep-frying
bunch of fresh herbs (flat-leaf
    parsley, thyme, basil)

First begin the savoury lentils: drop the lentils into a saucepan of lightly salted boiling water and simmer for 15–20 minutes or until just tender. Drain well and set aside.

Season the mallard on both sides. Heat a frying pan until hot, add the oil and butter and as soon as it is foaming, add the mallard, skin-side up, and cook for about 2 minutes. Turn and cook for a further 5–10 minutes, depending on how thick the breasts are and how pink you like your duck. Turn skin-side up and leave in a warm place to relax for 10 minutes.

To finish the lentils, heat the olive oil in a saucepan, add the shallot, garlic, carrot, parsnip and swede and cook for a few minutes, until soft. Add the cooked lentils, chicken stock, rosemary and thyme and simmer for 5 minutes. Add the tarragon, cream and butter and simmer for a further 2–3 minutes, by which time the lentils should have a loose sauce consistency – not too wet, not too dry. Stir in any juices from the duck and season to taste.

For the garnish, heat about 5–8 cm/2–3 inches of sunflower oil in a deep pan to 190°C/375°F, or until a cube of bread browns in 30 seconds. Drop in small handfuls of the herbs and deep-fry until the bubbling has subsided. Using a slotted spoon, lift out and drain on paper towels.

To serve, spoon the lentils into four warmed large soup plates. Carve the mallard breasts into slices, rest them on top and garnish with a pile of deep-fried herbs.

Relax with a first course and pudding that you can prepare ahead. How about baby leeks vinaigrette with crisp Parmesan biscuits, then a soft chocolate cake with mascarpone cream and espresso coffee sauce?

BREAST OF DUCK

with dauphinoise potatoes and Madeira sauce

SERVES 4

125 g/4 oz butter

450 g/1 lb Cara potatoes,
   sliced into thin discs

4 garlic cloves, crushed

4 pinches of freshly grated
   nutmeg

salt and pepper

300 ml/½ pint double cream

300 ml/½ pint milk

4 duck breasts, about
   175–200 g/6–7 oz each

Madeira sauce

2 tablespoons olive oil

175 g/6 oz meat, diced (use the
   duck leg meat)

4 shallots, sliced

12 button mushrooms, sliced

4 garlic cloves, sliced

2 sprigs of thyme

1 small bay leaf

6 black peppercorns,
   coarsely crushed

1 tablespoon red wine vinegar

300 ml/10 fl oz Madeira

300 ml/10 fl oz veal stock

300 ml/10 fl oz chicken stock

First make the Madeira sauce. Heat half the oil in a saucepan, add the meat and cook over high heat until the meat is sealed and browned, turning frequently. Heat the remaining oil in a frying pan over moderate to high heat, add the shallots, mushrooms, garlic, thyme, bay leaf and peppercorns and sauté until lightly browned. Add the vinegar and boil until all the moisture has evaporated. Add the shallot mixture to the meat, pour over the Madeira and boil to reduce by half. Add the stocks and bring to the boil, then skim and reduce the heat. Simmer for 30–40 minutes. Remove from the heat and leave to stand for 5 minutes. Strain several times through a muslin-lined sieve to remove impurities and make a wonderful clear sauce.

Preheat the oven to 200°C/400°F/Gas Mark 6.

Melt the butter in a large deep saucepan over a low heat. Add the potatoes, garlic, nutmeg, salt and pepper. Cook over a low heat for 3–5 minutes, stirring frequently, then add the cream and milk and simmer gently for 7–8 minutes. Transfer to an ovenproof dish and place in the oven for 25 minutes or until golden brown on top. Leave to rest for 10–15 minutes.

Season the duck breasts with salt and pepper. Place the breasts skin side down in a cold frying pan and bring up to a high heat; this will allow a lot of the fat to be released from the skin. Turn over and cook until sealed and golden. Transfer the breasts to a baking sheet and place in the oven for 6 minutes. Remove from the oven and leave to rest.

To serve, slice the duck breasts on to four dinner plates. Serve with some dauphinoise potatoes (if you like, you can use a round pastry cutter to cut out small gateaux of potato) and roasted shallots and pour the sauce over.

Serve as a dinner party main course with roasted shallots, buttered carrots and asparagus . Alternatively, the dauphinoise potatoes topped with cheese and bacon make a meal in themselves.

AGRA HARSHA PASANDA

Creamy duck curry

SERVES 4

600 g/1¼ lb duck breast, fat removed

3 tablespoons vegetable oil

1 teaspoon fennel seeds

4–6 garlic cloves, finely chopped

2.5 cm/1 inch cube of fresh ginger, finely chopped

1 large onion, finely chopped

1 fennel bulb, finely chopped

400 ml/14 fl oz crème fraîche

2 tablespoons chopped fresh coriander leaves

1 teaspoon garam masala

salt

Marinade

100 ml/3½ fl oz red wine

2 tablespoons ground fennel seeds

2 tablespoons ground coriander

1 tablespoon brown sugar

½ teaspoon chilli powder

½ teaspoon salt

Cut the duck breast into slices about 8 mm/ ⅓ inch thick. Beat the slices with a rolling pin or the side of a cleaver until they form escalopes about 4 mm/¹⁄₁₆ inch thick. Place in a shallow, non-metallic bowl. Mix the marinade ingredients together and pour over the duck escalopes. Cover and refrigerate for a minimum of 1 hour, up to a maximum of 24 hours.

When you are ready to cook, preheat the oven to 190°C/375°F/Gas Mark 5.

Heat the oil in a wok or karahi until hot, but well below smoking point. Add the fennel seeds and stir-fry briskly for about 30 seconds. Add the garlic and ginger and continue to stir-fry briskly for a further 30 seconds. Add the onion and mix in well. Keeping the heat high at first, stir-fry until the onion caramelizes. This will take 10–15 minutes, and the heat will need to be lowered gradually during this time.

Transfer the caramelized onion mixture to a lidded casserole dish, add the duck with its marinade, and place in the oven.

After 20 minutes, stir in the fennel and cream and return to the oven.

After a further 20 minutes, stir in the coriander, garam masala and salt to taste. Return to the oven for a final 20–30 minutes, until the duck is tender. If the dish looks dry during the cooking, stir in a little water. Serve hot.

Superb with rice and curried vegetables, or try it in an unconventional way, with creamed mashed potatoes and asparagus tips.

BRAISED DUCK LEGS WITH CABBAGE

SERVES 4

8 duck legs
salt and pepper
500 ml/16 fl oz duck fat*
200 g/7 oz golden syrup
50 ml/2 fl oz dry white wine
300 ml/10 fl oz soy sauce
6 tablespoons sesame oil
2.5 cm/1 inch piece of fresh ginger, sliced
8 cloves
1 fresh red chilli, sliced
5 star aniseed
5 cardamom pods
5 coriander seeds
1 teaspoon Chinese five-spice powder
50 g/2 oz garlic, very thinly sliced
1 kg/2¼ lb Chinese cabbage, large stalks removed
3 tablespoons vegetable oil
50 g/2 oz sugar
125 ml/4 fl oz duck or chicken stock

*Whenever you cook duck, strain off and reserve the fat. It can be kept in the refrigerator for up to 2 months, and is delicious for other dishes, such as sautéed potatoes.

Preheat the oven to 160°C/325°F/Gas Mark 3. Season the duck legs and place in a flameproof casserole. Add the duck fat, golden syrup, wine, 100 ml/3½ fl oz of the soy sauce, 3 tablespoons of the sesame oil, the spices and one-third of the garlic. Bring to the boil, then place in the oven and simmer gently for 1½–2 hours, until the legs are very tender.

Using a slotted spoon, transfer the legs to a baking sheet and brown in the oven, basting occasionally with a little of their cooking liquid. When they are browned, leave to cool slightly, then trim 2 cm/¾ inch of the skin from the top of the legs. Keep warm.

While the duck is browning, blanch the cabbage in boiling water for 10 seconds. Refresh in iced water and drain well. Heat the vegetable oil in a small frying pan and fry the remaining garlic over a low heat until golden brown. Drain on paper towels.

Put the sugar in a small, heavy saucepan with 3 tablespoons water and cook over medium heat until it turns golden brown. Then add 100 ml/3½ fl oz of the soy sauce and the duck stock, and boil until syrupy.

Heat the remaining sesame oil in a large sauce-pan, add the cabbage and the remaining soy sauce. When hot, place the cabbage on four warmed plates, top with the duck and drizzle a little of the sauce around it. Sprinkle with the garlic crisps and serve hot.

As an accompaniment, serve rösti potatoes. A scallop and potato salad would make a good starter, with a simple rhubarb compote for pudding.

HONEY DUCK
AND CRACKLING

SERVES 4

450 g/1 lb duck breast
1 teaspoon Chinese five-spice
    powder
2 tablespoons honey
2 tablespoons light soy sauce
2 tablespoons Worcestershire
    sauce
1 tablespoon pale dry sherry
1 teaspoon cornflour
1 tablespoon groundnut oil
1 garlic clove, crushed
1 teaspoon grated fresh ginger
2 spring onions, thinly sliced
    diagonally
2 tablespoons sesame seeds,
    roasted
1 teaspoon sesame seed oil

Remove the skin from the duck and cut it into 5 mm/¼ inch strips. Cut the meat into 1 cm/½ inch thick slices and season with the five-spice powder. In a small jug, combine the honey, soy and Worcestershire sauces, sherry and cornflour.

Heat a wok or large pan, then add the oil. When the oil is hot and begins to smoke, add the duck skin and stir-fry for 2–3 minutes, until crisp and golden. Remove with a slotted spoon and drain on paper towels.

Reheat the wok and add more oil if necessary. Add the garlic and ginger and stir for 30 seconds. Add the duck meat and stir-fry for 3 minutes. Remove the wok from the heat and add the cornflour mixture, return to the heat and stir for 2 minutes. Add the spring onions and stir-fry for 1 minute. Add half the sesame seeds and stir for 30 seconds. Add the sesame seed oil and stir for 1 minute. Remove from the heat, sprinkle with the remaining sesame seeds and serve immediately.

This dish is quite rich and would be best served with fresh green beans and steamed rice or sliced boiled potatoes. Follow with a fresh fruit sorbet or homemade citrus fruit ice-cream and almond bread.

RABBIT WITH GINGER, MUSTARD AND POLENTA

SERVES 4

1 rabbit

salt and pepper

4 tablespoons wholegrain
 mustard

2 tablespoons plain flour

2 tablespoons groundnut oil

100 g/3½ oz unsalted butter

1 onion, finely chopped

1 garlic clove, crushed

1 teaspoon freshly grated ginger

2 tablespoons medium-sweet
 sherry

2 tablespoons tarragon vinegar

900 ml/1½ pints chicken stock

100 ml/3½ fl oz double cream

100 g/3½ oz polenta
 (coarse maize flour)

4 plum tomatoes, skinned,
 seeded and diced

2 tablespoons chopped
 fresh tarragon

8 fresh sage leaves, chopped

85 g/3 oz taleggio cheese,
 cut into thin slices

Ask your butcher to joint the rabbit so that you have 10 pieces: the legs cut in half, the saddle cut into four pieces and the shoulders.

Preheat the oven to 180°C/350°F/Gas Mark 4. Season the rabbit, then brush the mustard on generously and dust with the flour. Heat half the oil in a flameproof casserole; add the rabbit and 25 g/1 oz of the butter. Turn the rabbit until it is golden brown all over.

Remove the rabbit from the casserole and pour away the fat. Add 25 g/1 oz of the remaining butter and then the onion and sweat over a low heat until soft. Add the garlic and ginger and sweat for a further minute. Stir in the sherry and vinegar and boil over high heat until reduced by half. Add 400 ml/14 fl oz of the stock and boil until reduced by two-thirds. Add the cream and return the rabbit to the casserole. Cover with a lid and cook in the oven for about 30 minutes, until the meat is tender.

Meanwhile, heat the remaining stock in a saucepan, add another 25 g/1 oz of the butter and stir in the polenta in a thin, steady stream, stirring continuously with a whisk so that no lumps form. Reduce the heat and stir frequently until the polenta starts to come away from the sides of the pan; this will take about 40 minutes.

Using a slotted spoon, remove the rabbit to a warmed plate. Boil the sauce until slightly thickened. At the last minute, add the tomatoes and tarragon, and taste and adjust the seasoning. Add the remaining butter, sage and cheese to the polenta and serve with the rabbit and its sauce.

Serve in spring or summer, preceded by a fish soup with aïoli and followed by a light orange dessert such as a cold soufflé.

LAPIN AUX PRUNEAUX

Rabbit with prunes

SERVES 4

1 rabbit, about 1.8 kg/4 lb*
175 g/6 oz pitted prunes
1 tablespoon vegetable oil
1 tablespoon butter
1 tablespoon plain flour
250 ml/8 fl oz red wine
375 ml/12 fl oz veal
   or chicken stock
1 garlic clove, chopped
salt and pepper
1 tablespoon chopped
   fresh parsley

Marinade
500 ml/16 fl oz red wine
large bouquet garni
1 onion, chopped
1 carrot, chopped
1 teaspoon crushed black
   peppercorns
1 tablespoon vegetable oil

*Or 1 large chicken, cut into
eight pieces

You will need to start this dish at least a day before you want to eat it. To prepare the rabbit: trim and discard the flaps of skin, tips of forelegs and any excess bone. Using a heavy knife or cleaver, divide the rabbit into three sections: back legs, back, and forelegs including the rib cage. Cut between the back legs to separate them; trim the end of the backbone. Chop the front of the rabbit in half to separate the forelegs. Cut the back crossways into two or three pieces depending on the size, giving six or seven pieces. Leave the kidneys (if present) attached to the ribs.

Stir all the marinade ingredients except the oil together in a deep, non-metallic bowl. Add the pieces of rabbit, pushing them down into the liquid. Spoon over the oil, cover and refrigerate for 1–2 days.

Pour boiling water over the prunes to cover and leave to soak. Remove the rabbit from the marinade and pat dry. Strain the marinade into a jug and reserve the liquid and the vegetables.

Heat the oil and butter in a sauté pan or shallow flameproof casserole and brown the rabbit pieces on all sides, 5–7 minutes. Remove the rabbit, add the onion and carrot from the marinade and sauté until starting to brown, 5–7 minutes. Stir in the flour and continue cooking, stirring constantly, until well browned. Stir in the reserved marinade and the red wine and bring to the boil. Add the stock, garlic, any liquid from the prunes, the bouquet garni, salt and pepper. Replace the rabbit pieces, cover and simmer for 30 minutes.

Add the prunes and continue simmering – removing the lid if the sauce is thin and needs reducing – until the rabbit is very tender. Transfer the rabbit to a serving dish, spoon the prunes on top, cover and keep warm. If necessary, boil the sauce to reduce until it just coats a spoon. Discard the bouquet garni, taste the sauce and adjust the seasoning. Spoon the sauce over the rabbit, sprinkle with parsley and serve.

Rabbit with prunes just asks for the comfort of potato purée and a dish of glazed carrots or turnips. Begin with a soup of peppery greens such as watercress or spinach, and end with a caramelized rice pudding (page 325).

SLOW-ROAST HAUNCH OF VENISON

with red cabbage and the best-ever roast potatoes

SERVES 8

3 kg/7 lb haunch of venison on the bone
12 garlic cloves, peeled
3 sprigs of rosemary, broken into small pieces
2 onions, quartered
300 ml/10 fl oz red wine
salt and pepper
125 g/4 oz unsalted butter

Red cabbage

50 g/2 oz butter
450 g/1 lb red cabbage, cored and thinly sliced
2 tablespoons redcurrant jelly
3 tablespoons sherry vinegar
finely grated zest and juice of 1 orange
125 ml/4 fl oz port
250 ml/8 fl oz red wine
85 g/3 oz raisins

Best-ever roast potatoes

1.5 kg/3 lb large, floury potatoes, such as Cyprus,
    Golden Wonder or Kerr's Pink, peeled and cut in
    half only if very large
6 tablespoons sunflower oil

Preheat the oven to 190°C/375°F/Gas Mark 5. Line a roasting tin with enough foil to fold over and cover the venison. Tuck the garlic, rosemary and onion quarters around the venison, pour on the wine and season well. Melt the butter until foaming and pour over the venison. Seal the edges of the foil together, then roast for 3 hours.

For the red cabbage, melt the butter in a large saucepan. Add the cabbage and stir to coat in the butter. Add the redcurrant jelly, sherry vinegar, orange zest and juice, port, red wine and some seasoning. Simmer for about 1 hour, until the cabbage is tender. Set aside for 1 hour.

Remove the venison from the oven and leave in a warm place to relax for about 40 minutes. Increase the oven temperature to 240°C/475°F/Gas Mark 9. Boil the potatoes for about 15 minutes, until almost cooked, but still a bit hard in the middle. Drain in a colander. Pour the oil into a large roasting tin and slide the tin into the top of the oven. Return the potatoes to a dry pan and shake to rough up the edges. Add the potatoes to the roasting tin and turn them over to coat them in the hot oil. Roast at the top of the oven for about 40 minutes, turning regularly until crisp and golden all over.

Meanwhile, stir the raisins into the cabbage and simmer gently for another 30 minutes. To serve, unwrap the venison and lift on to a carving tray. Strain the juices into a small saucepan and check the seasoning. Carve the venison and spoon some of the juices over the meat.

Serve a light starter such as trout fillet with avocado and sauce vierge (page 231). Afterwards, poached pears with a champagne syrup would slip down nicely.

MEDALLIONS OF VENISON

with roasted root vegetables and a rich game sauce

SERVES 4

450 g/1 lb venison fillet, trimmed of fat and
    membrane (reserving the trimmings) and
    cut into 12 slices
2 tablespoons sunflower oil
4 small shallots, chopped
50 g/2 oz button mushrooms, sliced
½ garlic clove, crushed
1 bay leaf
1 sprig of thyme
6 white peppercorns, crushed
300 ml/10 fl oz red wine
1 teaspoon redcurrant jelly
600 ml/1 pint chicken stock
300 ml/10 fl oz beef stock
50 g/2 oz butter
1 tablespoon double cream

Roasted root vegetables
3 tablespoons sunflower oil
40 g/1½ oz butter
¼ swede, cut into 8 slices
2 large carrots, cut into 8 slices
4 sticks of celery, cut into 5 cm/2 inch pieces
12 new potatoes, boiled until tender,
    drained and cut in half

To garnish
deep-fried thyme (page 233)

Lightly flatten the venison slices to about 1 cm/
½ inch thick. Cover and set aside. Heat the oil in
a large saucepan and fry the meat trimmings
over high heat until browned. Add the shallots,
mushrooms, garlic, bay leaf, thyme and
peppercorns and fry until golden. Add the wine
and boil until reduced to about 2 tablespoons.
Add the redcurrant jelly, chicken and beef stock
and boil until reduced to about 300 ml/10 fl oz.

For the roasted vegetables, preheat the oven to
230°C/450°F/Gas Mark 8. Heat 2 tablespoons
of the oil and 25 g/1 oz of the butter in a cast-
iron casserole. Fry the swede, carrots and celery
for 5–6 minutes over high heat, until well
coloured. Season and add just enough water to
cover the vegetables. Bring to the boil and
reduce by two-thirds. Transfer to the oven and
cook for about 12 minutes until the vegetables
are just tender. Meanwhile, heat the rest of the
oil and butter in a frying pan and fry the
potatoes, cut side down, for a few minutes until
crisp. Turn off the oven, leave the door ajar and
leave the vegetables and potatoes inside.

Season the venison on both sides. Heat a large
frying pan until very hot, add a little oil and
25 g/1 oz of the butter, then fry the venison – in
two batches – for about 2 minutes on each side.
Bring the sauce back to a simmer and whisk in
the remaining butter and the cream. Put the
potatoes and vegetables on four warmed plates.
Rest three medallions on the vegetables, spoon a
little sauce over the meat and garnish with deep-
fried thyme.

*For a winter feast, start with filo baskets of mussels
with bacon and Brie; finish with Armagnac parfait
with prunes.*

ROAST SADDLE OF HARE

with parsnip purée and a game and chocolate sauce

SERVES 4

8 loins of hare from 2 saddles;
   reserve the bones for
   the sauce
sea salt and white pepper
1 tablespoon sunflower oil
50 g/2 oz butter

Parsnip purée
450 g/1 lb parsnips,
   cut into chunks
600 ml/1 pint milk
50 g/2 oz butter

Game and chocolate sauce
1 carrot, roughly chopped
2 tablespoons sunflower oil
4 shallots or 1 small onion,
   chopped
50 g/2 oz mushrooms, sliced
2 bay leaves
2 sprigs of thyme
6 white peppercorns, crushed
300 ml/10 fl oz red wine
600 ml/1 pint chicken stock
300 ml/10 fl oz beef stock
50 g/2 oz blueberries
1 tablespoon crème de cassis
7 g/¼ oz bitter plain chocolate
15 g/½ oz butter

To garnish
baby parsnips, cut lengthways
   into four
sunflower oil for deep-frying

First make the sauce. Preheat the oven to its highest temperature. Chop the hare bones and spread in a roasting tin, together with the carrot. Roast for 20–30 minutes, until well browned. Heat the oil in a large saucepan, add the shallots or onion, mushrooms, bay leaves, thyme and peppercorns and fry for a few minutes, until golden. Add the wine and boil until reduced to a couple of tablespoons. Add the roasted bones and both stocks and simmer for about 1 hour. Strain into another saucepan, leave to stand for a few minutes and then spoon off any fat from the surface. Bring back to the boil and boil until reduced to 300 ml/10 fl oz. Set aside.

For the parsnip purée, simmer the parsnips in the milk for 20–25 minutes, until very tender. Drain well. Purée the parsnips. The purée should be very thick; if necessary, return to a clean pan and cook, stirring, until the excess liquid has evaporated. Beat in the butter, season well and keep warm.

Season the hare. Heat a large frying pan until hot, add the oil and butter and fry the hare for 2–3 minutes on each side, until well browned. Leave in a warm place for about 10 minutes.

For the garnish, blanch the parsnips in boiling salted water for a few minutes until tender, then drain and dry well on paper towels. Heat about 5–8 cm/2–3 inches of sunflower oil in a deep pan to 190°C/375°F, or until a cube of bread browns in 30 seconds. Deep-fry the parsnips for a few minutes until crisp and golden. Using a slotted spoon, lift out and drain on paper towels.

Reheat the parsnip purée. Bring the sauce to a simmer, add the berries, crème de cassis and any juices from the hare. Cook until the berries are just tender. Spoon the parsnip purée on to four warmed plates. Slice the hare and arrange on the purée with the deep-fried parsnips on top. Whisk the chocolate and butter into the sauce and check the seasoning. Spoon some sauce over the meat and the rest, together with the blueberries, around the purée.

Begin with tartare of salmon, perhaps with cucumber 'spaghetti'. Finish with a caramelized apple tart.

MEAT

*In all aspects of life,
in no place should indifference
be allowed to creep;
and nowhere less than
the domain of the culinary arts.*

YUAN MEI
(18th-century Chinese gourmet and philosopher)

POT-AU-FEU À L'ANCIENNE

SERVES 8

1.5 kg/3 lb piece of beef or veal shank, with bone

1 kg/2¼ lb piece of beef chuck or brisket

1 kg/2¼ lb beef short ribs

1 onion, studded with 4 cloves

large bouquet garni

salt

1 tablespoon black peppercorns

1 stick of celery

1 cinnamon stick

8 beef marrow bones

1 kg/2¼ lb carrots, quartered and cut into
   8 cm/3 inch sticks

1.5 kg/3 lb leeks, trimmed, halved lengthways
   and cut into 8 cm/3 inch sticks

675 g/1½ lb turnips, cut into eighths

To serve

125 g/4 oz angel hair pasta

sea salt, gherkin pickles, mustard

Note: cooking takes a day from start to finish, and I
like to start 2 days ahead so the flavours mellow.

Put all the meat into a large stockpot with
enough water to cover generously. Bring slowly
to the boil, skimming often. Add the onion,
bouquet garni, salt, peppercorns, celery and
cinnamon stick. Tie each marrow bone in muslin
and add to the pot. Simmer very gently,
uncovered, skimming occasionally, for 3 hours.

Wrap the carrots, leeks and turnips in separate
bundles in muslin. Add to the pot, pushing them
down into the broth. Simmer for another hour
or until the meats and vegetables are very tender.
If some are done before others, remove them.
Be sure there is always enough broth to cover
the meats and vegetables; add water if necessary.

Transfer the bones, meats and vegetables to a
board. Strain the broth into a clean saucepan,
then boil it until reduced by half, or until
well flavoured. Taste and adjust the seasoning.
If preparing ahead, replace the meats and
vegetables in the broth and refrigerate. (Reheat
all in the broth.)

Unwrap the bones and arrange them on a
very large platter. Slice the meats and arrange
them overlapping on the platter. Unwrap the
vegetables and pile them in mounds on the
platter. Cover it with foil and keep warm.

For the first course, add the pasta to the reduced
broth and simmer for 3–5 minutes. Taste the
broth and adjust the seasoning, then transfer to
a tureen and serve. For the main course, serve
the platter of meats and vegetables with sea salt,
gherkins and mustard.

*Don't let dessert be an anticlimax – serve your very
best fruit pie.*

SWEET AND SOUR BRAISED BEEF

SERVES 4–6

1 leek, sliced

2 carrots, sliced

2 sticks of celery, sliced

3 onions, sliced

250 ml/8 fl oz red wine

250 ml/8 fl oz red wine vinegar

1.5 kg/3 lb kg chuck of beef, in one piece

½ bunch parsley

salt and pepper

3 tablespoons vegetable oil

1 bay leaf

2 cloves

4 juniper berries, crushed

½ teaspoon black peppercorns, crushed

2 tablespoons raisins

100 g/3½ oz unsalted butter, cut into cubes

Put the vegetables, wine and vinegar in a saucepan, bring to the boil and then leave to cool. Place the meat in a large bowl, pour on the vegetable mixture and its liquid and add the parsley. Cover and leave in the refrigerator to marinate for at least 48 hours (the longer you leave it in the marinade the more tender the meat becomes).

Preheat the oven to 160°C/325°F/Gas Mark 3.

Remove the meat from the marinade, pat dry and season with salt and pepper. Heat the oil in a flameproof casserole over high heat, add the meat and brown well on all sides. Pour in enough of the marinade to half cover the meat. Wrap the bay leaf, cloves, juniper berries and peppercorns in a piece of muslin and add to the casserole. Cook in the oven for about 3 hours, adding more marinade if necessary, until the meat is tender.

Remove the meat from the liquid, wrap in foil and keep warm. Press the liquid through a fine sieve into a saucepan and boil until it thickens slightly. Add the raisins and whisk in the butter. Slice the meat and pour over the sauce.
Serve hot.

Serve with braised red cabbage and dumplings. A fresh-looking first course might be grilled asparagus with Parma ham, followed by a fresh-tasting pudding such as lemon posset.

RICH BEEF CASSEROLE

SERVES 4

1 kg/2¼ lb boneless beef
    such as brisket or chuck,
    trimmed and cut into
    5 cm/2 inch cubes
150 g/5 oz button mushrooms,
    quartered if large
2 onions, thickly sliced
2 carrots, thickly sliced
2 sticks of celery, thickly sliced
1 large leek, white and pale green
    parts only, sliced
3 garlic cloves, peeled
1 bottle of red wine
salt and pepper
flour for coating
100 ml/3½ fl oz vegetable oil
25 g/1 oz unsalted butter
100 g/3½ oz tomato purée
500 ml/16 fl oz chicken stock
3 sprigs of thyme
1 bay leaf

Place the beef in a large bowl with the vegetables and garlic and add the wine. Cover and leave to marinate in the refrigerator for 2 days.

Drain the meat and vegetables in a colander set over a bowl. Reserve the marinating liquid. Separate the beef, vegetables and mushrooms. Preheat the oven to 150°C/300°F/Gas Mark 2.

Pat the beef dry with paper towels. Season, then coat lightly with flour. Heat a flameproof casserole over high heat and add enough oil to make a film on the bottom. Fry the cubes of beef, a few at a time, until well browned. When all the beef has been browned and removed from the casserole, pour off the fat.

Add a little more oil to the casserole with half the butter and reduce the heat to moderate. Cook the marinated vegetables and garlic (but not the mushrooms) until soft and lightly browned, stirring often. Stir in the tomato purée. Add a ladleful of the marinating liquid and bring to the boil. Boil until reduced to a glaze. Add another ladleful of the liquid and boil to reduce again. Continue adding the liquid little by little. When all the liquid has been added and reduced, stir in the stock and bring to the boil. Return the beef to the casserole and add the herbs. Cover and transfer to the oven. Cook for 2½–3 hours or until the beef is very tender, stirring frequently.

To serve, sauté the reserved mushrooms in butter. Reheat the casserole if necessary and serve with the mushrooms.

Serve with vegetables roasted in olive oil. Roast for the following times: corn on the cob and whole garlic bulbs 50 minutes; celeriac 45 minutes; carrots 40 minutes; cauliflower 35 minutes; parsnips 30 minutes.

CARI BO

Beef curry

SERVES 6–8

900 g/2 lb stewing beef,
    cut into 5 cm/2 inch cubes
2 tablespoons grated fresh ginger
1 large onion, finely chopped
6 large garlic cloves,
    finely chopped
3 fresh red chillies,
    finely chopped
3 tablespoons curry powder,
    preferably Madras
2 teaspoons turmeric
1 teaspoon sugar
½ teaspoon ground black pepper
2 teaspoons salt
3 tablespoons peanut
    or vegetable oil
4 tablespoons fish sauce
4 carrots, cut into 2.5 cm/
    1 inch chunks
2 tablespoons cornflour
500 ml/16 fl oz canned
    unsweetened coconut milk,
    well stirred

Combine the beef, ginger, onion, garlic, chillies, curry powder, turmeric, sugar, pepper and 1 teaspoon of the salt. Cover and leave to marinate for 2 hours, or overnight in the refrigerator.

Heat the oil in a large, heavy-bottomed saucepan over high heat. Add the marinated beef and stir quickly to seal, about 3 minutes. Add 750 ml/1¼ pints hot water, the fish sauce, and the remaining 1 teaspoon salt. Bring to the boil, reduce the heat, cover and simmer until the beef is almost tender, about 1 hour.

Add the carrots and simmer, stirring occasionally, for a further 15 minutes.

Dissolve the cornflour in the coconut milk and stir the mixture into the stew. Continue simmering, uncovered, stirring to prevent sticking, until the sauce thickens slightly, about 15 minutes. Ladle the curry into a soup tureen and serve immediately.

Serve as a buffet-style dish, accompanied by steamed rice, rice noodles or French bread. A mixed green salad, tomato salad, or steamed vegetables would also be appropriate.

BO XAO KHOI TAY

Stir-fried beef with potatoes

Combine the beef with the fish sauce, half of the garlic and some freshly ground black pepper and leave to marinate for 30 minutes.

Slice the potatoes about 1 cm/½ inch thick, then sprinkle the salt over them. Heat 8 cm/3 inches of oil in a deep-fryer or heavy-bottomed sauce-pan until very hot (about 190°C/375°F – a cube of bread should brown in 30 seconds) and deep-fry the potatoes until golden brown and tender. Remove with a slotted spoon and drain on paper towels.

Heat 2 tablespoons of oil in a large frying pan over high heat and brown the remaining garlic. Add the onion and the beef mixture and stir-fry until the beef is medium-rare, about 1 minute. Add the potatoes and cornflour mixture and stir briefly until the juices thicken. Transfer to a serving dish, sprinkle with freshly ground black pepper and serve immediately.

Accompany with rice or bread and a simple green vegetable, such as broccoli. A mixed green salad would be fine too. Pass chilli dipping sauce (page 375) separately.

SERVES 4–6

675 g/1½ lb beef flank steak or sirloin,
    cut against the grain into 3 mm/⅛ inch slices,
    about 5 x 2.5 cm/2 x 1 inch
2 tablespoons fish sauce
8 large garlic cloves, finely chopped
pepper
4 potatoes
1 teaspoon salt
peanut or vegetable oil for deep-frying
1 large onion, thinly sliced
1 tablespoon cornflour dissolved in
    3 tablespoons water

BEEF RIB STEAK

with a mustard and shallot topping

SERVES 4

25 g/1 oz unsalted butter
325 g/12 oz shallots, chopped
1 garlic clove, chopped
1 tablespoon white wine vinegar
1 tablespoon Dijon mustard
1 tablespoon chopped fresh coriander
salt and pepper
2 beef rib steaks on the bone,
    about 675 g/1½ lb each
vegetable oil for brushing

Heat the grill or barbecue.

Heat the butter in a saucepan, add the shallots and cook over a low heat until softened. Add the garlic and cook slowly for 20 minutes. Add the vinegar and cook until reduced to a dry consistency. Stir in the mustard and coriander and season to taste.

Brush the steaks with oil and grill, turning regularly, until cooked rare. Cut the beef off the bone, slice and serve hot, covered with the shallot mixture.

Whenever I think of this dish I think of garlic roast potatoes and green beans. First I might serve hot grilled prawns or a prawn salad, with a lemon posset and raspberries to finish.

BEEF WITH CITRUS SAUCE

SERVES 4

2 tablespoons freshly squeezed
    orange juice
grated rind of ½ orange
1 tablespoon pale dry sherry
    or dry vermouth
2 tablespoons dark soy sauce
1 teaspoon cornflour
1 teaspoon five-spice powder
2 teaspoons soft brown sugar
1 tablespoon groundnut oil
1 garlic clove, crushed
1 teaspoon grated fresh ginger
450 g/1 lb fillet steak, cut into
    1 cm/½ inch thick rounds
150 g/5 oz asparagus tips
150 g/5 oz chestnut mushrooms,
    sliced
salt and pepper

In a small jug, combine the orange juice and rind, sherry, soy sauce, cornflour, five-spice powder and sugar. Mix well to dissolve the sugar.

Heat a wok or large pan, then add the oil. When the oil is hot and begins to smoke, add the garlic and ginger and stir for 30 seconds. Add the beef and stir-fry for 3 minutes, or until the meat is browned. (The beef may need to be cooked in batches, in which case more oil may need to be added.) Remove with a slotted spoon and keep warm.

Add the asparagus and mushrooms and stir-fry for 2–3 minutes. Remove the wok from the heat, add the beef and the cornflour mixture and stir well. Return to the heat and stir-fry for a further 3 minutes, until the vegetables are cooked but still crisp. Season to taste with salt and pepper. Serve immediately.

This has a lovely fresh flavour and needs only plain rice as an accompaniment. As it is light and not too rich, you could serve almost any dessert afterwards; summer pudding or pears poached in red wine would echo the freshness of the flavours.

BEEF WITH GREEN AND RED PEPPERS

**SERVES 3–4, OR 5–6 AS PART OF
A MULTI-COURSE MEAL**

450 g/1 lb flank steak
2 tablespoons dark soy sauce
1 teaspoon rice wine or
   dry sherry
1 teaspoon cornflour
1 teaspoon sugar
3 tablespoons groundnut
   or corn oil
1 red pepper, seeded,
   cored and cut into
   5 x 1 cm/2 x ½ inch strips
1 green pepper, seeded,
   cored and cut into
   5 x 1 cm/2 x ½ inch strips
2 slices of fresh ginger
2 garlic cloves, crushed
salt

Trim the fat from the meat and cut along the grain into long strips, about 5 cm/2 inches wide. Then slice the strips across the grain into thin slices, about 3 mm/⅛ inch. Place the beef in a bowl, add the soy sauce, rice wine, cornflour and sugar and mix well. Set aside.

Heat 1 tablespoon of the oil in a wok over medium–high heat until hot. Add the peppers and stir for 1 minute. Transfer to a platter.

Heat the remaining oil in the same wok and add the ginger and garlic. Stir a few times until fragrant, then stir the beef mixture again and pour into the wok. Stir constantly for about 2 minutes, or until the beef is almost done. Return the peppers to the wok and give a few big stirs with a spatula until mixed and heated. Taste and add salt if necessary. Serve immediately.

As a meal in its own right, this needs no accompaniment other than rice or noodles.

STEAK, KIDNEY AND POTATO PIE

SERVES 4

300 g/11 oz stewing steak, cut into 1 cm/½ inch dice
150 g/5 oz ox kidney, cut into 1 cm/½ inch pieces
200 g/7 oz onion, chopped
200 g/7 oz peeled potato, diced
2 teaspoons plain flour
salt and pepper
1 small egg, beaten

Pie pastry

150 g/5 oz dripping or lard, very cold from the
   refrigerator and cut into small pieces
300 g/11 oz plain flour, sifted
salt
4–5 tablespoons iced water

First make the pastry. Rub together the fat, flour and salt until it resembles coarse breadcrumbs. Quickly mix in the water, knead lightly and put into a plastic bag. Leave to rest in the refrigerator for 30 minutes.

Preheat the oven to 200°C/400°F/Gas Mark 6 and put a baking sheet on the middle shelf to heat up. Lightly butter a 20 cm/8 inch diameter loose-bottomed tin, 4 cm/1½ inches deep.

Put the steak, kidney, onion, potato, flour, salt and pepper into a large bowl and mix together.

Cut off about two-thirds of the pastry and roll out on a lightly floured surface to form a circle about 3 mm/⅛ inch thick. Line the tin with the pastry, leaving it overhanging at the edges. Roll out the rest of the pastry for the lid and set aside. Pile the filling into the tin and carefully pour in 125 ml/4 fl oz cold water. Brush the overhanging pastry with water and put the pastry lid on top. Press the edges together and then slice off the excess pastry with a knife.

Brush the pastry with beaten egg, then decorate with pastry trimmings and crimp the edges together with a fork. Make two incisions in the centre of the pie and place on the hot baking sheet. Cook for 25 minutes, and then turn the temperature down to 160°C/325°F/Gas Mark 3. Bake for a further 1½ hours; if the pastry is browning too much turn the oven down further. Remove from the oven and leave to rest for 10 minutes before serving.

There really isn't any room for anything else here, except something sharp such as pickled red cabbage or piccalilli; I might also reach for the ketchup bottle.

CORNED BEEF HASH

SERVES 4

450–500 g/16–18 oz Pentland Dell potatoes,
    quartered
125 g/4 oz butter
225 g/8 oz onions, sliced
125 g/4 oz leeks, roughly chopped
2 x 350 g/13 oz cans of corned beef, diced
8 tablespoons Worcestershire sauce
25 g/1 oz flat-leaf parsley, chopped
salt and pepper

To serve
4 eggs, poached
hollandaise sauce (page 373)

Boil the potatoes in salted water until tender.
Melt the butter in a frying pan, add the onions
and leeks and cook over a low heat until soft
but not browned.

When the potatoes are cooked, drain and add to
the onions and leeks. Add the diced corned beef,
Worcestershire sauce, parsley and seasoning to
taste, and mix together.

Divide the hash between four plates, top each
with a poached egg and coat with hollandaise
sauce.

*Comfort food at its best, great for breakfast, lunch
or supper.*

BREADCRUMBED VEAL SWEETBREADS
with sauce gribiche

SERVES 4

600–800 g/1¼–1¾ lb veal
    sweetbreads
juice of 1 lemon
1 onion, sliced
1 large carrot, sliced
2 sprigs of thyme
2 bay leaves
salt
a few peppercorns
1 tablespoon plain flour
1 large egg, beaten
3–4 tablespoons fresh white
    breadcrumbs
2 tablespoons olive oil
50 g/2 oz butter

Sauce gribiche

1 tablespoon smooth
    Dijon mustard
2 tablespoons tarragon vinegar
salt and pepper
275–325 ml/9–11 fl oz
    groundnut or sunflower oil
1½ tablespoons capers,
    drained, squeezed dry
    and coarsely chopped
5 sprigs of tarragon, leaves only,
    finely chopped
5 hard-boiled eggs, yolks only,
    sieved

To serve

1 lemon, cut into quarters
sprigs of watercress or tarragon

First prepare the sweetbreads. Trim off any unsightly bits and pieces from the sweetbreads and rinse under cold running water for a few minutes. Drain, then put into a stainless steel or other non-reactive saucepan. Just cover with cold water and add the lemon juice, onion, carrot, herbs, a little salt and the peppercorns. Bring to a simmer, then simmer very gently for about 7–10 minutes. Drain in a colander and refresh under cold water, then lay out on a plate or chopping board. Pick over each piece and peel off the thin membrane using a small, sharp knife.

To make the sauce, blend the mustard, vinegar, salt and pepper in a liquidizer or whisk together in a bowl. With the motor running (or still whisking), start pouring in the oil in a thin stream. When you have added about three-quarters of the oil, switch off and taste for acidity and seasoning. Continue adding more oil if necessary. The finished sauce should have the consistency of thick, just pourable, double cream; it may need thinning down with a little lukewarm water. When the basic dressing is complete, stir in the capers, tarragon and egg yolks.

Cut the prepared sweetbreads into approximately twelve pieces. Put the flour, beaten egg and breadcrumbs in three saucers. Coat each piece of sweetbread in the flour, then the egg and finally the breadcrumbs.

Heat the oil and butter together in a large frying pan, until foaming. Gently lay in the sweetbreads and cook over a low heat for about 4–5 minutes on each side, until crusted and golden. Remove with a slotted spoon and drain on paper towels.

Put the sweetbreads into a warmed serving dish and garnish with lemon wedges and watercress or tarragon. Hand the sauce separately.

Excellent served with chips and perhaps a fiery rocket salad. As an alternative to sauce gribiche, make a rich béarnaise (page 373). Follow with apple or pear tart and whipped cream.

CALVES' LIVER VENETIAN STYLE

SERVES 4

3 tablespoons light olive oil
3 mild Spanish onions, very thinly sliced
salt and pepper
40 g/1½ oz butter
8 very thin slices of calves' liver,
    cut into small squares
1 tablespoon chopped fresh parsley
1–2 tablespoons red wine vinegar

Heat the olive oil in a frying pan, add the onions and cook over a low heat until meltingly tender and soft. It doesn't matter if they take on a little colour, but the most important thing is that they cook slowly – which can take up to 30 minutes. Season with salt and pepper.

The final assembly of the dish should not take more than about 1 minute. Heat the butter in a large frying pan until foaming. Season the liver with salt and pepper and toss in the butter for about 20 seconds. Transfer to a colander. Put the onions into the pan and toss briefly until golden brown. Return the liver to the pan together with the parsley, and stir in the vinegar. Serve at once, on warmed plates.

This dish is good served with wet polenta (page 274), or perhaps some buttery mashed potatoes. A green salad dressed with lemon juice and good olive oil, and eaten with ripe gorgonzola cheese, would be a fitting follow-up.

MEAT

GRILLED CALVES' LIVER
with guacamole

First make the guacamole. Mix all the ingredients in a bowl, press a piece of cling film over the surface and set aside.

Heat a ribbed stove-top grill pan (not a radiant grill, as this results in a steaming slice of hot liver) until very hot. Season the liver, brush with olive oil and place on the hot grill. Cook for about 1 minute on each side, so the surfaces are nicely striped from the grill.

Serve at once on four warmed plates and pile some of the guacamole alongside each serving. Garnish with coriander sprigs, sprinkle a little extra virgin olive oil over the liver and put a lime wedge on each plate.

Chips or fried potatoes with onions sounds good here – and maybe a crisp green salad dressed with olive oil and Parmesan cheese – even a Caesar salad, although that might be more fitting as a first course. How about a slice of lemon tart to finish with?

SERVES 4

4 slices of calves' liver,
    total weight 350–400 g/13–14 oz
salt and pepper
olive oil

Guacamole
2 ripe Hass avocados, coarsely chopped
juice of 1 lime
2 large green chillies, not too fiery,
    seeded and finely chopped
8 mint leaves, finely chopped
1 tablespoon finely chopped fresh coriander
2 tablespoons virgin olive oil
2 spring onions, finely chopped
2 ripe tomatoes, skinned, seeded and finely chopped
1 garlic clove, crushed to a paste with a little salt

To serve
sprigs of fresh coriander
a little extra virgin olive oil
4 lime wedges

CALVES' LIVER STEAK
with Cumberland sauce

SERVES 4

2 thick slices of calves' liver,
    about 350 g/13 oz each,
    cut in half
salt and pepper
olive oil

Cumberland sauce
2 oranges
2 lemons
1 small jar (about 175 g/6 oz)
    redcurrant jelly
150 ml/5 fl oz port
1 large piece of fresh
    ginger, grated
2 teaspoons English
    mustard powder
1 teaspoon arrowroot

First make the sauce. Thinly pare the rind of the oranges and lemons and cut into very thin strips. Blanch in a small saucepan of boiling water for 20 seconds, then drain and rinse under cold running water. Dry on paper towels and reserve. Squeeze the juice from the oranges and lemons and put into a stainless steel or other non-reactive saucepan. Add the jelly, port and ginger, bring to a simmer and cook for 10 minutes. Strain through a fine sieve and then pour back into the cleaned pan. Mix the mustard and arrowroot together with 2 tablespoons water until smooth. Add to the port/jelly liquid and whisk together. Bring back to a simmer and cook for a few minutes until shiny and thickened. Stir in the reserved orange and lemon rind and keep warm.

Heat a ribbed stove-top grill pan (not a radiant grill, as this results in a steaming slice of hot liver) until hot, but not red hot. Season the liver, brush with olive oil and place on the hot grill. Cook for about 1 minute, then turn through 45 degrees to give the meat the traditional criss-cross pattern; cook for 1 minute more. Repeat on the other side. If the liver is particularly thick, it will need slightly longer cooking times; the texture, when prodded with your finger, should still be bouncy. Place in a very low oven for a minute or two, so that the meat has a chance to rest. Slice the liver and spoon over the sauce.

Serve with a potato dish such as pommes boulangère (sliced potatoes and onions baked in stock) and perhaps a dish of buttered spinach. Follow with an English pudding, but something not too sweet, such as a milky rice pudding.

GRILLED CALVES' KIDNEYS

with coriander, lime and chilli butter

SERVES 4

2 small veal kidneys, trimmed
    and cored, then sliced 1 cm/
    ½ inch thick
salt and pepper
olive oil

Coriander, lime and chilli butter

125 g/4 oz butter, softened
3 tablespoons virgin olive oil
2 teaspoons Asian fish sauce
    (optional)
2 large red chillies, not too fiery,
    seeded and finely chopped
2 tablespoons chopped fresh
    coriander
grated zest of 1 lime
juice of 2 limes

To serve

sprigs of coriander
a little extra virgin olive oil

First make the coriander, lime and chilli butter. Place all the ingredients in a food processor, add a little salt and blend thoroughly (use the plastic mixing blade rather than the sharp metal one). Wrap in a sheet of dampened greaseproof paper and form a sausage shape by squeezing the ends together like a Christmas cracker. Place in the refrigerator for at least 30 minutes to firm up.

Heat a ribbed stove-top grill pan until very hot. Season the kidneys and brush with a little olive oil on each side. Place on the hot grill pan and cook for 1–2 minutes on each side – you may have to do this in two batches.

Serve the kidneys on four warmed plates. Unwrap the butter, cut into thin slices and place a slice on each piece of kidney. Garnish with sprigs of coriander and sprinkle with a little extra virgin olive oil. The residual heat of the kidneys will partly melt the butter as it goes to table.

The spicy flavours in this dish suggest the accompaniment of stir-fried vegetables: a single variety or perhaps a mixture. Onions, peppers, aubergines and courgettes, spiced with cumin and coriander, might be seen as Asian ratatouille, but would be delicious. Fresh lychees, peeled and eaten at table, would be a fitting conclusion.

BRAISED VEAL KNUCKLE

SERVES 4

1 veal knuckle, weighing
about 2 kg/4½ lb
salt and pepper
25 g/1 oz unsalted butter
1½ tablespoons groundnut oil
1 large onion, chopped
2 carrots, chopped
1 stick of celery, chopped
1 leek, white and pale green
parts only, chopped
2 garlic cloves, peeled and halved
50 g/2 oz tomato purée
200 g/7 oz ripe but firm plum
tomatoes, skinned and
seeded (reserve the skins
and seeds), diced
250 ml/8 fl oz dry white wine
500 ml/16 fl oz chicken stock
½ teaspoon black peppercorns,
lightly crushed
1 sprig of rosemary
1 sprig of thyme

Ask your butcher to trim off the meat, skin and gristle from the top 5 cm/2 inches of bone at the thin end of the knuckle. Trim the other end and season the meat. Preheat the oven to 180°/350°F/Gas Mark 4.

Heat a flameproof casserole just large enough to hold the knuckle comfortably. Add the butter and oil, then add the knuckle and brown it on all sides over moderate heat. Remove it from the pot. Add the onion, carrots, celery, leek and garlic to the casserole and cook until soft and lightly browned, stirring constantly. Stir in the tomato purée and the reserved tomato skins and seeds. Cook for 1 minute, stirring all the time. Stir a little of the wine into the vegetables and boil until evaporated. Add the remaining wine a little at a time and boil to evaporate, stirring frequently.

Return the knuckle to the casserole and add half the stock, the peppercorns and herbs. Cover and transfer to the oven for about 3 hours or until the meat is very tender and is falling off the bone. Turn the knuckle frequently during cooking and add the remaining stock a little at a time. Remove the lid for the last 20 minutes so the knuckle will have a good colour (check often, and add a little stock or water if necessary).

Remove the knuckle from the pot and keep warm. Strain the sauce through a sieve into a saucepan, pressing the vegetables. Bring to the boil, stir in the diced tomato, then taste and adjust the seasoning. Take the meat off the bone in one piece, slice it and serve hot, with the sauce.

Create a northern Italian-style menu with a first course salad of rocket with balsamic vinegar and Parmesan shavings and a dessert of sweet polenta with stewed fruit.

BROCHETTE OF LAMBS' KIDNEYS

with pancetta, thyme and polenta

SERVES 4

10 lambs' kidneys, skinned and cored,
   then cut into four equal chunks
7–8 thickish slices of rindless pancetta
   or streaky bacon, cut into 32 small squares
12–15 small sprigs of thyme
4–5 tablespoons olive oil
3–4 garlic cloves, bruised
sea salt and black pepper

Polenta
1.2 litres/2 pints water
1½ teaspoons salt
200 g/7 oz coarse polenta
50–85 g/2–3 oz butter, cut into cubes
freshly ground white pepper
40 g/1½ oz Parmesan cheese, grated

Soak 8 wooden skewers in warm water for
20 minutes.

Thread five kidney pieces on to each skewer,
alternating with pieces of bacon and adding the
sprigs of thyme intermittently. Put the skewers
in a shallow dish, pour over the olive oil, tuck in
the garlic cloves and grind over plenty of pepper
– do not add salt at this stage. Leave to marinate
for 45 minutes while you prepare the polenta.

Bring the water and salt to the boil in a large,
heavy-bottomed saucepan. Start to stir the water
with a balloon whisk. With your other hand,
trickle the polenta into the water in a steady,
fine, sand-like stream. Do not stop whisking
until all the polenta has been added. Lower the
heat and continue whisking for a few moments,
then turn the heat as low as possible and start
to stir with a wooden spoon. Continue stirring
over a very low heat for about 30–40 minutes;
the polenta is ready when it starts to come away
from the sides of the pan. Stir in the butter piece
by piece, add the pepper and Parmesan, and keep
warm in the pan.

Heat a ribbed stove-top grill pan until it is hot,
but not red hot. Lift the skewers from the oil,
shaking off any excess, and place on the hot grill.
Cook for about 10–12 minutes, depending on
how pink you like your kidneys, turning from
time to time until browned on all sides.

Pile the polenta on to four warmed plates and
place two brochettes on top. Sprinkle with sea
salt and serve at once.

*A salad of crisp chicory with a perky mustard
vinaigrette would go down very well. Serve a light
pudding such as a fresh fruit jelly or fruit salad.*

ROSEMARY AND GARLIC LAMB
with rice

SERVES 4

125 g/4 oz long-grain white rice
1 tablespoon groundnut oil
2 large garlic cloves, sliced
450 g/1 lb lean lamb fillet, cut into 5 cm/2 inch strips
3 large sprigs of rosemary
2 teaspoons Pernod
salt and pepper
3–4 spring onions, sliced diagonally into
    5 mm/¼ inch lengths
1 teaspoon rosemary oil

Cook the rice until it is tender. Drain well, spread on a plate, cover and refrigerate to allow the grains to cool and separate. This will prevent the rice from becoming sticky.

Heat a wok or large pan, then add the oil. When the oil is hot and begins to smoke, add the garlic and stir for 30 seconds. Add the lamb and rosemary and stir-fry for 3–4 minutes, until the lamb is browned. Add the Pernod and 2 teaspoons water and stir for 1 minute. Remove the rosemary. Season to taste with salt and pepper. Add the cold rice and stir-fry for 2 minutes. Add the spring onions and stir-fry for 1 minute. Add the rosemary oil and stir for a further 30 seconds, then serve immediately.

This is a strongly flavoured dish that includes rice, so all it needs to set it off is a fresh green salad, or perhaps bunches of thin green beans tied together with a chive. Follow with a refreshing lemon mousse, or oranges in Cointreau.

BLANQUETTE OF SWEETBREADS
with cream and lemon

SERVES 4

675 g/1½ lb lambs' sweetbreads
juice of 2 small lemons
salt
40 g/1½ oz butter
2 shallots, finely chopped
100 ml/3½ fl oz dry white wine
3 strips of thinly pared lemon rind
3 sprigs of thyme
100 ml/3½ fl oz chicken stock
2 egg yolks
150 ml/5 fl oz double cream
1 tablespoon chopped
    fresh parsley

First prepare the sweetbreads. Trim off any unsightly bits and pieces and rinse under cold running water for a few minutes. Drain, then put into a stainless steel or other non-reactive saucepan. Just cover with cold water and add the lemon juice and a little salt. Bring to a simmer, cook for 1 minute, then drain in a colander. Refresh under cold water, then lay out on a plate or chopping board. Pick over each piece and peel off the thin membrane using a small, sharp knife.

Melt the butter in a saucepan, add the shallots and cook over a low heat until soft but not browned. Add the wine, lemon rind and thyme and simmer for 5 minutes. Add the stock and bring back to the boil. Simmer over a low heat until reduced by half.

Add the prepared sweetbreads to the pan and simmer for 15–20 minutes, until they are firm, but give a little when squeezed (lift one out with a slotted spoon to test). When the sweetbreads are ready, transfer them to an ovenproof dish, shaking off any bits of shallot, cover the dish and keep warm in a low oven.

Strain the cooking liquid into a clean saucepan and bring back to a simmer. Beat together the egg yolks and cream and pour into the pan, whisking constantly until well blended. Cook over a very low heat until thickened: do not boil. Stir in the juice of the second lemon and the parsley and return the sweetbreads to the sauce to heat through. Turn into a warmed dish and serve at once.

A rich and creamy dish such as this cries out for a simple vegetable such as fresh peas or broad beans. A few sautéed button mushrooms might be another option. Follow with the first strawberries of the season, simply dressed with a little sugar and lemon juice.

LAMB STEAKS IN MINT OIL

with rice

SERVES 4

4 lamb chump chops, about 175 g/6 oz each
½ bunch of mint, chopped
½ bunch of parsley, chopped
125 ml/4 fl oz groundnut oil
1 teaspoon olive oil
½ onion, chopped
175 g/6 oz basmati rice
1 teaspoon turmeric
salt and pepper
15 g/½ oz butter

Heat the grill or barbecue. Preheat the oven to 200°C/400°F/Gas Mark 6.

Trim the lamb chops of excess fat and place in a shallow dish. Put the mint and parsley in a food processor and blend, gradually adding the groundnut oil. Pour over the lamb and leave to marinate for about 5 minutes, while you prepare the rice.

Heat the olive oil in a casserole, add the onion and cook over a low heat until softened. Add the rice and one and a half times its volume of water, stir and bring to the boil. Add the turmeric. Cover with greased greaseproof paper and bake in the oven for 15 minutes or until the rice is tender. Season to taste and stir in the butter.

Grill the lamb for about 3 minutes on each side; it should still be pink in the middle. Brush with the mint oil, season and leave to rest for 10 minutes. Serve on the rice.

To make this the most perfect meal, start with a simple asparagus salad with Parmesan cheese and freshly ground black pepper. Follow with coffee crème brûlée and vanilla ice cream.

NAVARIN OF LAMB

SERVES 4

8 pieces of lamb from the middle neck,
    each weighing about 85 g/3 oz
salt and pepper
3 tablespoons groundnut oil
1 large onion, roughly chopped
1 carrot, roughly chopped
5 garlic cloves, roughly chopped
1 leek, white and green parts only, roughly chopped
50 g/2 oz tomato purée
300 ml/10 fl oz red wine
25 g/1 oz plain flour
750 ml/1¼ pints chicken stock
1 sprig of thyme
1 sprig of marjoram

Preheat the oven to 180°C/35. ./Gas Mark 4.

Trim the lamb and season with salt and pepper. Heat a flameproof casserole over high heat and add the oil. Brown the lamb briskly on both sides. Remove and set aside.

Add the vegetables to the casserole and cook over moderately low heat until lightly browned, stirring often. Add the tomato purée and cook for 30 seconds, stirring well. Add one-third of the wine, stir well and bring to the boil. Boil until reduced to a thick glaze. Repeat with the remaining wine, adding it half at a time.

Add the flour and stir well for 1 minute, then gradually stir in the stock. Bring to the boil, add the herbs and some salt and pepper, then return the lamb to the casserole. Cover and transfer to the oven. Braise for about 2 hours or until the lamb is very tender, stirring occasionally.

Remove the pieces of lamb from the casserole and keep warm. Strain the sauce through a fine sieve into a jug or bowl, pressing the vegetables to extract the maximum flavour and liquid. Taste and adjust the seasoning. Spoon the sauce over the lamb and serve hot.

Navarin of lamb is often made with young spring or early summer vegetables, but this version can be made at any time of year. I like to serve it with couscous and chargrilled vegetables. I might begin with a cool crab and avocado salad and finish the meal with a rich almond tart served with crème fraîche.

LAMB PEPERONATA

SERVES 4

3 red peppers

3 yellow peppers

3 green peppers

1 aubergine

200 ml/7 fl oz extra virgin
   olive oil

2 onions, finely chopped

2 garlic cloves, finely chopped

3 plum tomatoes, skinned,
   seeded and diced

1 tablespoon tomato purée

200 ml/7 fl oz dry white wine

12 lamb cutlets, trimmed

200 ml/7 fl oz chicken
   or lamb stock

salt and pepper

Preheat the oven to 190°C/375°F/Gas Mark 5.

Grill the peppers until blackened and blistered on all sides. Transfer
to a polythene bag and leave for 5 minutes or until cool enough to
handle. Peel off the blackened skin, scrape out the seeds and cut the
flesh into 1 cm/½ inch strips. Cut the aubergine lengthways into
1 cm/½ inch slices, then cut into strips similar in size to the peppers.

Heat the olive oil in a large flameproof casserole, add the onions and
sweat over a low heat until soft. Add the garlic and sweat for a further
minute. Add the tomatoes and cook for 3−4 minutes, then add the
tomato purée and cook for 2−3 minutes. Add the wine and boil over
high heat until it is reduced by half. Add the peppers and aubergine
strips and stir to mix, then add the lamb cutlets and cover with the
pepper mixture. Pour in the stock and season generously. Bring
back to a simmer, then transfer to the oven and braise, uncovered,
for 45−60 minutes, stirring occasionally, until the meat is tender.
Taste and adjust the seasoning and serve hot.

*Serve with a potato purée flavoured with good olive oil. For a first course
I suggest a smoked haddock chowder with grilled bacon. To finish, how about
pears with butterscotch sauce?*

IRISH STEW

SERVES 4

8 lamb chops
25 g/1 oz lamb fat
25 g/1 oz butter
175 g/6 oz onions, sliced
175 g/6 oz carrots, sliced
125 g/4 oz leeks, sliced
2 garlic cloves, chopped
1 bay leaf
2 sprigs of rosemary
125 g/4 oz pearl barley
400–450 g/14–16 oz Wilja
    potatoes, cut into large dice
1.2 litres/2 pints chicken stock
salt and pepper
175 g/6 oz cabbage, shredded
25 g/1 oz flat-leaf parsley,
    chopped

Blanch the chops in a pan of boiling water, then remove and refresh in cold water.

Melt the lamb fat and butter in a casserole, add the onions, carrots, leeks and garlic and cook over a low heat until softened. Add the chops, bay leaf, rosemary, pearl barley and potatoes, then add the chicken stock and about 600 ml/1 pint water to cover. Bring to the boil, skim off any impurities, then cover and simmer for 35–40 minutes or until the meat is tender.

To serve, add the cabbage to the casserole and cook for a further 4–5 minutes. Add the chopped parsley and season with salt and pepper. Serve in deep bowls, pouring the cooking liquid over the meat and vegetables.

Serve a dish of buttered green beans to accompany the stew. When my grandmother made Irish stew it was always followed by a steamed pudding, usually spotted dick.

SHAH JEHANI KORMA

Classic mild lamb curry

SERVES 4

675 g/1½ lb lean lamb, cubed
2 teaspoons sugar
1 teaspoon salt
250 ml/8 fl oz natural yogurt
4 tablespoons ghee or vegetable oil
2 tablespoons finely chopped garlic
1 tablespoon finely chopped fresh ginger
½ teaspoon turmeric
2 teaspoons ground coriander
2 onions, finely chopped
20–30 saffron strands
4 tablespoons ground almonds
175 ml/6 fl oz single cream
toasted flaked almonds and fresh coriander, to garnish

Whole spices
15 cm/6 inch piece of cassia bark
12 green cardamom pods
10 cloves
8 bay leaves
1 teaspoon fennel seeds

Place the meat in a non-metallic bowl, add the whole spices, sugar, salt and yogurt, mix well and leave in the refrigerator to marinate for between 6 and 48 hours.

Preheat the oven to 190°C/375°F/Gas Mark 5.

Heat the ghee or oil in a wok or karahi until hot, but well below smoking point. Add the garlic and ginger and stir-fry briskly for about 30 seconds. Add the turmeric and coriander, stir briskly, then add the onions and mix in well. Keeping the heat high at first, stir-fry until the onion caramelizes. This will take 10–15 minutes, and the heat will need to be lowered gradually during this time.

Place the lamb and its marinade in a casserole, add the fried onion and spice mixture, stir well and place in the oven for 25 minutes.

Stir in the saffron, ground almonds and cream and return to the oven.

After 20 minutes, stir the curry and add a little water if it looks dry. Cook for a further 10–20 minutes, or until the lamb is very tender.

Serve at once, or cool, chill and reheat the next day. Garnish with toasted almonds and fresh coriander.

Accompany with either plain basmati rice or navrattan pullao (page 139), and with potatoes in a pickle sauce (page 158) and the Queen's lentils (page 154), to make a Moghulai feast for 6–8 people.

BUTTERFLIED LEG OF LAMB

SERVES 6–8

2 kg/4½ lb leg of lamb, boned*
3 large garlic cloves
2 sprigs of rosemary
3–4 tablespoons olive oil
salt and pepper

* Ask your butcher to take out the bone in one cut, so the lamb can be opened out flat.

Lay the lamb lay out flat. Make 12 incisions in the lamb using the tip of a sharp knife. Slice each of the garlic cloves into four pieces and break the rosemary into 12 smaller sprigs. Place a slice of garlic and a rosemary sprig into each of the incisions in the lamb. Leave to marinate for 4 hours at room temperature or overnight in the refrigerator.

Heat the grill or barbecue.

Brush the lamb with olive oil and season well. Grill for 12–20 minutes on each side; cooking time will depend partly on the heat of the grill, partly on how well done you like your lamb. Should the lamb blacken too quickly, raise the barbecue grid slightly or turn down the heat. Leave the lamb to rest for 10 minutes before slicing. Serve hot.

For an ideal menu, serve fresh mint sauce and new potatoes with this dish, and finish with a tarte tatin.

SHALIMAR RAAN

Spicy roast leg of lamb

SERVES 4–6 AS A STARTER

1.5–1.6 kg /3–3½ lb leg of
    lamb, on the bone
450–500 g /about 1 lb Greek-
    style yogurt
4 tablespoons vegetable oil
2 tablespoons garam masala
1 teaspoon ground cinnamon
1 teaspoon ground cloves
1 tablespoon bottled tandoori
    paste
1–3 fresh red chillies
50 g/2 oz bottled beetroot
2 tablespoons chopped fresh
    mint leaves
2 tablespoons chopped fresh
    coriander leaves
1 teaspoon salt

Preheat the oven to 180°C/350°F/Gas Mark 4.

Trim all the fat and membranes off the leg of lamb, then make a
number of small gashes in the flesh. Put all the remaining ingredients
in a food processor and grind to a paste.

Line a roasting tin with foil. Put the lamb in the tin and coat it
liberally all over with the spicy paste, using about half the mixture.
Loosely cover the lamb with more foil and roast in the centre of the
oven for about 2 hours.

Spread the lamb with about half the remaining spice paste and roast
(without the foil) for at least a further hour. The flesh should fall off
the bone, so it may need more time to achieve this.

Remove the lamb from the oven and let it rest in a warm place for
about 15 minutes, during which time you can make the gravy. Put
the remaining spice paste in a saucepan and add any cooked paste
from the roasting tin, together with a little water, salt and garam
masala. Simmer for about 3 minutes. Carve the lamb, pour the gravy
over it and serve hot.

*Traditionally, raan would be served with naan bread, liberally spread with
ghee. For a change, try it with roast potatoes and light vegetables such as
mangetout, courgette and celery, lightly sautéed with butter, wild onion seeds
(kalonji) and some cream. Garnish with chilli powder and chopped chives.
Cold raan with pickle makes a great sandwich filler.*

BARBUR'S BIRIANI

Meat with saffron rice

SERVES 4

225 g/8 oz basmati rice

6 tablespoons ghee or butter

5–6 garlic cloves, chopped

5 cm/2 inch cube of fresh ginger,
    finely chopped

2 onions, finely chopped

1–2 small fresh red chillies,
    shredded (optional)

450g/1 lb lean leg of lamb or
    beef, cubed

125 g/4 oz Greek-style yogurt

500 ml/16 fl oz vegetable stock

25–30 saffron strands

3 tablespoons chopped fresh
    coriander leaves

2 teaspoons garam masala

salt

Spices

4–5 green cardamoms

6–8 cloves

4–5 bay leaves

2–3 star anise pods

3–4 pieces of cassia bark

1½ teaspoons ground coriander

1 teaspoon ground cumin

1 teaspoon black peppercorns

½ teaspoon fennel seeds

½ teaspoon black cumin seeds

½ teaspoon turmeric

Preheat the oven to 190°C/375°F/Gas Mark 5. Rinse the rice, then soak for 10 minutes.

Heat 4 tablespoons of the ghee in a wok or karahi until hot, but well below smoking point. Add the spices and stir-fry briskly for about 30 seconds. Add the garlic and ginger and stir-fry for a further 30 seconds, then add the onions and mix in well. Keeping the heat high at first, stir-fry until the onions caramelize. This will take 10–15 minutes, and the heat will need to be lowered gradually during this time. Add the meat and stir-fry for about 5–6 minutes to seal it. Add the yogurt and take the pan off the heat.

In a separate pan, bring the stock to the boil. Heat the remaining ghee in a lidded casserole dish of at least 3.4 litres/6 pints capacity. Drain the rice and add to the casserole, with the saffron. Stir until sizzling, then add the boiling stock. Put the lid on and leave the casserole over high heat for 3 minutes.

Stir in the meat mixture, then put the lid on the casserole and place in the oven.

After 25 minutes, gently (so as not to break the rice grains) fork around the biriani to aerate it and allow the steam to escape.

Add the coriander, garam masala and salt to taste. If the dish looks dry, add a little stock or water, then return it to the oven for a further 25 minutes.

Fork through the rice again, and test whether the meat is tender. It might need a further 10–20 minutes in the oven, so add more water if necessary. Serve hot.

This is a meal in itself – all you need are some curry condiments, such as a spicy gravy, pickles, chutneys and Indian bread. Follow with fresh mango or mango sorbet.

PORK WITH MUSHROOMS AND OLIVES

SERVES 4

450 g/1 lb pork loin fillet, cut into
    5 mm/¼ inch thick slices
pepper
2 tablespoons oyster sauce
1 tablespoon soy sauce
1 tablespoon dry white vermouth
2 tablespoons cornflour
1 tablespoon groundnut oil
125 g/4 oz broccoli,
    cut into small florets
125 g/4 oz button mushrooms,
    sliced
½ orange pepper,
    cut into thin strips
12 black pitted olives,
    sliced into thirds

Prepare the meat and season with pepper. In a small jug, combine the oyster and soy sauces, vermouth, cornflour and 2 tablespoons water.

Heat a wok or large pan, then add the oil. When the oil is hot and begins to smoke, add the meat and stir-fry for 2 minutes, or until the meat is brown. (The pork may need to be cooked in batches, in which case more oil may need to be added.) Remove with a slotted spoon and keep warm.

Add the broccoli to the wok and stir-fry for 2 minutes. Add the mushrooms and pepper and stir-fry for 2 minutes. Remove the wok from the heat and add the cornflour mixture. Return to the heat and and stir for 1 minute. Add the olives and return the meat to the wok and stir-fry for 1–2 minutes, until the meat is hot. Serve immediately.

A colourful dish that needs only white or brown rice to make a complete meal. It is not rich so you could follow it with a fresh apple or pear tart.

MAIALE AL LATTE

Loin of pork braised in milk

SERVES 6–8

1.5 kg/3 lb neatly tied loin of pork,
   boned and rindless but with a thin layer of fat
4 tablespoons olive oil
2 cloves, bruised
pinch of ground cinnamon
1 sprig of rosemary
2 garlic cloves, bruised
salt and pepper
6–7 peppercorns, bruised
1 bay leaf
50 g/2 oz unsalted butter
300 ml/10 fl oz full–fat milk

Put the meat in a bowl and add 2 tablespoons of the oil, the cloves, cinnamon, rosemary, garlic, 1 teaspoon salt, the peppercorns and the bay leaf. Coat the pork all over in the marinade, cover and marinate for about 8 hours. Turn the meat over whenever you remember.

Heat the butter and the remaining oil in a heavy casserole into which the pork will fit snugly. When the butter foam begins to subside, add the meat and brown well on all sides and on the ends.

Heat the milk to boiling point and pour slowly over the meat. Sprinkle with salt, place the lid over the pan slightly askew and cook for about 3 hours at a steady low simmer. Turn the meat over and baste approximately every 20 minutes. By the end of the cooking the meat should be very tender and the sauce should be a rich dark golden colour, and quite thick.

Transfer the meat to a carving board and cover with foil. If the sauce is still too thin, boil briskly without the lid until it darkens and thickens.

Skim off as much fat as you can from the surface of the sauce, add 2 tablespoons hot water and boil over high heat for about 2 minutes, scraping the bottom of the pan with a metal spoon. Taste and adjust the seasoning. Remove the string and carve the pork into 1 cm/½ inch slices. Arrange on a large warmed plate and spoon the sauce over the pork.

This winter dish really calls out for a buttery potato purée to mop up the sauce. A bowl of spinach would be my choice for a second vegetable. For a first course I suggest a light soup or a salad of celeriac.

SUONG NUONG

Charcoal-grilled pork chops

SERVES 4

3 tablespoons fish sauce

2 tablespoons sugar

2 tablespoons peanut or vegetable oil

2 thick stalks of fresh lemongrass, peeled and thinly
    sliced, or 2 tablespoons grated fresh ginger

4 shallots, finely chopped

4 large garlic cloves, finely chopped

2 fresh red chillies, finely chopped

½ teaspoon ground black pepper

4 pork chops, about 2 cm/¾ inch thick

Place all the ingredients except the pork chops in a liquidizer or food processor and blend until finely puréed. Transfer to a shallow dish large enough to accommodate the chops in a single layer.

Add the chops and turn to coat evenly with the paste. Cover and leave to marinate at room temperature for at least 2 hours, or overnight in the refrigerator.

Prepare the barbecue or preheat the grill.

Grill the chops until they are browned on both sides and just cooked through (the juices near the bone should run clear when pierced with the tip of a sharp knife), about 6–7 minutes on each side. Serve immediately.

Accompany these succulent chops with sliced fresh cucumbers or pickled vegetables (page 375) and steamed rice. Pass chilli dipping sauce (page 375) separately.

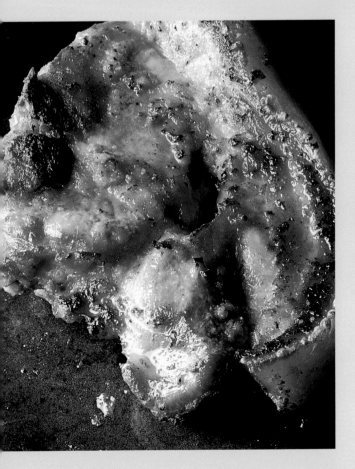

BLACK PUDDING AND CHAMP

with shallots and red wine sauce

SERVES 4

325 g/12 oz Pentland Hawk
    potatoes, chopped
325 g/12 oz black pudding
2 tablespoons olive oil
85 g/3 oz butter
2 bunches of spring onions,
    finely chopped
4 tablespoons double cream
salt and pepper

Red wine sauce
1 tablespoon olive oil
2 shallots, finely sliced
1 bottle red wine
175 ml/6 fl oz ruby port
600 ml/1 pint veal stock
85 g/3 oz unsalted butter, diced

Glazed shallots
16–20 shallots or button onions
85 g/3 oz butter
50 g/2 oz caster sugar
2 sprigs of thyme

For the red wine sauce, heat the oil in a saucepan, add the shallots and cook over a low heat until soft but not browned. Add the red wine and port and boil to reduce by three-quarters. Add the stock and boil to reduce to about 200 ml/7 fl oz. Set aside.

For the glazed shallots, put the shallots in a saucepan of cold water, bring to the boil for about 1 minute, then drain. Melt the butter and sugar in a frying pan, add the shallots, a splash of water and the thyme. Cover the shallots with a butter paper or foil and cook over a low heat until all the liquid has evaporated and the shallots are tender.

Meanwhile, place the potatoes in a saucepan of cold salted water, bring to the boil, then turn down the heat and simmer until tender. Drain and mash.

Slice the black pudding into small discs, then fry lightly in the olive oil.

The shallots should by now be coated in a light caramelized glaze. If they are not, turn up the heat and gently roll the shallots around the pan. Season to taste.

For the champ, melt the butter in a large saucepan, add the spring onions and cook for just long enough to soften them, then add the mashed potato and cream, season to taste and beat well.

Reheat the sauce to boiling point, then remove from the heat, add the butter and whisk vigorously. Season to taste.

To serve, spoon the champ on to four plates, scatter the glazed shallots around and lay the black pudding on top. Finally, pour over the red wine sauce.

All you need by way of accompaniment is a large plate of Irish oysters and a pint of Guinness.

DESSERTS

Blessed be he that invented pudding...
oh what an excellent thing is an English pudding!
To come in pudding-time is as much as to say
to come in the most lucky moment in the world.

H. MISSON DE VALBOURG
(A French visitor to Britain in 1690)

SEMIFREDDO DI CASSATA

Cassata semi freddo with strawberry sauce

First make the hazelnut brittle. Brush a baking sheet with vegetable oil to coat evenly. Put the sugar in a heavy-bottomed saucepan over a very low heat and heat gently, without stirring, until the sugar starts to melt. As soon as the sugar has liquefied and turned a caramel colour, add the hazelnuts and stir in. Pour the mixture on to the oiled baking sheet and leave to cool and harden.

For the sauce, purée the strawberries with the caster sugar and then pass the mixture through a fine sieve to make a smooth sauce. Cover and store in the refrigerator.

Line a 900 g/2 lb loaf tin with cling film.

Beat the egg whites until stiff. In a heavy-bottomed saucepan, heat the sugar to 120°C/250°F or the hard ball stage. (If you do not have a sugar thermometer, test by dropping a little syrup into a bowl of iced water, then kneading it between your fingers: it should form a firm, pliable ball.) Slowly pour the hot syrup on to the egg whites, whisking all the time. Continue whisking until the meringue is cold.

Break off a 50 g/2 oz piece of the hazelnut brittle and chop finely. Add the pistachios, candied fruits, sultanas and hazelnut brittle to the meringue and fold in well. Whip the cream until very thick, but not too stiff, then fold into the mixture. Pour into the lined tin and freeze for 5 hours. Serve sliced, with the strawberry sauce.

SERVES 6–8

50 g/2 oz egg whites (2 small eggs or 1 large egg)
125 g/4 oz sugar
25 g/1 oz pistachio nuts, chopped
25 g/1 oz candied fruits, chopped
1 tablespoon sultanas
250 ml/8 fl oz double cream

Strawberry sauce
150 g/5 oz very ripe strawberries
25 g/1 oz caster sugar

Hazelnut brittle
a little vegetable oil
85 g/3 oz sugar
85 g/3 oz hazelnuts, skinned

STRACCIATTELLA

Rich vanilla ice cream with chocolate chips

MAKES 2.3 LITRES/4 PINTS

1.2 litres/2 pints milk
1 vanilla pod, split
15 egg yolks
350 g/13 oz caster sugar
350 ml/13 fl oz whipping cream
125 g/4 oz chocolate, finely chopped

In a heavy-bottomed saucepan, heat the milk with the vanilla pod just to boiling point; set aside.

In a bowl, beat the egg yolks and sugar together until pale and creamy. Slowly add the hot milk, stirring all the time with a wooden spoon. Return the mixture to the cleaned saucepan over a low heat and stir gently until the custard thickens enough to coat the back of the spoon. Strain the custard into a clean bowl and leave to cool, preferably over ice.

Whip the cream until thick, but not too stiff, then fold into the custard. Churn the mixture in an ice cream machine. When the ice cream is almost frozen, add the chocolate and stir in evenly.

SEMIFREDDO ALLO ZABAIONE

Semi freddo with Marsala

SERVES 4–6

8 egg yolks
200 g/7 oz caster sugar
250 ml/8 fl oz dry Marsala
500 ml/16 fl oz double cream

Line a 900 g/2 lb loaf tin with cling film.

Put the egg yolks and sugar in a large bowl and whisk until they are thick, creamy and almost white. Add the Marsala, 1 tablespoon at a time, whisking well after each addition.

Place the bowl over a saucepan of barely simmering water and continue whisking the mixture until it is stiff. Transfer the mixture to a clean bowl and leave until cold, stirring from time to time.

Whip the cream until thick, but not too stiff, then gently fold into the egg mixture. Pour into the lined tin and freeze for 5–6 hours.

GELATO ALLA GIANDUIA
Chocolate and hazelnut ice cream

MAKES 2.3 LITRES/4 PINTS

600 ml/1 pint milk
300 ml/10 fl oz Jersey
   or double cream
1 vanilla pod, split
15 egg yolks
350 g/13 oz caster sugar

Gianduia paste
200 g/7 oz hazelnuts
50 g/2 oz pure cocoa powder

First make the gianduia paste. If your hazelnuts are still in their skins, spread them on a baking sheet and preheat the oven to 180°C/350°F/Gas Mark 4. Roast the nuts in the oven for 8–10 minutes, turning them after 5 minutes. Tip them on to a clean tea towel and rub until the skins flake off. Roast the hazelnuts until deep brown, but not burnt. Put the nuts into a food processor and grind until the oil runs from the nuts. Add the cocoa powder and process until a paste forms.

In a heavy-bottomed saucepan, heat the milk and cream together with the vanilla pod just to boiling point; set aside.

In a bowl, beat the egg yolks and sugar together until pale and creamy. Slowly add the hot milk, stirring all the time with a wooden spoon. Return the mixture to the cleaned saucepan over a low heat and stir gently until the custard thickens enough to coat the back of the spoon. Strain into a clean cold bowl and leave until cold, preferably over ice.

Add the gianduia paste a little at a time until it has all been incorporated into the custard. Churn in an ice cream machine.

GELATO DI CARAMELLO PRALINATO

Caramel ice cream with praline

MAKES 2.3 LITRES/4 PINTS

600 ml/1 pint milk
400 ml/14 fl oz Jersey
    or double cream
500 g/1 lb 2 oz caster sugar
15 egg yolks

Praline
a little vegetable oil
125 g/4 oz sugar
125 g/4 oz whole almonds

First make the praline. Brush a baking sheet with vegetable oil to coat evenly. Put the sugar in a heavy-bottomed saucepan over a very low heat, and do not stir until the sugar starts to melt. As soon as the sugar has liquefied and turned a caramel colour, add the almonds and stir in. Taking great care, as it is very hot, pour the mixture on to the oiled baking sheet and leave to harden.

Heat the milk and cream together to boiling point; set aside.

Caramelize the sugar as for the praline, then add the hot milk and cream to the caramel – never the other way round – stirring all the time.

In a bowl, beat the egg yolks together lightly. Slowly add the milk and caramel mixture to the egg yolks, stirring continuously with a wooden spoon. Return the mixture to the cleaned saucepan over a low heat and stir continuously until the caramel custard thickens enough to coat the back of the spoon. Leave to cool.

Churn in an ice cream machine. When the ice cream is almost frozen, crush the praline and fold in.

GELATO DI FRAGOLE E YOGURT

Strawberry and yogurt ice cream

SERVES 6–8

500 g/1 lb 2 oz strawberries
125 g/4 oz caster sugar
1 tablespoon strained lemon juice
200 g/7 oz full cream yogurt
4 tablespoons milk
finely grated zest of 1 lemon

Wash the strawberries with the stalks on and pat dry on paper towels. Hull the strawberries and purée them, then pass through a fine, non-metallic sieve. Add half of the sugar and the lemon juice to the purée.

In a bowl, mix the yogurt with the remaining sugar, milk and grated lemon zest, beating with a balloon whisk. Add the strawberry purée and mix well. Churn the mixture in an ice cream machine.

This refreshing gelato is not a true ice cream but is very good for people who cannot eat eggs.

GELATO DI MIELE E NOCI

Honey and walnut ice cream

SERVES 6–8

a little vegetable oil
85 g/3 oz sugar
85 g/3 oz walnuts
6 egg yolks
300 ml/10 fl oz milk
6 tablespoons clear honey

Brush a baking sheet with vegetable oil to coat evenly. Put the sugar in a heavy-bottomed saucepan over a very low heat, and do not stir until the sugar starts to melt. As soon as the sugar has liquefied and turned to a caramel colour, add the walnuts and stir in. Taking great care, as it is very hot, pour the mixture on to the oiled baking sheet and leave to harden.

In a bowl set over a pan of gently simmering water, beat the egg yolks with a balloon whisk until thickened. Meanwhile, heat the milk and honey together to boiling point. Slowly add the hot milk to the eggs, stirring continuously. Return the mixture to the saucepan over a low heat and stir gently with a wooden spoon until the custard thickens enough to coat the back of the spoon. Leave to cool.

Churn in an ice cream machine. When the ice cream is almost frozen, crush the walnut praline and fold into the ice cream.

GELATO DI CAPPUCCINO
Cappuccino ice cream

MAKES 2.3 LITRES/4 PINTS

250 ml/8 fl oz milk
500 ml/16 fl oz double cream
3 teaspoons instant espresso
    coffee powder
10 egg yolks
150 g/5 oz caster sugar

To serve
whipped cream
powdered chocolate

In a heavy-bottomed saucepan, bring the milk, cream and coffee to the boil; set aside.

In a bowl, beat the egg yolks and sugar together until pale and creamy. Slowly add the hot milk, stirring continuously with a balloon whisk. Return the mixture to the cleaned saucepan over a low heat and stir with a wooden spoon until the custard thickens enough to coat the back of the spoon. Strain the custard into a bowl and leave to cool.

Churn in an ice cream machine. Serve with fresh whipped cream and a sprinkling of powdered chocolate.

MASCARPONE AND LEMON ICE CREAM

SERVES 6

grated zest and juice of 2 lemons
125 g/4 oz caster sugar
4 large egg yolks
500 g/1 lb 2 oz mascarpone cheese

Make the lemon juice up to 150 ml/5 fl oz with water, then put into a saucepan with the lemon zest and sugar. Heat gently until the sugar has dissolved, then boil until syrupy – about 4 minutes.

Meanwhile, in a large heatproof bowl, whisk the egg yolks until they are quite thick and pale. Whisking continuously, strain the hot syrup over the egg yolks. Set the bowl over a pan of simmering water and whisk for a further 5 minutes or so, until very thick and pale. Leave to cool slightly, then whisk in the mascarpone.

Pour the mixture into a plastic container and freeze until firm; or use an ice cream machine. Remove from the freezer for 15 minutes or so before serving, to allow the ice cream to soften a little.

Serve on its own or with fresh fruit such as raspberries to finish off a special summer meal; perhaps a mixed rice pilaf with fresh asparagus and summer vegetables and a garden herb salad.

LA MOUSSE AU CHOCOLAT DE CHEF CHAMBRETTE

SERVES 4–6

175 g/6 oz good-quality plain chocolate, chopped
250 ml/8 fl oz fresh orange juice
2 tablespoons Grand Marnier
4 egg whites
25 g/1 oz caster sugar
cocoa powder for sprinkling

Candied zest
pared zest of 1 orange
2 tablespoons sugar
2 tablespoons water

In a heavy saucepan melt the chocolate in the orange juice, stirring gently. Bring to the boil and simmer for 3–4 minutes, stirring constantly until it has the consistency of double cream. Let it cool to tepid, then stir in the Grand Marnier.

Whisk the egg whites until stiff. Add the sugar and continue beating until glossy, about 30 seconds. Stir about a quarter of the whites into the chocolate until well mixed and light. Add this mixture back into the remaining whites and fold together as lightly as possible. Spoon the mousse into small pots or ramekins and tap them on the work surface to level the mixture. Cover and chill until set – at least 6 and up to 24 hours.

Not more than 1 hour before serving, candy the zest: cut the orange zest into the finest possible julienne strips. In a small saucepan heat the sugar and water until dissolved. Add the orange strips and simmer very gently, stirring occasionally, until the zests are translucent and the syrup has evaporated, 7–10 minutes. Spread the zests on a sheet of greaseproof paper and leave to dry for 15–30 minutes.

Just before serving, sprinkle the mousses with cocoa and top each with a pinch of candied zest. Serve chilled.

I was given this recipe by Chef Fernand Chambrette, who in the long-ago 1950s was awarded two Michelin stars for his mastery of bistro dishes such as duck confit and rum babas. He liked to melt the chocolate in strong black coffee; here I use orange juice. To precede this chocolate mousse I'm opting for grilled fillets of sole or John Dory with a tarragon butter sauce, asparagus on the side, and as opener a classic onion soup.

RHUBARB AND GINGER FOOL

SERVES 4

150 ml/5 fl oz double cream
1 teaspoon icing sugar
2 pieces of stem ginger
600 g/1¼ lb early season
    forced rhubarb
225 g/8 oz caster sugar
2–3 drops of pink food colouring
    (optional)
150 ml/5 fl oz vanilla custard
    (page 377), chilled

Whisk the cream with the icing sugar until firm, but not stiff and dry. Chill.

Slice the ginger thinly and then slice across into thin strips.

Top, tail and wash the rhubarb, leaving the pink skin on. Put the rhubarb in a wide shallow pan with the caster sugar and 3 table-spoons water, and simmer until softened to a pulp. If the colour is not pink enough from the skins, add two or three drops of colouring (it should be pale pink, but as the rhubarb gets older the purée will be less pink and may need a little help).

Press the purée through a very coarse sieve, just to remove any stringy bits but leaving some texture in the fruit. Stir in the ginger and chill well.

Place alternate spoonfuls of the custard, cream and fruit purée in a wide bowl. Using a spatula, draw them lightly together to make a marbled fool. Spoon into glasses to show off the marbled effect, and serve with shortbread fingers.

A gutsy February dish of braised oxtail with mashed potatoes would be a perfect foil for this light fool made with the new season's rhubarb.

SUMMER PUDDINGS

SERVES 4

175 g/6 oz blackcurrants
175 g/6 oz redcurrants
175 g/6 oz blueberries
    or bilberries
175 g/6 oz small strawberries
175 g/6 oz raspberries
175 g/6 oz cherries, pitted
4–6 tablespoons caster sugar
1 lemon, zest pared in
    large strips
1 large loaf of stoneground
    wholemeal bread, thinly sliced,
    crusts removed
mint leaves and icing sugar,
    to decorate

Begin making the puddings the day before you need them. Reserve a few little bunches of berries for decoration, then strip the stalks and hulls from all the fruit. Place the fruit in a saucepan with 4 tablespoons of the sugar and the strips of lemon zest. Heat gently, until the juices just begin to flow from the fruit, then remove from the heat. Taste and add more sugar if necessary. Pour the fruit into a colander set over a bowl to collect the juices. Remove the lemon zest.

Cut out four circles of bread to fit the bases of four individual pudding moulds. Cut strips of bread long enough to line the sides of the moulds with about 5 mm/¼ inch over. Dip the bread in the fruit juice, then line the moulds, putting the circles in first and then pressing the strips up the sides. Pack the fruit into the moulds, right to the top of the bread. Cut four more circles of bread to cover the fruit, first dipping them in the fruit juice. Cover with cling film and place on a small tray. Cover with another tray and press it in place with heavy weights. Chill overnight.

Purée any remaining fruit with its juices, pass through a fine sieve into a container and chill.

Before serving, trim away any excess bread. Run a thin-bladed knife around each pudding and invert on to a serving plate. Shake to remove the puddings from the moulds. Pour a little sauce over and around each pudding, and decorate with the reserved berries and some small mint leaves. Dust lightly with icing sugar. Serve with pouring cream or crème fraîche.

Chargrilled fillet of cod with pesto and a rocket salad is a lovely dish to precede a classic summer pudding.

RASPBERRY QUEEN OF PUDDINGS

SERVES 4–6

50 g/2 oz fresh white
   breadcrumbs
grated zest of 1 lemon
600 ml/1 pint hot vanilla custard
   (page 377)
3 tablespoons raspberry jam
175 g/6 oz raspberries,
   washed and dried

Meringue
5 egg whites
pinch of salt
4 tablespoons caster sugar
1 tablespoon flaked almonds
   (optional)

Raspberry coulis
175 g/6 oz raspberries
50 g/2 oz icing sugar

Sprinkle the breadcrumbs and grated lemon zest into a 1 litre/ 1¾ pint ovenproof serving dish and pour the hot custard over. Leave to cool, then chill in the refrigerator for 2 hours.

Preheat the oven to 120°C/250°F/Gas Mark ½.

Warm the jam with 1 tablespoon cold water. Pass through a fine sieve to remove the seeds, then spread the jam over the custard and top with the raspberries.

To make the meringue, whisk the egg whites in a bowl with a pinch of salt, until they form stiff peaks. Whisk in 3 tablespoons of the sugar and whisk to form stiff, glossy peaks. Pile the meringue on top of the raspberries in rough peaks – do not attempt to spread the meringue, but make certain the raspberries are completely covered. Scatter the remaining sugar and the flaked almonds over the meringue. Bake for 25–30 minutes, until the meringue is crisp with light golden peaks.

Meanwhile, make the coulis: toss the raspberries in the icing sugar, then press through a sieve to remove the seeds. Serve the pudding hot or cold, with the raspberry coulis.

As a main course, how about a summery fish dish such as baked red mullet with a tomato and chilli salsa?

GOOSEBERRY AND ELDERFLOWER CRUMBLE

SERVES 4–6

butter for preparing the dish
900 g/2 lb gooseberries
4 heads (umbels) of elderflowers
225 g/8 oz caster sugar
175 g/6 oz plain flour
pinch of salt
85 g/3 oz unsalted butter, chilled and diced
25 g/1 oz hazelnuts (or cobnuts), chopped

Preheat the oven to 200°C/400°F/Gas Mark 6. Butter a 1.2 litre/2 pint ovenproof shallow dish.

Top and tail the gooseberries and put them in the dish. Gently wash the elderflowers and shake dry, holding them upside down to remove any insects. Sprinkle 150 g/5 oz of the sugar over the gooseberries and tuck the elderflowers among the fruit.

Sift the flour and salt into a mixing bowl and rub in the butter until it resembles fine bread-crumbs. Stir in the remaining sugar and the chopped nuts.

Beginning at the outer edges (which helps to prevent the juices from rising up the sides), spoon the topping evenly over the fruit. Firm the crumbs down with the back of the spoon and then mark lines with a fork to help make the top crisp.

Bake for 40–45 minutes, until the top is crisp and golden brown and the gooseberries tender. Serve hot or cold, with custard or crème fraîche.

A light fish dish such as sea bass roasted over fennel with roasted vegetables would be an excellent main course to precede this early summer dessert.

BLACKBERRY SOUFFLÉ

SERVES 4

butter and caster sugar for preparing the dishes
500g/1 lb 2 oz fresh ripe blackberries
1 teaspoon lemon juice
85 g/3 oz caster sugar
3 egg whites
pinch of salt
3 tablespoons caster sugar
icing sugar for dusting

Preheat the oven to 200°C/400°F/Gas Mark 6. Lightly butter four individual soufflé dishes and sprinkle a little caster sugar in each. Shake the dishes to coat the insides evenly with caster sugar.

Press the blackberries through a medium sieve into a bowl. Add the lemon juice and caster sugar to the thick purée of blackberries. Taste and add a squeeze more lemon juice if necessary: it should taste very fruity but quite sharp. Chill well.

Put 1 dessertspoon of blackberry purée in the bottom of each soufflé dish.

In a perfectly clean bowl, whisk the egg whites with a pinch of salt until they form stiff peaks. Fold in half the caster sugar and whisk to form stiff, glossy peaks. Repeat with the remaining sugar.

Using a balloon whisk, carefully fold in the blackberry purée until evenly mixed. Pile into the soufflé dishes. Smooth the sides and top with a palette knife, allowing the mixture to stand about 2 cm/¾ inch above the rims.

Bake until well risen and golden, about 4–5 minutes. Dust with icing sugar and serve immediately. Some blackberry sorbet would be a rather nice accompaniment.

Blackberry soufflé makes a light autumn pudding to follow a traditional roast such as a loin of pork with apple sauce.

STRAWBERRY AND ROSE PETAL SHORTCAKES

SERVES 6

225 g/8 oz unsalted butter
125 g/4 oz vanilla-flavoured
   caster sugar
225 g/8 oz plain flour
125 g/4 oz semolina

Rose cream
2 teaspoons lemon juice
3 large red old-fashioned
   scented roses*
300 ml/10 fl oz double cream
1 tablespoon icing sugar, sifted
½ teaspoon rosewater

Filling and decoration
2–3 rose buds*
1 egg white, lightly beaten
caster sugar
450g/1 lb ripe strawberries,
   sliced
sprigs of mint

Pick the rose petals in the morning on a dry day and examine them carefully for insects before use. Do not use roses that have been sprayed with insecticide.

For the decoration, prepare the crystallized rose petals several hours before you need them. Take the petals from the rose buds (or use small petals from the centre of an open rose) and leave to dry on paper towels for about 1 hour. Paint the dry petals with lightly beaten egg white, using a clean artist's paintbrush – do not leave any blobs of egg white on the petals. Dredge with caster sugar from a fine dredger and leave on absorbent paper to become firm and crisp but retain their natural appearance.

Cream the butter and vanilla sugar together in a large bowl until pale and fluffy. Sieve the flour and semolina together, then gradually work into the creamed mixture. Finish the mixing with your hands, then gently knead on a lightly floured surface until smooth. Roll out quite thinly and prick with a fork. Using a fluted cutter about 8 cm/3 inches in diameter, cut out two circles for each shortcake and lift on to a lightly floured baking sheet. Chill for about 30 minutes; this helps the shortcakes to retain their shape. Preheat the oven to 180°C/350°F/Gas Mark 4.

To make the rose cream, place the lemon juice in a bowl, crush the rose petals in your hand and drop them into the lemon juice. Turn the petals gently in the juice to keep their colour bright. Add the cream, icing sugar and rosewater, stir to blend, then leave in a cool place for 30 minutes for the flavours to infuse the cream.

Bake the shortcakes in the oven for 10–12 minutes, until just tinged golden (they will become crisp only when cold). Using a palette knife, lift on to a wire rack and leave to cool.

Strain the cream through a sieve, discarding the petals. Whisk the cream until firm but not stiff.

To assemble the shortcakes, spread half the circles fairly thickly with rose cream, top with sliced strawberries and then the second layer of shortbread. Top with crystallized rose petals and a sprig of mint.

A fragrant dessert for summer entertaining. Why not begin with poached wild salmon with mayonnaise, new potatoes and a herby green salad?

APPLE AND CINNAMON BROWN BETTY

SERVES 4

butter for preparing the dish
600 g/1¼ lb Bramley apples
125 g/4 oz demerara sugar, plus 1 tablespoon extra
grated zest and juice of 1 lemon
1 cinnamon stick, broken into 5 or 6 pieces
85 g/3 oz unsalted butter
175 g/6 oz fresh brown breadcrumbs

Preheat the oven to 180°C/350°F/Gas Mark 4. Butter a 1.2 litre/2 pint ovenproof dish.

Peel, core and thinly slice the apples into a bowl. Mix in 125 g/4 oz demerara sugar, the zest and juice of the lemon and the cinnamon stick.

Melt the butter in a heavy-based frying pan and tip in the breadcrumbs. Cook over a medium heat, stirring constantly with a wooden spoon, until all the butter has been absorbed into the bread and the crumbs have separated out again and are golden in colour.

Layer the apples and crumbs in the buttered dish, finishing with a layer of crumbs. Press down with the back of the spoon and sprinkle the extra tablespoon of demerara sugar on top.

Bake in the centre of the oven for 45–50 minutes, until the apples are soft (test with a skewer) and the top is crisp and brown. If it seems to be getting too brown before the apples are cooked, cover the surface lightly with a piece of baking parchment or foil. Do not tuck it round the dish as this will spoil the crispness of the topping. Serve hot, with clotted cream.

The autumnal flavours of pot-roasted pheasant with tangerine zest and thyme, with roasted parsnips, would be just right before this spicy apple pudding.

MULLED PLUMS
with crème fraîche

SERVES 4

300 ml/10 fl oz soft red wine (e.g. Merlot)
100 ml/3½ fl oz ruby port
pared zest of 1 lemon
2 cinnamon sticks, broken into 2 or 3 pieces
5 cloves
10 juniper berries
2–3 tablespoons unrefined molasses sugar
325 g/12 oz dessert plums
3 teaspoons arrowroot

To serve
crème fraîche
a little ground cinnamon

Heat the wine and port in a saucepan and bring to the boil. Reduce the heat and add the lemon zest, cinnamon sticks, cloves, juniper berries and sugar. Leave to simmer steadily while you prepare the plums.

Wash, dry, halve and stone the plums.

In a small bowl, blend the arrowroot with 2–3 teaspoons cold water until smooth. Pour some of the hot wine over the arrowroot, stirring all the time. Return to the pan and cook until thickened and clear. Pour the hot wine mixture over the plums and leave to cool with all the aromatics. Store in the refrigerator overnight. The juices from the plums will add to the liquid.

Before serving, discard the cloves, lemon zest and cinnamon. The juniper berries can be left in for visual impact if you like. Serve in pretty glasses, with a separate bowl of crème fraîche dusted with cinnamon.

It's very difficult to follow outdoor barbecue food with a dessert, but I think these mulled plums with their aromatic flavours are just right.

BAKED BANANAS IN RUM

SERVES 4

4 bananas
2 tablespoons brown sugar
grated zest of 2 oranges
2 tablespoons dark rum
25 g/1 oz butter

To serve
clotted cream

Heat the barbecue or preheat the oven to 180°C/350°F/Gas Mark 4.

Cut each banana into three. Mix the sugar and orange zest with a splash of rum, then mix with the bananas.

Butter a rectangle of foil, about 40 x 30 cm/ 16 x 12 inches. Fold it in half and seal two of the three edges. Pour in the banana mixture and add the extra rum. Seal and put on the barbecue or bake in the oven for 5 minutes. Serve hot, with clotted cream.

A simple pudding for any occasion. Beef with a mustard and shallot topping (page 257) would be particularly good before these bananas.

POUDING DE RIZ CARAMELISÉ AUX RAISINS MACÉRÉS

Caramelized rice pudding with tipsy raisins

SERVES 4

3 tablespoons raisins
2 tablespoons rum
1 litre/1¾ pints milk, or more if needed
100 g/3½ oz round-grain rice
1 vanilla bean, split
pinch of salt
3 tablespoons sugar, or to taste
2 eggs

Caramel
100 g/3½ oz sugar
5 tablespoons cold water

To serve
125 ml/4 fl oz double cream

Note: I find the flavour improves if the puddings
are chilled for 1–2 days.

Put the raisins and rum in a saucepan, heat until quite hot, then remove from the heat and leave to macerate.

Bring the milk to the boil in a heavy saucepan and stir in the rice, vanilla bean and salt. Simmer, uncovered, stirring occasionally, until the rice is very tender, 30–40 minutes. If necessary add more milk during cooking – when done the milk should just be absorbed.

Meanwhile, make the caramel. Heat the sugar and water in a heavy saucepan until the sugar dissolves. Bring to the boil and boil steadily without stirring until the syrup starts to colour. Lower the heat and boil until the syrup cooks to a dark caramel. Remove from the heat, let the bubbles subside and then pour the caramel into four ramekins: beware, it is very hot. Leave to set.

Preheat the oven to 180°C/350°F/Gas Mark 4. When the rice is cooked, remove the vanilla bean, stir in the raisins, rum and sugar and taste, adding more sugar if needed. Whisk the eggs until pale and stir into the rice. Spoon the rice into the ramekins. Set the ramekins in a roasting pan of hot water and bring to the boil on top of the stove. Transfer to the oven and bake until the puddings are just set, 20–25 minutes. Remove from the water bath and leave until cold. To serve, run a knife around the edge of each pudding and turn out on to individual plates. Spoon cream around them

Roast meat, for me, is the right partner for rice pudding. In France the beef would probably come with little fried potatoes and baked tomatoes topped with garlic, parsley and breadcrumbs à la Provençale, or the lamb with green beans or flageolet beans.

GULA MELAKA

Sago pudding with palm sugar and coconut milk

SERVES 6

100 g/3½ oz palm sugar
1 cup (250 ml/8 fl oz) pearl
  (small seed) sago
125 ml/4 fl oz thick coconut milk
pinch of salt

Put the palm sugar in a small saucepan with 250 ml/8 fl oz water and place over medium heat, stirring until the sugar has dissolved. Simmer until the liquid reduces to around 175 ml/6 fl oz. Leave to cool.

Bring 1.5 litres/2½ pints water to the boil in a saucepan. When it bubbles, add the sago in a slow, steady stream, stirring constantly. Cook, stirring, for 10–15 minutes, until the sago is soft and transparent. Drain and rinse under cold running water to wash off excess starch. Drain well.

Mix the sago with half the palm sugar syrup, half the coconut milk and the salt, and ladle into six 125 ml/4 fl oz moulds. Cover and chill for at least 1–2 hours.

To serve, unmould the chilled sago on to individual serving plates, and top each one with a spoonful of the remaining palm sugar syrup and a spoonful of chilled coconut milk.

Serve on its own, or surrounded by fresh tropical fruits: mango, starfruit, papaya, pineapple. This pudding also goes well with a small espresso coffee!

AKBARI SHAHI TUKRI

Aromatic bread and butter pudding

SERVES 4

8 slices of white bread
vegetable oil for deep-frying
1 litre/1¾ pints milk
250 ml/8 fl oz sweetened condensed milk
½ teaspoon saffron strands
a few drops of vanilla essence
½ teaspoon ground green cardamom
a few drops of rosewater

Garnish

1 tablespoon flaked almonds, roasted
1 tablespoon pistachio nuts, chopped
4 silver or gold leaf sheets (optional)

Preheat the oven to 190°C/375°F/Gas Mark 5.

Remove and discard the crusts from the bread. Heat the oil to 190°C/375°F or until a cube of bread browns in 30 seconds. Deep-fry the bread until golden, then drain on paper towels.

Using a non-stick saucepan to prevent burning, bring the milk to the boil, then reduce to a simmer. Add the condensed milk and simmer for 15 minutes to thicken it, stirring occasionally. Add the saffron, vanilla essence, cardamom and rosewater, and remove from the heat.

Arrange four of the fried bread slices to cover the base of a small roasting tin. Place the remaining four slices on top. Pour the milk mixture over the bread, ensuring that the bread is thoroughly soaked.

Immediately place the tray in the oven and bake for 15 minutes. Serve hot or cold, garnished with the nuts and the silver or gold leaf.

Since this is quite a rich and filling pudding, I would serve it after a light curry such as the chilli chicken (page 229) or the fenugreek prawn curry (page 185).

MADEIRA TIPSY TRIFLE

SERVES 6–8

vanilla custard (page 377)

225 g/8 oz raspberries and 2 tablespoons icing sugar
    or 200 g/7 oz canned apricots, drained, and the
    juice of ½ lemon

150 ml/5 fl oz Madeira

2 tablespoons fresh orange juice

1 tablespoon brandy

3 tablespoons caster sugar

1 layer of orange sandwich cake, plain sponge cake
    or sponge fingers

2–3 tablespoons good-quality raspberry or apricot jam

1 tablespoon flaked almonds, toasted, to decorate

Chantilly cream

1 vanilla pod

450 ml/15 fl oz double cream

2 heaped teaspoons icing sugar, sifted

First, assemble all the parts. Make the custard. Mix the raspberries and sugar together in a bowl, then press through a sieve to remove the seeds. Alternatively, purée the apricots and sharpen the taste with a little lemon juice. Mix the Madeira, orange juice, brandy and caster sugar together, taste and add more sugar if necessary.

For the Chantilly cream, split the vanilla pod and scoop the seeds into the cream. Add the icing sugar and whisk together lightly to form a soft, spreadable consistency.

Slice the sponge in half horizontally, spread thickly with the jam, and sandwich the layers back together. Cut into pieces and arrange in a glass dish. Pour over enough of the Madeira mixture to moisten the sponges well.

Top with the fruit purée, then spread with the custard. Spread about two-thirds of the Chantilly cream thickly on top. Whisk the remaining cream until stiff and pipe on to the trifle. Decorate with toasted flaked almonds.

A luxurious trifle is traditionally part of a Christmas high tea. What about rum-roasted gammon, Waldorf salad and some homemade chutney to start?

BAKED CHOCOLATE PUDDING
with hot chocolate fudge sauce

SERVES 4

100 g/3½ oz self-raising flour
½ level teaspoon baking powder
¼ level teaspoon bicarbonate of soda
1 rounded tablespoon cocoa powder
70 g/2½ oz caster sugar
1 extra-large egg, beaten
1 tablespoon golden syrup
100 ml/3½ fl oz milk
100 ml/3½ fl oz sunflower oil

Chocolate fudge sauce
25 g/1 oz unsalted butter
85 g/3 oz extra bitter dark chocolate
    (Meunier or Valrhona)
200 ml/7 fl oz double cream
225 g/8 oz icing sugar, sifted

To serve
vanilla custard (page 377)

Preheat the oven to 150°C/300°F/Gas Mark 2. Grease four individual 175 ml/6 fl oz pudding moulds.

Sift the flour, baking powder, bicarbonate of soda, cocoa and caster sugar together into a mixing bowl. Make a well in the centre. Pour the egg into the well with the golden syrup, milk and oil. Gradually draw the dry ingredients in from the sides of the bowl and beat to make a smooth batter. Pour into the prepared moulds and bake in the oven for about 30 minutes, until springy to the touch.

To make the sauce, melt the butter, chocolate and cream together in a double boiler. Gradually beat in the icing sugar until glossy.

To serve, unmould the puddings on to four dessert plates and pour the fudge sauce over and around the puddings. Pour hot custard around the edges of the plates and – using the point of a small knife or a wooden skewer – swirl the custard and fudge sauce together.

Although appearing to be rich, this pudding is actually very light and would make a good second course to follow a simple chicken dish, maybe cooked with lemon, ginger and coriander.

WALNUT AND ORANGE PUDDING
with toffee sauce

SERVES 4

butter for preparing the dish
50 g/2 oz walnuts
50 g/2 oz self-raising flour
¼ teaspoon baking powder
pinch of salt
125 g/4 oz unsalted butter, softened
125 g/4 oz soft brown sugar
grated zest of 1 orange
2 eggs, beaten

Toffee sauce
50 g/2 oz walnuts
85 g/3 oz caster sugar
150 ml/5 fl oz double cream
50 g/2 oz unsalted butter

Preheat the oven to 160°C/325°F/Gas Mark 3.
Lightly butter four individual pudding moulds.

Grind the walnuts in a liquidizer or food
processor. Sift the flour, baking powder and salt
into a bowl and mix in the ground walnuts.

Cream the butter, brown sugar and orange
zest together in a bowl until pale and fluffy.
Gradually beat in the eggs. Gently fold in the
flour mixture until evenly mixed; it should have
a soft, dropping consistency. Divide the mixture
between the prepared pudding moulds. Bake for
about 25 minutes, until the puddings are well
risen and firm to touch.

While the puddings are baking, prepare the
toffee sauce. First, blanch the walnuts: place in a
saucepan and cover with cold water. Bring to the
boil, then drain. Rub the skins from the nuts,
then chop roughly.

Place the caster sugar in a saucepan with
3 tablespoons water. Heat gently until the sugar
is dissolved, then bring to the boil. Boil rapidly
until the syrup becomes a deep caramel colour.
Quickly whisk the cream and butter into the
caramel. The sauce will be lumpy at first but
keep whisking – it will become smooth and
glossy. Stir the chopped walnuts into the sauce.

Carefully turn the puddings out on to serving
plates. Serve with the toffee sauce poured over,
ideally with a scoop of caramel ice cream.

*Pot-roasted duck with fresh figs and a watercress
salad followed by this pudding would make a lovely
winter meal.*

TORTA DI RICOTTA

Ricotta cake

SERVES 4–6

(the quantities can be doubled for
a 25 cm/10 inch diameter cake)

85 g/3 oz sultanas
70 g/2½ oz unsalted butter,
   at room temperature
150 g/5 oz granulated sugar
2 large eggs, at room
   temperature
grated rind of ½ organic lemon
3 tablespoons potato flour
1½ teaspoons baking powder
pinch of salt
450 g/1 lb fresh ricotta cheese
icing sugar

Soak the sultanas in hot water for 15 minutes to plump them up.
Preheat the oven to 180°C/350°F/Gas Mark 4.

Beat the butter until creamy. Set aside 1 tablespoon of the sugar
and beat the rest with the butter. Beat in the eggs, one at a time.
When the eggs have been incorporated, mix in the lemon rind,
potato flour, baking powder and salt. Pass the ricotta through the
small hole disc of a food mill, or through a sieve, directly on to the
other ingredients. Do not use a processor as this would not aerate
the ricotta. Fold the ricotta thoroughly into the mixture.

Generously butter a 15 cm/6 inch diameter spring-clip tin and
sprinkle with the reserved sugar. Spoon the ricotta mixture into the
tin and bake for about 1 hour, until a small skewer inserted into the
centre comes out clean. Leave to cool.

Unmould the cake when it is cold. Just before serving, sprinkle with
plenty of icing sugar.

*This is suitable for serving at the end of any meal, because it is quite light –
much lighter than American-style cheesecake.*

TARTE AUX POIRES NORMANDE

Pear and almond tart

SERVES 6–8

3–4 ripe pears, about
    600 g/1¼ lb
caster sugar for sprinkling

Pie pastry
200 g/7 oz flour
100 g/3½ oz unsalted butter
1 egg yolk
½ teaspoon salt

Almond frangipane
100 g/3½ oz unsalted butter
100 g/3½ oz caster sugar
1 egg
1 egg yolk
1 tablespoon Calvados or Cognac
100 g/3½ oz ground blanched
    almonds
2 tablespoons plain flour

First make the pastry. Sift the flour on to a work surface and make a well in the centre. Pound the butter with your fist to soften it slightly. Add the butter, egg yolk, salt and 3 tablespoons cold water to the well and work with your fingertips until mixed. Using a pastry scraper, draw in the flour and work until coarse crumbs are formed. If the crumbs seem dry, add 1–2 tablespoons more water. Gently press into a ball; it should be soft but not sticky. Lightly flour the work surface and blend the dough by pushing it away with the heel of your hand and gathering it up with a scraper. After 1–2 minutes it should be smooth and peel easily from the work surface. Press it into a ball, wrap in greaseproof paper and chill for 30 minutes.

Roll out the chilled pastry to 5 mm/¼ inch thick and use to a line a buttered 25 cm/10 inch tart tin with a removable base. Prick the base of the pastry so air bubbles do not form during cooking. Chill until firm, 15–30 minutes. Preheat the oven to 200°C/400°F/Gas Mark 6 and place a baking sheet in the lower third of the oven.

For the frangipane: cream the butter, gradually beat in the sugar, then beat until the mixture is soft and light, 2–3 minutes. Beat in the egg and egg yolk. Add the Calvados or Cognac, then stir in the almonds and flour. Spread the frangipane in the chilled pastry shell.

Peel the pears, halve them and scoop out the cores. Set the halves flat on a board and slice very thinly, retaining the pear shape. Flatten them slightly, then lift with a palette knife and carefully place on the frangipane. Set the tart on the heated baking sheet and bake until the pastry starts to brown, 10–15 minutes. Lower the heat to 180°C/350°F/Gas Mark 4 and continue baking for 10–15 minutes. Sprinkle the tart with sugar and bake for a further 10 minutes, until the pears are tender, the frangipane is set and the sugar is slightly caramelized. The tart will shrink from the sides of the tin. Leave on a wire rack to cool for 5 minutes, then remove the sides of the tart tin. Let the tart cool to tepid before removing the base. Serve at room temperature.

Pears are an autumn fruit, the seasonal partner of goose, turkey or game simmered with red wine and onions. With the game I would serve braised red cabbage and a purée of chestnuts or celeriac. Cheese must come somewhere in the meal, perhaps toasted on croûtes to serve with salad.

CARAMELIZED APPLE TARTS

SERVES 4

1½ teaspoons lemon juice
1 egg
2 tablespoons iced water
225 g/8 oz plain flour
1 teaspoon icing sugar
½ teaspoon salt
150 g/5 oz unsalted butter, chilled and diced

Pastry cream
300 ml/10 fl oz single cream
½ split vanilla pod
2 egg yolks
1 tablespoon plain flour
½ teaspoon cornflour
1 tablespoon caster sugar

Apple purée
2 Bramley apples, peeled, cored and sliced
1½ tablespoons caster sugar
1 strip of lemon zest
1 tablespoon water
1 tablespoon Calvados

Apple topping
40 g/1½ oz butter
1 tablespoon caster sugar
3 Cox's apples, peeled, cored and thinly sliced
icing sugar for dusting

First make the pastry. Beat the lemon juice, egg and iced water; chill until thickened. Sift the flour, icing sugar and salt into a bowl, then rub in the butter until the mixture resembles bread-crumbs. Add the chilled liquid and stir until the mixture forms a loose dough. Knead lightly until smooth, then wrap and chill for 30 minutes.

Preheat the oven to 190°C/375°F/Gas Mark 5. Roll out one-third of the pastry (chill or freeze the rest) and use to line four individual tart tins. Bake blind for about 20 minutes. Leave to cool.

For the pastry cream, put the cream in a sauce-pan. Scrape the vanilla seeds into the cream, add the pod, then bring to the boil. Blend the yolks, flour, cornflour and sugar in a bowl. Pour the hot cream on to the yolks, whisking steadily. Rinse the pan and return the mixture to a low heat. Cook gently, stirring, until thickened. Remove the vanilla pod and cover with buttered greaseproof paper to prevent a skin forming.

For the apple purée, stew the Bramleys gently in a heavy-based pan with the sugar, lemon zest and water until the apples collapse and form a purée. Add the Calvados, then taste and add a little more sugar if necessary.

Turn the oven to 220°C/425°F/Gas Mark 7. For the topping, heat the butter and sugar in a sauce-pan with 1 tablespoon water. Bring to the boil, add the apples and cook until soft, 2–3 minutes. Divide the pastry cream between the tart bases and top with 1 tablespoon of apple purée, then the apple slices. Bake for 10–12 minutes. If the edges are not golden brown, dredge lightly with icing sugar and caramelize under a hot grill. To serve, dredge with icing sugar.

DESSERTS

RAISIN AND CURD CHEESE TART

SERVES 6–8

225 g/8 oz curd cheese or low-fat soft cheese
125 g/4 oz caster sugar
150 ml/5 fl oz double cream
3 eggs, beaten
50 g/2 oz raisins

Shortcrust pastry
85 g/3 oz plain flour
85 g/3 oz wholewheat flour
85 g/3 oz butter, chilled and diced

First make the pastry. Sift the flours together into a bowl or food processor, adding the residue of bran left in the sieve. Add the butter, then whizz the mixture in the food processor or rub the butter in with your fingertips until the mixture resembles breadcrumbs. Add 6 teaspoons of ice-cold water and mix briefly until the mixture comes together to make a dough. Wrap and chill for 20–30 minutes.

Preheat the oven to 190°C/375°F/Gas Mark 5. Roll out the pastry and use to line a 22 cm/ 9 inch flan dish; ease the pastry into the dish, press it down and trim off any excess. Prick the base lightly with a fork, then put a circle of greaseproof paper on top of the pastry and weigh it down with baking beans or pastry trimmings. Bake for 10–15 minutes, then remove the paper and beans or pastry trimmings and bake for a further 5–10 minutes, until the pastry is crisp.

Leave the pastry to cool slightly while you make the filling. Beat together the cheese, sugar, cream and eggs, until smooth. Scatter the raisins evenly over the pastry base, then pour the cheese mixture on top. Put the tart into the oven, turn the temperature down to 160°C/ 325°F/ Gas Mark 3 and bake for 30–35 minutes, until set. Leave to cool. Serve the tart at room temperature or chilled, with some pouring cream or crème fraîche.

Serve after a main course that includes plenty of colourful vegetables; perhaps spinach lasagne with steamed carrots. This tart also makes a delicious mid-morning or afternoon treat with a cup of tea or coffee.

CAKES AND COOKIES

*Dost thou think,
because thou art virtuous,
there shall be no more
cakes and ale?*

SIR TOBY BELCH, FROM *TWELFTH NIGHT*
WILLIAM SHAKESPEARE

CHEDDAR CHEESE BISCUITS

MAKES 20

85 g/3 oz plain wholewheat flour
pinch of cayenne pepper
50 g/2 oz butter,
    at room temperature
50 g/2 oz strongly flavoured
    Cheddar cheese, grated

Preheat the oven to 200°C/400°F/Gas Mark 6.

Sift the flour and cayenne pepper into a bowl, adding any residue of bran left in the sieve. Add the butter to the bowl, then use a fork to mix it thoroughly with the flour. Mix in the grated cheese to make a dough.

Roll the dough into a sausage shape, then, using a sharp knife, cut off slices about 5 mm/¼ inch thick and place these on a baking sheet, pressing them gently into shape if necessary. Leave a little space between them, but they won't spread much. Bake for about 10 minutes, or until the biscuits are golden brown.

Leave on the baking sheet to cool slightly, then transfer to a wire rack to become completely cold and crisp.

If you make small biscuits, they are good nibbles to have with drinks. They could also be served as an accompaniment to a soup such as watercress. Alternatively, for a light lunch, offer them with a cheese board, nuts and celery, perhaps followed by little coffee custards.

APRICOT AND SUNFLOWER FLAPJACKS

MAKES 8 BARS

125 g/4 oz margarine
125 g/4 oz demerara sugar
1 tablespoon golden syrup
175 g/6 oz rolled oats
50 g/2 oz no-soak apricots,
    snipped into pieces
50 g/2 oz sunflower seeds

Preheat the oven to 160°C/325°F/Gas Mark 3. Lightly grease an 18 cm/7 inch square shallow cake tin.

Put the margarine, sugar and golden syrup in a saucepan and melt over a low heat. Stir in the oats, apricots and sunflower seeds and mix well. Turn into the prepared tin and level the surface. Bake in the oven for about 35 minutes, until golden brown.

Leave to cool in the tin for 10 minutes. Mark into eight bars and leave to cool until they are firm enough to lift out of the tin with a palette knife. Transfer to a wire rack and leave to cool completely.

SOUR CHERRY MUFFINS

MAKES 12 MUFFINS

275 g/10 oz plain flour

3 teaspoons baking powder

2 eggs

85 g/3 oz caster sugar

250 ml/8 fl oz milk

125 g/4 oz butter, melted and cooled

few drops of vanilla essence

175 g/6 oz dried sour cherries,* roughly chopped

nibbed sugar, preserving sugar or crushed sugar cubes

*Available from large supermarkets and health food shops. Substitute dried cranberries or dried blueberries if you wish.

Preheat the oven to 200°C/400°F/Gas Mark 6. Lightly grease a 12-hole muffin tray, or line with paper muffin cases.

Sift the flour and baking powder into a bowl. Put the eggs, caster sugar, milk, melted butter and vanilla essence into a separate large bowl and stir until well mixed. Quickly stir the flour and baking powder into the egg mixture, mixing only until the ingredients have just come together and no longer, so as not to knock out too much air. Carefully fold in the cherries. Divide the mixture between the muffin cases and sprinkle with nibbed sugar. Bake in the oven for about 30 minutes or until well risen, firm and golden. Serve warm.

ORANGE FORK BISCUITS

MAKES ABOUT 30 BISCUITS

225 g/8 oz butter, softened
125 g/4 oz caster sugar
grated zest of 2 small oranges
275 g/10 oz self-raising flour

Preheat the oven to 180°C/350°F/Gas Mark 4. Lightly grease three baking sheets.

Put the butter, sugar and grated orange zest into a mixing bowl and cream together until soft. Sift in the flour and work to a stiff paste, using your hands to bring the mixture together. Divide the mixture into walnut-sized pieces and place on the baking sheets, leaving room for the biscuits to spread. Press the biscuits with a fork to flatten them, then bake in the oven for about 15–20 minutes, until pale golden. Lift the biscuits off the baking tray with a palette knife or fish slice and leave to cool completely on a wire rack.

LEMON SHORTBREAD

MAKES ABOUT 18–20 PIECES

175 g/6 oz butter, softened
85 g/3 oz caster sugar
175 g/6 oz plain flour, sifted
85 g/3 oz ground rice*
grated zest of 2 lemons
caster sugar to sprinkle

*Ground rice gives a good short texture to the shortbread. If you like a more crunchy shortbread, replace the ground rice with semolina.

Preheat the oven to 160°C/325°F/Gas Mark 3. Lightly grease a 30 x 23 cm/12 x 9 inch shallow tin (about 4 cm/1½ inches deep).

Put the butter and sugar into a mixing bowl and cream together with a wooden spoon until light and fluffy. Work in the flour, ground rice and lemon zest and knead well until smooth. Press the mixture into the prepared tin and level the surface. Bake in the oven for about 35 minutes, until pale golden brown.

Mark the shortbread into fingers or wedges and leave in the tin until quite cold. Using a palette knife, lift out on to a wire rack and sprinkle with caster sugar.

MINCEMEAT TRAYBAKE

Preheat the oven to 180°C/350°F/Gas Mark 4. Lightly grease a 30 x 23 cm/12 x 9 inch shallow tin (about 4 cm/1½ inches deep) and line the base with greased greaseproof paper.

Put the margarine, sugar, flour, baking powder, eggs and milk into a large mixing bowl and beat well for about 2 minutes, until well blended. Gently mix in the mincemeat and currants. Turn the mixture into the prepared tin and level the top. Bake in the oven for about 40–45 minutes, until the cake has shrunk from the sides of the tin and springs back when lightly pressed with a finger. Leave to cool in the tin. To serve, cut into 18 squares.

MAKES 18 SQUARES

225 g/8 oz soft baking margarine
225 g/8 oz caster sugar
275 g/10 oz self-raising flour
2 teaspoons baking powder
4 eggs
1 tablespoon milk
225 g/8 oz mincemeat
125 g/4 oz currants

RICH FRUITED TEA LOAF

MAKES TWO 450 G/1 LB LOAVES

175 g/6 oz currants
175 g/6 oz sultanas
175 g/6 oz light muscovado sugar
300 ml/10 fl oz strong hot tea
275 g/10 oz self-raising flour, sifted
1 egg, beaten
2 tablespoons fine-cut marmalade

Start making this tea loaf the night before you want to bake it. Put the currants, sultanas and sugar into a bowl, pour over the hot tea, cover and leave overnight.

Preheat the oven to 150°C/300°F/Gas Mark 2. Lightly grease two 450 g/1 lb loaf tins and line the bases with greased greaseproof paper (it is best cooked in two smaller tins, rather than one 900 g/2 lb tin).

Stir the flour, egg and marmalade into the fruit mixture, mix thoroughly, then turn into the prepared tins and level the surface. Bake in the oven for about 1–1¼ hours, until well risen and firm to the touch; a fine skewer inserted into the centre should come out clean. Leave to cool in the tins for about 10 minutes, then turn out and leave to cool completely on a wire rack. Serve sliced and buttered.

SPICED GINGER CAKE

MAKES 9 PIECES

125 g/4 oz soft baking margarine
85 g/3 oz caster sugar
125 g/4 oz black treacle
150 g/5 oz self-raising flour
1 teaspoon baking powder
1 teaspoon ground ginger
2 eggs
2 tablespoons milk

Icing
125 g/4 oz icing sugar
2 tablespoons stem ginger syrup
1 cm/½ inch piece of stem
   ginger, thinly shredded

Preheat the oven to 180°C/350°F/Gas Mark 4. Lightly grease an 18 cm/7 inch square shallow cake tin and line the base with greased greaseproof paper.

Put all the cake ingredients into a large bowl and beat well for about 2 minutes, until well blended. Turn the mixture into the prepared tin and level the top. Bake in the oven for about 30−35 minutes, until the cake has shrunk from the sides of the tin and springs back when pressed lightly with the fingertips. Leave to cool in the tin for a few minutes, then turn out, peel off the lining paper and leave to cool completely on a wire rack.

For the icing, sift the icing sugar into a bowl and add the stem ginger syrup and 2−3 teaspoons water. Mix until smooth, then stir in the shredded stem ginger. Pour the icing over the cake and leave to set. To serve, cut into nine squares.

LIGHT TROPICAL FRUIT CAKE

MAKES AN 18 CM/7 INCH CAKE

125 g/4 oz soft baking margarine

125 g/4 oz caster sugar

2 eggs, beaten

175 g/6 oz self-raising flour

1 teaspoon baking powder

1 tablespoon milk

225 g/8 oz mixed ready-to-eat
  dried fruits, such as mango,
  papaya, pear, pineapple,
  chopped

To decorate

85 g/3 oz icing sugar, sifted

about 5 teaspoons boiling water

50 g/2 oz mixed dried fruits
  (as above), chopped

Preheat the oven to 180°C/350°F/Gas Mark 4. Lightly grease an 18 cm/7 inch deep round cake tin and line the base with greased greaseproof paper.

Put the margarine, caster sugar, eggs, flour, baking powder and milk into a mixing bowl and beat well for about 2 minutes, until evenly blended. Fold in the chopped fruit, then spoon the mixture into the prepared cake tin and level the surface. Bake in the oven for about 1 hour, until golden and firm to the touch. Leave to cool in the tin for about 10 minutes, then turn out, peel off the lining paper and leave to cool completely on a wire rack.

To decorate, mix the icing sugar with the water until smooth. Drizzle over the top of the cake and scatter over the chopped dried fruits.

COFFEE ALMOND CAKE

MAKES A 20 CM/8 INCH CAKE

3 eggs
125 g/4 oz caster sugar
85 g/3 oz self-raising flour

Coffee buttercream icing
325 g/12 oz icing sugar, sifted
200 g/7 oz butter, softened
2 teaspoons instant coffee
    dissolved in 2 tablespoons
    hot water

To decorate
175 g/6 oz flaked almonds,
    toasted

Preheat the oven to 190°C/375°F/Gas Mark 5. Lightly grease a 20 cm/8 inch deep round cake tin and line the base with greased greaseproof paper.

Put the eggs and caster sugar into a large bowl and whisk at full speed with an electric whisk until the mixture is pale and thick enough to just leave a trail when the whisk is lifted from the bowl. Sift the flour over the surface of the mixture and gently fold in using a metal spoon or spatula. Turn into the prepared cake tin, tilting the tin to level the surface. Bake in the oven for about 30 minutes, until well risen and golden brown. Turn out, peel off the lining paper and leave to cool on a wire rack.

For the icing: put the sugar, butter and coffee into a bowl and beat until smooth. Cut the cake in half horizontally and use about two-thirds of the icing to fill and cover the cake. Press the toasted flaked almonds all over the top and sides of the cake. Put the remaining buttercream icing into a piping bag and pipe rosettes on to the cake.

Fatless whisked sponges do not keep, so either freeze, or eat on the day it is made.

VICTORIA SANDWICH CAKE

MAKES A 20 CM/8 INCH CAKE

225 g/8 oz soft baking margarine
225 g/8 oz caster sugar
4 eggs
225 g/8 oz self-raising flour
2 teaspoons baking powder

To finish
about 4 tablespoons raspberry or strawberry jam
150 ml/5 fl oz double cream, whipped
caster sugar to sprinkle

Preheat the oven to 180°C/350°F/Gas Mark 4. Lightly grease two 20 cm/8 inch sandwich tins and line the bases with greased greaseproof paper.

Put the margarine, sugar, eggs, flour and baking powder into a large bowl and beat well until thoroughly blended. Divide the mixture between the prepared cake tins and level the surfaces. Bake in the oven for about 25 minutes, until well risen and the tops of the cakes spring back when lightly pressed with a finger. Leave to cool in the tins for a few moments, then turn out, peel off the lining paper and leave to cool completely on a wire rack.

When completely cold, sandwich the cakes together with the jam and whipped cream and sprinkle with caster sugar.

LIME MERINGUE ROULADE

SERVES 8–10

5 egg whites
275 g/10 oz caster sugar
50 g/2 oz flaked almonds

Lime filling
grated zest and juice of 2 large limes
40 g/1½ oz cornflour
2 egg yolks
85 g/3 oz caster sugar
3 tablespoons double cream

Preheat the oven to 220°C/425°F/Gas Mark 7. Line a 33 x 23 cm/13 x 9 inch Swiss roll tin with greased nonstick baking paper.

First make the filling: put the lime zest and juice in a small bowl, add the cornflour and stir until blended. Bring 300 ml/10 fl oz water to the boil in a saucepan and stir into the cornflour mixture. Return the mixture to the pan and simmer gently, stirring constantly until it forms a thick custard. Mix the egg yolks and sugar together and stir into the lime mixture. Bring back to the boil, stirring until just bubbling. Remove from the heat and leave to cool, stirring occasionally.

For the roulade, whisk the egg whites in an electric mixer on full speed until very stiff. With the mixer still on high speed, gradually add the sugar, a teaspoon at a time, whisking well between each addition. Whisk until very stiff and all the sugar has been added. Spread the meringue mixture into the prepared tin and sprinkle with the almonds. Place the tin fairly near the top of the oven and bake for about 8–10 minutes, until very golden. Then lower the temperature to 160°C/325°F/Gas Mark 3 and bake the roulade for a further 15 minutes, until firm to the touch.

Turn the meringue on to a sheet of nonstick baking paper, almond side down. Peel off the paper from the base of the meringue and leave to cool for about 10 minutes.

Lightly whip the cream and fold into the cooled lime custard. Spread evenly over the meringue. Roll up the meringue fairly tightly from one of the long sides to form a roulade. Wrap in nonstick baking paper and chill well before serving.

SPECIAL CHOCOLATE CAKE

MAKES A 20 CM/8 INCH CAKE

50 g/2 oz cocoa, sifted
5 tablespoons boiling water
3 eggs
150 g/5 oz low-fat natural yogurt
125 g/4 oz soft baking margarine
275 g/10 oz caster sugar
175 g/6 oz self-raising flour
1 rounded teaspoon baking
    powder

White chocolate ganache
300 g/11 oz white chocolate,
    chopped
300 ml/10 fl oz double cream

To decorate
about 125 g/4 oz dark chocolate

Preheat the oven to 180°C/350°F/Gas Mark 4. Lightly grease two 20 cm/8 inch sandwich tins and line the bases with greased greaseproof paper.

Sift the cocoa into a large mixing bowl, add the water and blend until smooth. Leave to cool slightly. Add the eggs, yogurt, margarine and sugar, sift in the flour and baking powder and beat well until smooth. Divide the mixture between the two tins and level the surface. Bake in the oven for 25–30 minutes, until the cakes are well risen, firm to the touch and just beginning to shrink away from the sides of the tins. Leave to cool in the tins for a few minutes, then turn out, peel off the lining paper and leave to cool completely on a wire rack.

To decorate the cake, make chocolate caraque or curls. For caraque, as shown, melt the dark chocolate in a bowl over a saucepan of hot water and pour a thin layer on to a smooth, scratch-proof surface. Spread the chocolate thinly using a palette knife and leave until nearly set. Hold a long, sharp, flexible knife at an angle and shave the chocolate off the surface. For chocolate curls, use a swivel peeler along the flat side of a chocolate bar at room temperature. Chocolate-flavoured cake covering is particularly good for this.

For the white chocolate ganache, put the chocolate in a heatproof bowl. Bring the cream to the boil, pour over the chocolate and leave to stand, without stirring, for about 5 minutes, then stir until smooth. Leave to cool. Whisk the cooled mixture until it has the consistency of thickly whipped cream.

When completely cold, sandwich the cakes with half the ganache and spread the rest over the sides and top of the cake. Decorate with the chocolate caraque or curls.

WHITE CHOCOLATE ANGEL GATEAU

SERVES 10

85 g/3 oz self-raising flour
2 teaspoons cream of tartar
175 g/6 oz caster sugar
6 egg whites
¼ teaspoon salt
1 tablespoon lemon juice
1 teaspoon vanilla essence

Filling

275 g/10 oz white chocolate, chopped
275 g/10 oz light cream cheese
3 egg whites
85 g/3 oz caster sugar

Preheat the oven to 190°C/375°F/Gas Mark 5. Grease and flour a 20 cm/8 inch round cake tin. Sift the flour, add half of the cream of tartar and sift again; set aside. Sift the sugar and set aside.

Whisk the egg whites until they form soft peaks, then add the salt and the rest of the cream of tartar. Beat in the sugar, 2 tablespoons at a time, then add the lemon juice and vanilla. Fold in the flour lightly, 2 tablespoons at a time. Turn into the prepared cake tin and bake for 20 minutes. Turn the heat down to 160°C/325°F/Gas Mark 3 and cook for a further 20 minutes. Leave in the tin on a wire rack for 10 minutes, then carefully turn out and leave to cool completely.

For the filling, melt the white chocolate in a bowl set over a pan of simmering water. Mash the cream cheese and stir into the melted chocolate. Whisk the egg whites until they form stiff peaks, then gradually whisk in the sugar until very stiff and shiny. Fold into the cream cheese and white chocolate mixture.

Slice the cake into four layers and spread each layer with some of the filling. Stack up the gateau, and dust the top with icing sugar.

For a vegetarian dinner party, start with mushroom and pesto tartlets (page 53), and follow with penne with red and yellow pepper sauce (page 109) served with stir-fried mangetout and mushrooms (page 164). Then linger over a mixed leaf salad, and finish with this exquisite angel gateau that my American mother used to make.

CHOCOLATE TRUFFLE CAKE

First make the ganache: put the cream in a saucepan, bring to the boil, then stir in the chocolate until smooth. Remove 2 tablespoons of the mixture and set aside. Leave the mixture to cool, whisking occasionally to prevent a skin from forming. When cool, whisk thoroughly and beat in the softened butter.

Slice the sponge into three layers. Sprinkle the bottom layer with 2 tablespoons of the Grand Marnier, if using, and spread with one-third of the ganache, then put the second layer on top. Sprinkle with Grand Marnier and spread with ganache as before, then add the third layer of sponge. Sprinkle with the remaining Grand Marnier, then spread the remaining ganache all over the cake.

Place a tiny amount of ganache into a piping bag and pipe an abstract design on top of the cake. Dust with cocoa powder. Coat the sides in chocolate strands and place in the refrigerator to set for 10–15 minutes.

Put the reserved chocolate cream in a piping bag and fill in the abstract design. Decorate the cake with chocolate curls and fruit.

20 cm/8 inch round chocolate sponge (page 377)
5 tablespoons Grand Marnier (optional)
1–2 tablespoons cocoa powder
50 g/2 oz chocolate strands

Ganache
300 ml/10 fl oz double cream
325 g/12 oz plain chocolate, chopped
85 g/3 oz butter, softened

To decorate
chocolate curls
fresh fruit

WHITE CHOCOLATE WEDDING CAKE

30 cm/12 inch, 22 cm/9 inch
and 15 cm/6 inch round
chocolate sponges (page 377)
2.2 kg/5 lb ready-to-roll icing
225 g/8 oz royal icing (page 377)
1.5 kg/3 lb white chocolate drops

Buttercream
1.1 kg/2½ lb butter, softened
1.7 kg/3 lb 12 oz icing sugar
300 ml/10 fl oz hot water
1 teaspoon vanilla essence

To decorate
fresh, silk or dried flowers
and leaves

Equipment
45 cm/18 inch round cake
board/drum; 22 cm/9 inch
round thin (4 mm) board;
15 cm/6 inch round thin
(4 mm) board; 8 plastic
dowels; palette knife;
metal scraper

First make the buttercream. Beat the butter until light and fluffy. Gradually beat in the icing sugar and then the hot water and vanilla.

Slice each of the sponge cakes into three layers. Sandwich the layers with buttercream and spread a thin layer over the top and sides. Place the large sponge on the 45 cm/18 inch cake board, the 22 cm/9 inch sponge on the 22 cm/9 inch card and the small sponge on the 15 cm/6 inch card.

Divide the ready-to-roll icing into three and roll out thinly to cover all three cakes separately.

Place four plastic dowels into each of the two larger cakes, to support the boards on top. Remove the dowels, trim to be flush with the top of the cake and reinsert. Place the 22 cm/9 inch cake on top of the 30 cm/12 inch one and the 15 cm/6 inch cake on top of the 22 cm/9 inch one, making sure they are all in the centre. Secure using a little royal icing.

Melt the white chocolate drops in a bowl over a saucepan of hot water. Using a palette knife, spread the chocolate, in small amounts at a time, evenly and thinly on to a clean, dry, smooth surface (a marble slab is ideal). Leave to set. Using a metal scraper, holding it at an angle, push along the top of the chocolate to form curls. Store in the refrigerator. If there is any chocolate left on the surface, scrape it off and melt it down again.

Place the chocolate curls all around the sides of the cakes, securing with royal icing. Sprinkle any broken bits on the tops of the cakes. Decorate with flowers or leaves of your choice.

CAT NAPPING!

20 cm/8 inch round fruit cake (page 377)
125 g/4 oz apricot jam, boiled
icing sugar for dusting
675 g/1½ lb marzipan
1.5 kg/3 lb ready-to-roll icing: 650 g/1 lb 6 oz pale
    brown, 325 g/12 oz black, 225 g/8 oz ivory,
    125 g/4 oz bottle green, 50 g/2 oz white
food colours: brown, black, cream, green, pale pink

Equipment

pastry brush; 30 cm/12 inch round cake board;
    basketweave rolling pin; fishbone tool;
    fine paintbrush

Trim the cake to an oval. Brush all over with
the apricot jam. Dust a work surface with icing
sugar, roll out the marzipan and use to cover
the cake. Place on the board and leave to dry.

Roll out a quarter of the pale brown icing and
cover the top of the cake. Roll out the rest of the
brown icing into a strip long enough to encircle
the cake. Indent with the basketweave rolling
pin, then stick around the sides of the cake,
attaching with a little water; trim. Knead the
trimmings together and roll out two long
sausages. Twist them together and stick around
the top of the cake.

Knead and roll out the ivory icing, dampen the
cake board and drape the icing around the
basket. Trim off any excess.

Using half of the black icing, make a teardrop
shape for the cat's body and stick on top of the
cake. Make a tapering sausage shape for the tail
and attach to the body. Make two shorter sausage
shapes for the paws and attach. Roll a large ball
for the cat's head, stick in place and add two
triangles for ears.

Using the white icing, add a little to the end of
the cat's tail and paws, using the fishbone tool
to blend and mark. Make the features for the
cat's face from the white icing, then colour the
trimmings pink and make the nose and inner
ears. Paint the eyes.

Roll out the green icing and mark the quilted
pattern with the fishbone tool. Trim to a
rectangle and stick to the top of the cake with
a little water.

CHRISTENING CAKE

Brush the cake with the apricot jam. Dust a work surface with icing sugar, roll out the marzipan and use to cover the cake. Place on the board and leave to dry.

Roll out the white icing and cover the cake. Knead the trimmings together and roll out a long strip of icing to cover the board, sticking with a little water.

Using a no.3 piping nozzle, pipe a royal icing snail's trail around the base of the cake.

Roll out half the yellow icing and cut six equal strips about 15 cm/6 inches long and 5 mm/¼ inch wide. Twist each strip, and stick to the sides of the cake with a little water. Reroll the trimmings and more yellow icing to make the bows and tails: the bows are made from strips of icing, the ends folded into the centre and a small piece of icing wrapped around the join. Stick to the top of each swag.

Model the rabbit, teddy, building blocks and balls from the remaining icing, and paint on the details. Stick on to the cake with water or a little royal icing.

Colour the remaining royal icing pale yellow. Using the no.1 piping nozzle, write the name and pipe a simple pattern around the board.

20 cm/8 inch round fruit cake (page 377)
125 g/4 oz apricot jam, boiled
icing sugar for dusting
900 g/2 lb marzipan
1.1 kg/2½ lb ready-to-roll icing: 850 g/1 lb 14 oz
    white, 225 g/8 oz yellow, 50 g/2 oz brown
food colours: yellow, brown, pink, black
125 g/4 oz royal icing (page 377)

Equipment
pastry brush; 30 cm/12 inch round cake board;
    fine paintbrush; piping nozzles (no.1 and no.3)

PORSCHE 911

25 cm/10 inch square fruit cake
  (page 377)
125 g/4 oz apricot jam, boiled
icing sugar for dusting
1.5 kg/3 lb marzipan
2 kg/4½ lb ready-to-roll icing:
  1.5 kg/3 lb dark green,
  450 g/1 lb white,
  225 g/8 oz black
food colours: green, black,
  silver*, orange, yellow, red

Equipment
pastry brush; 40 x 36 cm/
  16 x 14 inch cake board;
  fishbone tool; 4 cm/1½ inch
  round cutter; fine paintbrush

* Although the silver colour is
non-toxic, it is not suitable for
consumption and should be
removed before eating.

Cut the cake into two 25 x 12 cm/10 x 5 inch cakes. Cut a 5 cm/ 2 inch slice off one of the cakes, and stick this piece to the end of the other half of the cake with apricot jam. Brush the top with apricot jam and place the remaining 20 x 12 cm/8 x 5 inch piece on top. Place on the board.

Dust a work surface with icing sugar, roll out the marzipan and use to cover the cake. Knead the trimmings together and use to build up the wings and wheel arches, attaching them with a little water. Leave to dry.

Roll a small amount of black icing into a long strip, approximately 2.5 cm/1 inch wide. Stick all around the bottom of the car. Brush the whole cake with water. Roll out the green icing, lay over the car and smooth into place. Trim off the icing where it reaches the black strip and trim around the wheel arches. Using the fishbone tool, mark the windows, doors and bonnet. Using a sharp knife, carefully remove the green icing in the windows and replace with thinly rolled black icing. Cut out four wheels of black icing. Paint the wire wheels or hub caps with silver food colour and leave to dry.

Using the green icing trimmings, mould the front and back bumpers and wing mirrors; attach with a little water. Roll out a little white icing and cut out the headlights, indicators and registration plates; paint appropriately and stick to the car. Using black icing, mould the window trims, door handles and windscreen wipers and stick to the car.

Knead and roll out the remaining white icing, dampen the cake board and cover with the icing. If you like, crimp the edges of the iced board. Finally, stick the wheels in place.

SWEET CASCADE

20 cm/8 inch round chocolate
    sponge (page 377)
about 200 g/7 oz sweets
about 200 g/7 oz soft fruits

Stock syrup
50 g/2 oz sugar
1 lemon, sliced
1–2 tablespoons rum
    or amaretto

Chocolate buttercream
125 g/4 oz butter
175 g/6 oz icing sugar
2 tablespoons hot water
50 g/2 oz dark chocolate, melted

Boiled chocolate icing
275 g/10 oz caster sugar
125 g/4 oz plain chocolate,
    chopped
50 g/2 oz cocoa powder, sifted

Equipment
pastry brush; 25 cm/10 inch
    round cake board;
    sugar thermometer

For the stock syrup: put the sugar and lemon in a small saucepan with 150 ml/5 fl oz water. Bring to the boil, boil for 5 minutes, then leave to cool. Add the rum or amaretto, if using.

For the chocolate buttercream: beat the butter in a bowl until light and fluffy. Gradually beat in the icing sugar and then beat in the hot water and melted chocolate.

Slice the sponge into three layers and brush all three layers with the syrup. Place the bottom layer on the cake board. Spread with buttercream, add the second layer, spread with buttercream, then add the top layer. Spread a thin layer of buttercream over the top and sides of the cake and place in the refrigerator to set.

Make the chocolate icing: put the sugar, chocolate and cocoa into a heavy-bottomed saucepan. Add 8 tablespoons water and stir thoroughly with a wooden spoon. Stirring all the time, bring to the boil. Place a sugar thermometer in the mixture and cook until it reaches 108°C/220°F or the long thread stage, brushing the edge of the saucepan frequently with water to prevent the mixture from crystallizing. Pour into a heatproof bowl and beat well until thick and glossy. To cool quickly, pour half on to a clean, dry work surface and work with a palette knife, then return to the bowl.

Place the cake on a wire rack, pour over the cooled chocolate icing and spread with a palette knife. Leave to set.

Place the cake back on the board and decorate: stick on the sweets and fruits with a little of the chocolate icing and pipe around the base.

BASKET OF WINE

25 cm/10 inch square fruit cake (page 377)
125 g/4 oz apricot jam, boiled
icing sugar for dusting
900 g/2 lb marzipan
1.3 kg/2 lb 12 oz ready-to-roll icing: 1.1 kg/2½ lb
    cream, 125 g/4 oz black, 25 g/1 oz red
food colours: cream, black, red, brown
225 g/8 oz pastillage (page 377)
450 g/1 lb royal icing (page 377)

Equipment
pastry brush; 40 x 25 cm/16 x 10 inch cake board;
    piping nozzles (basketweave and no.4);
    fine paintbrush

Cut the cake into two 25 x 12 cm/10 x 5 inch cakes. Slice one of the cakes in half horizontally. Stick half on top of the 25 x 12 cm/10 x 5 inch cake with apricot jam. Trim the other half to a domed bottle shape and stick on top of the rectangular cake. Brush all over with apricot jam. Dust a work surface with icing sugar, roll out the marzipan and use to cover the cake. Place on the board and leave to dry.

Roll out 800 g/1¾ lb of the cream icing and cover the cake. Cut the icing off the bottle and replace with thinly rolled black icing. Form the neck of the bottle from the red icing – it should overhang the edge of the cake. Roll out the pastillage into two long sausages and form the handles for the basket. Leave to dry for at least 24 hours.

Roll out a little cream icing, cut out a rectangle for the label and stick to the bottle. Paint on a suitable design. Colour the royal icing pale brown and, using the piping nozzles, pipe the basketweave around the cake.

Roll out some more cream icing and form the folds of the napkin around the bottle and on the board, sticking with a little water. Finally, paint and stick on the handle of the basket, supporting it with cocktail sticks until it dries.

CHRISTMAS CAKE

20 cm/8 inch round fruit cake (page 377)
125 g/4 oz apricot jam, boiled
icing sugar for dusting
900 g/2 lb marzipan
1.1 kg/2½ lb ready-to-roll icing
1 tablespoon royal icing (page 377)
food colours: gold*, red, green
85 g/3 oz petal paste (page 377): 25 g/1 oz red,
     25 g/1 oz green, 25 g/1 oz white

Equipment

pastry brush; cake smoother; 30 cm/12 inch round
     cake board; garrett frill cutter; piping nozzle (no.1);
     poinsettia cutter; ball tool; grooved petal board;
     holly cutter; 26-gauge floristry wire; ivy cutter;
     floristry tape

* Although the gold colour is non-toxic, it is not
suitable for consumption and should be removed
before eating.

Brush the cake with apricot jam. Dust a work
surface with icing sugar, roll out the marzipan
and use to cover the cake. Place on the board
and leave to dry.

Roll out the icing and cover the cake. Knead
the trimmings together and roll out a long strip
of icing to cover the board, sticking with a little
water. Dust the work surface generously with
icing sugar, roll out some white icing thinly and
cut out six frills. Ruffle the edges of each one
with a cocktail stick and attach to the sides of
the cake with a little water. Add a second layer
of frills. Using the no.1 piping nozzle and a little
royal icing, pipe a holly pattern around the top
of the frills. Leave to dry, then paint gold.

Roll out the red petal paste and cut out five
large poinsettia petals. Indent the veins and thin
the edge slightly with the ball tool. Leave to dry
in a foil cup. Make five smaller red petals and five
large green petals. Add a pinch of white petal
paste to a pinch of green, roll out and cut the
calyx. When all the petals are dry, stick together
with a little red royal icing.

Using the grooved petal board, roll out the
green petal paste very thinly, cut out the holly
and insert the floristry wire. Thin the edges
slightly and leave to dry. Using the white petal
paste, repeat the process to make the ivy. When
dry, paint the ivy gold. The holly berries are made
from small balls of red petal paste, on wires.

To assemble, tape the leaves together in small
sprigs. Make a small mound of icing on top of
the cake and push the leaves into it, sticking the
poinsettia in the centre. Using the no.1 piping
nozzle, write the message.

THE BASICS

vegetable stock

MAKES ABOUT 1 LITRE/1¾ PINTS

2 tablespoons vegetable oil
2 onions, finely chopped
2 carrots, finely chopped
1 small fennel bulb, chopped
2–3 sticks of celery with leaves,
    chopped
2 leeks, rinsed and sliced
finely pared zest and juice of 1 lemon
150 ml/5 fl oz dry white wine
¼ teaspoon white peppercorns
½ teaspoon coriander seeds
1 bay leaf
salt

Warm the oil in a large saucepan, add
the onions and fry until softened but
not browned. Stir in the remaining
vegetables and let them warm
through, then add the lemon zest,
wine and 150 ml/5 fl oz water, stir,
and bring to the boil. Turn down the
heat, cover loosely and simmer gently
for 30 minutes.

Roughly crush the peppercorns
and coriander and add to the pan
together with the bay leaf, a little salt
and 1 litre/1¾ pints water. Bring back
to the boil. Cover loosely and simmer
for a further 20 minutes or so.

Take the pan off the heat, stir in
the lemon juice and leave to infuse
in a cold place, preferably overnight.
Strain and keep in the refrigerator for
a day or two or freeze.

chicken stock

MAKES ABOUT 2.5 LITRES/4½ PINTS

1.5 kg/3 lb chicken backs,
    necks and bones
1 onion, quartered
1 carrot, quartered
1 stick of celery, chopped
bouquet garni
1 teaspoon peppercorns

Put all the ingredients into a large
saucepan with about 4 litres/6½ pints
water. Bring slowly to the boil,
skimming often. Simmer uncovered
for 2–3 hours, skimming occasionally.

Strain the stock, taste, and if the
flavour is not concentrated, boil it
until well reduced. Leave to cool,
then refrigerate it. Before using, lift
any solidified fat from the surface.
Keep in the refrigerator for up to
3 days or freeze.

dashi

8 cm/3 inch square piece of konbu (kelp)
25 g/1 oz dried bonito flakes

Put the konbu in a saucepan with
1 litre/1¾ pints cold water and heat.
Just before the water comes to the
boil, remove the konbu and add the
bonito flakes. Bring back to the boil,
then immediately remove the pan
from the heat. Leave for 30 seconds to
1 minute, then strain through muslin
and leave to cool. Keep, well covered,
in the refrigerator for up to 3 days.

fish stock

MAKES ABOUT 2 LITRES/3½ PINTS

6 tablespoons olive oil
1 small leek, chopped
1 small onion, chopped
1 stick of celery, chopped
½ small fennel bulb, chopped
2 garlic cloves, unpeeled
about 1.5 kg/3 lb white fish bones
    or carcasses (eyes and gills removed)
300 ml/10 fl oz dry white wine
bouquet garni
½ lemon, sliced
¼ teaspoon black peppercorns

Heat the oil in a large saucepan,
add the leek, onion, celery, fennel
and garlic and cook over a low heat
for 7–10 minutes or until softened
but not coloured.

Add the fish bones and wine
and cook until evaporated, then add
2 litres/3½ pints water and slowly
bring to the boil. Using a slotted
spoon, skim off any scum that rises
to the surface, then add the bouquet
garni, lemon and peppercorns.
Simmer for 20 minutes, then remove
the pan from the heat and leave to
stand for 10 minutes.

Strain carefully through a muslin-
lined sieve and leave to cool. Keep,
well covered, in the refrigerator for
up to 3 days or freeze.

vinaigrette

MAKES ABOUT 300 ML/10 FL OZ

50 ml/2 fl oz sherry vinegar
250 ml/8 fl oz extra virgin olive oil
50 ml/2 fl oz groundnut oil
juice of ½ lemon
sea salt and ground white pepper

Simply whisk or shake everything together until emulsified. Store in the refrigerator in a screw-topped jar and shake again before serving.

aïoli

SERVES 4–6

1 garlic clove, pounded to a paste
1 egg yolk
about 150 ml/5 fl oz olive oil
1 tablespoon wine vinegar
salt

Make sure all the ingredients are at room temperature. Put the crushed garlic and egg yolk in a deep plate and work together with a fork. Trickle in the oil, drop by drop at first, beating steadily with the fork. As the sauce thickens, you can increase the trickle of oil. If the aïoli looks as if it might be about to separate, fork furiously at one corner until it becomes smooth and thick again, and then work in the rest. Finish with vinegar and salt to taste.

béarnaise sauce

MAKES 250 ML/8 FL OZ

3 tablespoons white wine vinegar
3 tablespoons dry white wine
1 shallot, finely chopped
10 peppercorns
2 tablespoons chopped fresh tarragon
2 egg yolks
125 g/4 oz butter, cut into small pieces
½ lemon
salt and cayenne pepper

Put the vinegar, wine, shallot, peppercorns and half the tarragon into a small saucepan (not aluminium), and boil until reduced to 2 tablespoons. Leave to cool.

Bring a large saucepan of water to the boil. Beat the egg yolks with 1 tablespoon water, then whisk them into the reduced liquid. Whisking constantly, lower the small saucepan into the pan of boiling water and whisk until the yolks begin to thicken. Whisk in the butter, piece by piece, to make a thick sauce. Strain the sauce, stir in the remaining tarragon, then taste and adjust the seasoning with lemon juice, salt and cayenne pepper. Serve warm.

hollandaise sauce

SERVES 4

225 g/8 oz butter
4 egg yolks
juice of ½ lemon
salt and cayenne pepper

Melt the butter in a small saucepan (preferably one with a pouring lip).

Put the egg yolks and 4 teaspoons water into a mixing bowl and whisk until the yolks become almost white in colour and are very light and foamy.

Place the bowl over a pan of simmering (not boiling) water and whisk vigorously while you gently pour in the melted butter, a little at a time, in a thin stream. When the sauce is creamy, stop whisking and beat in the lemon juice, salt and cayenne pepper to taste.

tomato sauce

MAKES ABOUT 700 G/1½ LB,
ENOUGH FOR 450 G/1 LB PASTA

1 kg/2¼ lb ripe tomatoes, quartered
1 stick of celery, strings removed,
    cut into pieces
1 onion, coarsely chopped
½ carrot, chopped
2 garlic cloves
3–4 sprigs of parsley
2 fresh sage leaves
1 sprig of thyme, leaves only
1 teaspoon tomato purée
1 teaspoon sea salt
1 teaspoon sugar
freshly ground black pepper
4 tablespoons extra virgin olive oil
    or 50 g/2 oz unsalted butter

If you want to use a food processor
you must skin the tomatoes before
you start.

Put all the ingredients – except
the pepper and the oil or butter – in
a fairly wide saucepan and bring to
the boil. Cook over lively heat for
10 minutes or so, while mashing the
tomatoes down with a spoon. Turn
down the heat and continue cooking
for 40 minutes, stirring occasionally.
By the end of cooking any liquid
should have evaporated.

Put the sauce through a food
mill or a sieve, or blend in a food
processor. Taste, add a generous
grinding of pepper and adjust the salt.

For dressing pasta, add the oil or
the butter. For other dishes, such as
soups and stews, use as it is. You can
make larger quantities and freeze it.

TO SKIN, SEED AND CHOP TOMATOES

Pull off the tomato stalks and mark a
small cross at the opposite end with
the tip of a knife. Put the tomatoes in
a small bowl, pour boiling water over
them and leave for 10 seconds or until
the skin starts to curl away at the
cross. Drain and peel them. Halve
them crossways like a grapefruit and
squeeze to remove the seeds. The
seeds can be rubbed in a sieve to
extract the juice. Cut the tomato
halves in slices, then chop them.

pesto

MAKES ABOUT 300 ML/½ PINT
6 garlic cloves, peeled
300 ml/½ pint fresh basil leaves
50 g/2 oz pine kernels, toasted
50 g/2 oz Pecorino
    or Parmesan cheese, grated
1 teaspoon salt
about 150 ml/5 fl oz olive oil

Put the garlic, basil, pine kernels,
grated cheese, salt and a little less
than 150 ml/5fl oz of the oil into
a food processor and process to a
purée. With the motor running,
trickle in enough extra oil to make
a thick sauce.

TO CLEAN MUSSELS

Wash the mussels under cold running
water, scraping the shells clean with
a knife. Discard any mussels with
broken shells and any that do not
close when tapped because this
indicates that the mussel may be dead.
The 'beard', or tough seaweed-like
thread dangling from inside the shell,
should be removed only just before
cooking the mussels.

TO SEGMENT CITRUS FRUIT

Using a sharp knife, cut a slice from
the top and bottom of the fruit,
right through to the flesh. Cut away
the skin and pith, working from top
to bottom, following the curve of
the fruit.

Holding the fruit in the palm
of one hand over a bowl to catch
the juice, cut down between the
membrane and the orange segment.
As you reach the centre of the fruit,
twist the knife and cut up the other
side of the segment, letting the piece
fall into the bowl. Repeat with the
remaining segments.

sichuan chilli oil

250 ml/8 fl oz peanut oil
3 tablespoons dried red chillies, crushed
1 teaspoon Sichuan peppercorns

Heat the oil in a wok until almost smoking, then turn off the heat. Add the chillies and peppercorns and leave to cool. Strain through a fine sieve or muslin into a screw-topped bottle and store in a cool, dark place.

nuoc cham
VIETNAMESE CHILLI DIPPING SAUCE

MAKES 250 ML/8 FL OZ

1 fresh red chilli, finely chopped
2 tablespoons sugar
2 tablespoons fresh lime juice
4 tablespoons rice vinegar
    or distilled white vinegar
4 tablespoons fish sauce
2 large garlic cloves, finely chopped

In a bowl, mix all the ingredients with 4 tablespoons hot water. Stir to dissolve the sugar. Transfer to a jar, cover and store in the refrigerator for up to 1 week.

dua chua
VIETNAMESE PICKLED VEGETABLES

MAKES ABOUT 1.5 LITRES/2½ PINTS

250 ml/8 fl oz distilled white vinegar
4 tablespoons sugar
2½ tablespoons salt
2 carrots, sliced 3 mm/⅛ inch thick
675 g/1½ lb white cabbage
    or Chinese leaves, cored and cut into
    long shreds about 1 cm/½ inch wide
bunch of spring onions, trimmed and cut
    into 5 cm/2 inch lengths

Put the vinegar, sugar, salt and 600 ml/1 pint water in a large saucepan and bring to the boil, stirring to dissolve the sugar. Remove from the heat and leave to cool until just warm to the touch.

Put the carrots, cabbage and spring onions in a large ceramic bowl and pour the brine over the vegetables. (Cover with a small dish to keep the vegetables from floating.) Cover and leave to stand at room temperature until the vegetables turn sour, 4–6 hours or overnight.

The pickled vegetables will keep in the refrigerator for up to 1 month. Drain before serving.

Broccoli, cauliflower florets or green beans (halved lengthways) can be used instead of cabbage.

nasi lemak
MALAYSIAN COCONUT RICE

SERVES 4–6

275 g/10 oz long-grain rice
500 ml/16 fl oz coconut milk
½ teaspoon salt

Wash the rice under cold running water until the water runs clear. Drain well.

Put the coconut milk, salt and 250 ml/8 fl oz water in a saucepan and bring slowly to the boil, stirring constantly. Add the rice, stir, then cover and leave over the lowest possible heat (use a heat-diffusing mat if necessary) for about 20 minutes, until the rice has absorbed all the liquid and small holes have formed in the top. Remove from the heat and fluff up with a fork. Cover and leave in a warm place for up to 20 minutes.

| Square | 12 cm/5 inch | 15 cm/6 inch | 18 cm/7 inch | 20 cm/8 inch | 22 cm/9 inch | 25 cm/10 inch | 28 cm/11 inch |
Round/hexagonal	15 cm/6 inch	18 cm/7 inch	20 cm/8 inch	22 cm/9 inch	25 cm/10 inch	28 cm/11 inch	30 cm/12 inch
RICH FRUIT CAKE							
Mixed dried fruit	425 g/15 oz	650 g/1 lb 7 oz	800 g/1 lb 14 oz	1 kg/2 lb 6 oz	1.5 kg/3 lb 5 oz	1.8 kg/4 lb 2 oz	2.2 kg/5 lb 2 oz
Glacé cherries	50 g/2 oz	85 g/3 oz	150 g/5 oz	175 g/6 oz	250 g/9 oz	275 g/10 oz	325 g/12 oz
Mixed peel	25 g/1 oz	50 g/2 oz	85 g/3 oz	125 g/4 oz	150 g/5 oz	200 g/7 oz	250 g/9 oz
Flaked almonds (optional)	25 g/1 oz	50 g/2 oz	85 g/3 oz	125 g/4 oz	150 g/5 oz	200 g/7 oz	225 g/8 oz
Ground mixed spice (teaspoons)	½	1	1½	2	2½	3	5
Lemon zest (grated)	½	½	1	1	1½	2	2½
Brandy (tablespoons)	1	1	1½	2	2½	3	5
Butter	160 g/5½ oz	175 g/6 oz	275 g/10 oz	325 g/12 oz	500 g/1 lb 2 oz	600 g/1 lb 5oz	675 g/1½ lb
Soft dark brown sugar	160 g/5½ oz	175 g/6 oz	275 g/10 oz	325 g/12 oz	500 g/1 lb 2oz	600 g/1 lb 5oz	675 g/1½ lb
Eggs (medium)	2	3	5	6	8	9	10
Plain flour	200 g/7 oz	225 g/8 oz	325 g/12 oz	400 g/14 oz	600 g/1 lb 5oz	675 g/1½ lb	800 g/1 lb 12oz
Cooking time (approx)	3¾ hours	3¾ hours	4¾ hours	5½ hours	6½ hours	7¾ hours	8½ hours
SPONGE CAKE							
Butter	50 g/2 oz	135 g/4½oz	175 g/6 oz	225 g/8 oz	325 g/12 oz	450 g/1 lb	500 g/1 lb 2 oz
Caster sugar	50 g/2 oz	135 g/4½oz	175 g/6 oz	225 g/8 oz	325 g/12 oz	450 g/1 lb	500 g/1 lb 2 oz
Eggs (medium)	1	2	3	4	6	8	9
Self-raising flour	50 g/2 oz	135 g/4½oz	175 g/6 oz	225 g/8 oz	325 g/12 oz	450 g/1 lb	500 g/1 lb 2 oz
CHOCOLATE SPONGE							
Replace these amounts of flour with cocoa powder	15 g/½ oz	20 g/¾ oz	25 g/1 oz	40 g/1½ oz	50 g/2 oz	125 g/4 oz	175 g/6 oz
Cooking time	30 minutes	40 minutes	50 minutes	1 hour	1¼ hours	1½ hours	1¾ hours

CUTTING AND SHAPING CAKES

Always use a sharp serrated knife. If you require height, pile up several cakes, sticking together with apricot jam or buttercream. Always start by carving off less than you think and trim until you get the correct shape. If gaps appear (very likely when using fruit cake) fill them with marzipan before covering.

COVERING THE CAKE BOARD

For a round board, roll out a long strip of icing (use a piece of string to measure the length). Roll up, dampen the board with water and unroll the icing around the cake. Trim the edge.

For a square board, cut out four strips of icing, one for each side. Dampen the board, lay on the icing and cut each corner, from the corner of the cake to the corner of the board. Trim the edges.

To cover the complete board, dampen and cover, trim the edges and crimp if desired.

rich fruit cake

Place the dried fruit, cherries, peel, almonds, spice and lemon zest in a large bowl. Pour over the brandy and mix well. Leave to soak overnight.

Double line the base and sides of an 8 cm/3 inch deep cake tin with greaseproof paper. Wrap the outside with double-thickness brown paper, secure with string. Place on a baking sheet lined with 3–4 thicknesses of brown paper or newspaper. Preheat the oven to 140°C/275°F/Gas Mark 1.

Cream the butter and sugar until light and fluffy. Add the eggs one at a time, beating well after each addition. Fold in the sifted flour, then the fruit mixture. Place in the prepared tin and smooth the top with the back of a wet metal spoon. Bake (see chart).

Leave the cake to cool in the tin. When cold, turn out and wrap in foil until required.

sponge cake

Double line the base and sides of an 8 cm/3 inch deep cake tin with greaseproof paper. Preheat the oven to 170°C/325°F/Gas Mark 3.

Cream the butter and sugar until light and fluffy. Add the eggs one at a time, beating well after each addition. Fold in the sifted flour, place in the prepared tin and bake (see chart).

Test by pressing the centre with your fingers – it will spring back and feel firm when cooked. Turn out on to a wire rack and leave until cold.

royal icing

2 egg whites
2 teaspoons lemon juice
450 g/1 lb icing sugar, sifted

Using a fork, beat the egg whites in a bowl, whisk in the lemon juice, then add the icing sugar a little at a time, beating well.

pastillage

450 g/1 lb icing sugar
125 g/4 oz cornflour
2 teaspoons gum tragacanth
2 leaves of gelatine
1 teaspoon liquid glucose

Sift the icing sugar, cornflour and gum tragacanth together into a bowl. Dissolve the gelatine in 5 tablespoons water, add the glucose and then add the liquid to the dry ingredients. Beat well to form a paste, then knead until smooth. Keep in a plastic bag until required.

petal paste

450 g/1 lb icing sugar
1 teaspoon gum tragacanth
2 teaspoons powdered gelatine
5 teaspoons white fat
2 teaspoons liquid glucose
1 egg white

Sift the icing sugar and gum tragacanth into a bowl and stand it over hot water to warm it a little. Soak the gelatine in

5 teaspoons water, then place in a saucepan with the white fat and glucose. Place over a low heat until smooth, add the egg white then pour on to the icing sugar. Beat with an electric mixer for 2–3 minutes, or until it becomes elastic. (If you are beating by hand, you will need to do it for at least 5–10 minutes.) Keep in a plastic bag in the refrigerator for at least 30 minutes before use.

vanilla custard

SERVES 4

600 ml/1 pint double cream
1 vanilla pod
5 egg yolks
1 teaspoon cornflour
1 tablespoon caster sugar

Put the cream into a saucepan. Split the vanilla pod in half lengthways, scrape out the seeds into the cream and add the pod as well.

Whisk the egg yolks, cornflour and sugar together in a bowl.

Bring the cream to boiling point, then remove the vanilla pod. Allow the cream to rise in the pan, then quickly pour on to the egg mixture, whisking continuously until the mixture thickens. Pour the custard through a fine sieve into a serving jug.

The cornflour should prevent the eggs from curdling. If you need to reheat the custard, do this very gently. Should it look like curdling at this stage, quickly whisk in a tablespoon of cold double cream.

GLOSSARY

BANANA LEAVES Long green leaves used in Southeast Asia to wrap food before steaming, frying or grilling, or as a plate decoration. Dip into boiling water for 2 minutes to soften if using for wrapping.

BEANCURD (TOFU) Beancurd, made from soybeans, is sold in vacuum packs in many supermarkets; for stir-frying look for firm rather than 'silken' tofu. Asian food stores also sell beancurd 'puffs', cubes of deep-fried beancurd.

BEANCURD CAKE, DRIED (MALAYSIAN, TAU KWA) Bought in squares from Asian food stores.

BEANCURD SKINS, DRIED (MALAYSIAN, TAU FU JUK) The skin that forms on heated soybean milk is dried on bamboo mats to form soft, translucent sheets, sold fresh or frozen in Asian food stores. Use for wrapping foods before steaming or frying.

BEAN PASTE A thick, salty paste made of fermented soy beans. Japanese bean paste is called miso.

BLACHAN Dried shrimp paste with a pungent smell; when cooked it gives a distinctive aromatic tang in Southeast Asian food. To use, either toast or grind and fry with onions. Available in butter-like blocks, it should be stored in a screw-topped jar.

BONITO FLAKES Dried shavings of a fish of the mackerel family, used in making dashi stock and for flavouring Japanese soups.

BOTTARGA Grey mullet roe, salted, pressed and sun-dried. A speciality of Sardinia, bottarga has a very savoury, fishy, sweet-salt flavour. To use, peel away the membrane and grate finely over pasta. It is sold whole or ready-grated from Italian shops.

BOUQUET GARNI A bundle of aromatic herbs used for flavouring stocks, braises and ragoûts. It should include a generous sprig of thyme, a bay leaf and several sprigs of parsley or parsley stalks, tied together with string. A piece of green leek and/or some celery tops may also be included.

CANDLENUTS (MALAYSIAN, BUAH KERAS) Used to thicken sauces and add creaminess and a nutty flavour to Thai and Malaysian food. If unobtainable, substitute macadamia nuts.

CHILLIES, DRIED RED (MALAYSIAN, CILI KERING) Soak in water for a few hours, then blend or pound with a little of the soaking water to make a reddish paste. If unobtainable, substitute fresh red chillies.

CHINESE RICE WINE A yellow wine made from glutinous rice.

CHINESE ROAST PORK (CHAR SIEU) Available from Asian food stores.

CURRY LEAVES (MALAYSIAN, DAUN KARI) Small dark green leaves, available fresh or dried, often used in fish curries.

FISH BALLS Cooked balls of minced fish, used in soups and stir-fries. Found in the refrigerated section of Asian food stores.

FISH SAUCE (THAI, NAM PLA, VIETNAMESE, NUOC MAM) A pungent, salty sauce made from fermented fish.

FIVE-SPICE POWDER A popular Chinese seasoning made of ground star anise, fennel, cloves, cinnamon and Sichuan pepper.

GALANGAL Also known as laos and Siamese ginger, galangal has a medicinal taste and is an essential flavour in Thai cooking.

GOLDEN NEEDLES The name describes the appearance of these dried lily flowers. They must be softened before use by soaking them in hot water for about 30 minutes. They should then be rinsed, drained and squeezed to remove most of the water, and trimmed of their tough ends. Used in vegetarian and many northern Chinese dishes.

HOISIN SAUCE A thick, spicy-sweet sauce made of fermented soy beans, garlic, vinegar, sugar and spices. Use for cooking or as a dipping sauce.

KAMABOKO White Japanese fishcake, pressed on to a thin board. Usually sold frozen in Asian food stores.

KONBU Giant sea kelp, usually sold dried. Along with bonito, it forms the basis of Japanese dashi stock.

LEMONGRASS (MALAYSIAN, SERAI, VIETNAMESE, XA) A fresh, tough reed grass with a strong lemon fragrance. Peel back and discard any dried, tough outer leaves from the stalk; trim the root end; slice paper-thin from the bulb portion up to where the leaves begin to branch, then finely chop to release more flavour during cooking.

MANDARIN PANCAKES These fine wheat pancakes are sold in Asian food stores. Steam to reheat.

MIRIN Japanese sweet rice wine with low alcohol content.

NOODLES, FRESH RICE Flat, glossy white noodles known as *pho* in Vietnam, *kueh teow* in Malaysia and *hor fun* in China. Available from Chinese food stores, cut or uncut.

NOODLES, HOKKIEN Round yellow egg noodles available fresh from Asian food stores. If unobtainable, substitute dried egg noodles.

NORI Dark green sheets of dried seaweed, used to wrap rice in rolls, and to garnish savoury dishes.

PALM SUGAR (MALAYSIAN, GULA MELAKA) Brownish-black rolls of tree sap, sold in some Asian food stores. Break off a piece and dissolve in a little water. Simmer until the sugar has melted, then strain. If unobtainable, substitute soft brown sugar with a touch of golden syrup.

PANCETTA Italian belly pork (the same cut as streaky bacon) cured with salt and spices, and sold smoked or unsmoked. For cooking, buy pancetta in a flat piece, with its rind attached. Cut into thick rashers, then cut across into chunky strips, or lardons. Store tightly wrapped in the refrigerator.

PRAWN CRACKERS (INDONESIAN, KROPOEK, VIETNAMESE, BANH PHONG TOM) Also known as shrimp chips; when you buy them, they are translucent, reddish-pink or white, hard, thin discs; they must be fried in hot oil before serving. As soon as they are added to the hot oil, they will puff up to triple their size, so add only a few at a time. When they puff up, immediately turn them over and keep them immersed in the oil, using a slotted spoon, for 10–15 seconds longer. Do not let them colour, or they will taste bitter. Remove and drain on paper towels while you cook the rest. Serve them the same day they are cooked, or store them in an airtight container for up to 4 days.

RICE PAPERS, DRIED (VIETNAMESE BANH TRANG) These very thin, dried pancakes, about 22 cm/9 inches in diameter, are essential in preparing the famous Vietnamese spring rolls. There is no substitute; thick Chinese spring roll wrappers will not do. Since they are very delicate and brittle they must be handled with care. They tend to

dry out and crack in contact with air, so you need to keep them covered with a barely damp towel while you are working. To use, they must be dipped briefly in hot water; they will become pliable within seconds.

RICE, GLUTINOUS OR SWEET (VIETNAMESE GAO NEP) Also known as sticky rice, this differs from regular, translucent, long-grain rice in that it has creamy white, sturdy kernels. It also has a higher starch content, so it needs to be washed, soaked overnight, then steamed.

SALTED RADISH A dried, salted root vegetable known as *hua pak gart kao* in Thai. It may be labelled 'salted turnip'.

SESAME PASTE A paste made from crushed sesame seeds. Substitute tahini or smooth peanut butter.

SESAME SEED OIL Chinese sesame seed oil is an aromatic, amber-coloured oil pressed from roasted sesame seeds. It is quite different from the cold-pressed sesame seed oil used in some Western cooking. A low smoking temperature and strong flavour make this oil unsuitable for stir-frying. It is usually sprinkled over the food just before serving.

SHRIMPS, DRIED (MALAYSIAN, UDANG KERING) Should be a bright orange-pink. Soak in a little hot water for 10 minutes before cooking. Drain and toss into stir-fries and rice.

SICHUAN PEPPER The seeds from the pepper-ash tree, with a peppery, prickly flavour.

SICHUAN PRESERVED VEGETABLE Mustard green roots preserved in salt and chilli, usually sold in cans.

SOYBEAN AND CHILLI PASTE A pungent, thick chilli sauce, chunky

with soybeans, sold in jars at Asian food stores.

SOY SAUCE Light soy sauce refers to the thin texture of the sauce; it may be replaced with a Japanese soy sauce. Dark soy sauce contains molasses or caramel, which give it a darker colour, sweeter taste and thicker texture. Look for naturally brewed soy sauce.

STAR ANISE Star-shaped spice with a haunting aniseed flavour.

TAMARIND (MALAYSIAN, ASSAM JAWA) Tamarind pulp is the pressed pods of the tamarind tree. To make tamarind water, soak the required amount of pulp in a little boiling water for 5 minutes, then squeeze until dissolved, and strain. Add to a chicken soup or fish curry for a tongue-curling lemon-lime sourness.

WAKAME Dark green dried seaweed which expands dramatically when soaked in water.

WASABI A green pungent root known as Japanese horseradish, it is grated to form a paste with the bite of English mustard. Available in Asian super-markets in tubes or powdered in tins.

WON TON WRAPPERS Thin sheets of dough, about 10 cm/4 inches square, made from eggs and wheat flour. Even professionals use the ready-made sheets, available at Asian food stores.

WOOD EARS A tree fungus, also known as cloud ears or black fungus, this is sold dried. Before use it must be soaked in hot water until soft and pliable – it will expand to many times its size. It should then be rinsed, drained and squeezed to remove most of the water. Trim off the hard stems before using.

INDEX

A

Agra harsha pasanda 236
aïoli 373
Akbari shahi tukri 328
almond frangipane 335
anchovy sauce, with baked hake 199
apple and cinnamon brown Betty 322
apple tarts, caramelized 336
apricot sauce, with deep-fried Camembert 55
apricot and sunflower flapjacks 343
Armagnac, with chicken liver pâté and
    sultanas 75
artichokes, with tagliardi and pancetta 115
Asher, Jane, recipes 361–71
aubergines
    aubergine caviar 50
    aubergine, mozzarella and tomato layer 165
    in ratatouille 148
    in sweet and sour sauce 145
avgolemono 21
avocado
    basil, feta and tomato salad 90
    with chicken and mango 217
    guacamole with tian of crab 65
    Mexican avocado soup 19
    and pear salad 89

B

bacon
    in avocado and pear salad 89
    with barbecued trout and spinach 191
    with cod fillet wrapped in potato 207
    in frisée aux lardons 85
    in homestyle spring onion pancakes 48
    with pheasant and sauerkraut 230
    with a salad of green lentils 99
    with spinach and mushrooms 151
    see also *pancetta*
balsamic vinaigrette 97
bananas
    baked in rum 324
    banana salsa 214
Barbur's biriani 288
barley, roast with wild mushrooms 231
basil
    in avocado, basil, feta and tomato salad 90
    in leek and potato soup 17
    and tomato coulis 188
basket of wine, cake 370
beancurd
    and crabmeat 182
    dau phu xao xa 163
    mee goreng 131
beans
    black bean sauce 194
    borlotti beans 29
    broad beans 21
    butter beans 49
    green beans 27, 108
    mung beans 221
beansprouts 92
beef
    chap chae (stir-fried noodles) 130
    with citrus sauce 259
    corned beef hash 263
    curry 254
    with fried rice noodles 127
    with green and red peppers 260
    in maharajah sheek kebab 80

pot-au-feu à l'ancienne 250
rib steak with mustard and shallot
    topping 257
rich beef casserole 253
with saffron rice 288
steak, kidney and potato pie 262
stir-fried with potatoes 256
sweet and sour braised 251
Berry, Mary, recipes 343–59
biscuits
    Cheddar cheese 340
    lemon shortbread 347
    orange fork 345
blachan kang kong 150
black pudding and champ, with shallots and
    red wine sauce 294
blackberry soufflé 319
blackcurrants, in summer pudding 314
blueberries, in summer pudding 314
bo xao khoi tay 256
bottarga, with fettucelle 112
Bramley, Tessa, recipes 313–23, 329–31, 336
bread and butter pudding, aromatic 328
brill, fillets with three mustard sauce 203
Bulgarian monastery soup 22

C

ca chien sot ca chua 197
cabbage
    with braised duck legs 237
    red with roast haunch of venison 244
cakes and cookies 339–71, 376–7
caponatina 145
cari bo 254
carrots
    carrot and ginger soup 16
    in linguine primavera 108
cassata semi freddo, with strawberry sauce 298
cat napping!, cake 364
caviar
    aubergine 50
    with baked new potatoes, smoked salmon
      and crème fraîche 72
    with tagliatelle and salmon 118
celery
    in caponatina 145
    Stilton and celery soup 15
cha gio 57
Chantilly cream 329
chap chae 130
Chapman, Pat, recipes 80, 139, 154, 158, 185,
    193, 229, 236, 284, 287–8, 328
char kuey teow 134
chaudrée de moules au fenouil et safran 186
cheese
    with baked polenta 156
    Cheddar cheese biscuits 340
    cream cheese in white chocolate angel
      gateau 360
    curd cheese 88, 337
    deep-fried Camembert 55
    feta 90, 168
    fontina 156
    goats' cheese en croûte 169
    goats' cheese in mezze plate 50
    gorgonzola 156
    Gruyère 52, 54
    halloumi 167
    mascarpone with lemon ice cream 310

mozzarella 159, 165
Parmesan 52, 54, 155, 156
    with polenta and sun-dried tomatoes 159
ricotta 332
Roquefort 86, 106
skimmed milk soft cheese 54
Stilton and celery soup 15
taleggio 156
cheesecakes, torta di ricotta 332
Chen, Helen, recipes 43, 48, 81, 91, 133, 138,
    178, 182, 220, 260
cherries
    sour cherry muffins 344
    in summer pudding 314
chestnuts, in pumpkin and leek soup 14
chicken
    chicken mole 225
    chilli chicken with seared garlic and
      lemon salad 98
    chilli chicken with spinach 229
    cucumber and chicken shreds 91
    with forty cloves of garlic 222
    in fried spring rolls 57
    in laksa lemak 40
    in maharajah sheek kebab 80
    with mango and avocado 217
    in nabeyaki udon 45
    satay 77
    skewered five-spice 79
    slow roast chicken thighs 219
    with walnuts 220
    see also *poultry and game*
chicken livers
    chicken liver pâté 75
    pan-fried 70
    substitute for foie gras 71
chickpeas
    with orecchiette 117
    Spanish chickpea and pepper soup 24
chillies
    in blachan kang kong 150
    chilli prawns 184
    fried with squid 179
    in Hokkien mee 124
    Hungarian paprika soup 33
    in Mexican avocado soup 19
    in otak otak 61
    with spaghettini con aglio e olio 113
    with stir-fried beancurd and
      lemongrass 163
chimichangas with salsa 160
Chinese greens, stir-fried with glazed duck
    skewers 215
chocolate
    baked chocolate pudding 330
    boiled chocolate icing 369
    chocolate mousse 311
    chocolate truffle cake 361
    ganache 359, 361
    special chocolate cake 359
    sweet cascade chocolate sponge 369
    white chocolate angel gateau 360
    white chocolate wedding cake 363
chowder, cod and mussel 186
christening cake 365
Christmas cake 371
Chungking noodles 132
cili udang 184
citrus fruit, to segment 374